T5-BAH-797

Sex and Psyche

CROSS-CULTURAL RESEARCH AND METHODOLOGY SERIES

Series Editors

Volumes in this series:

Volume 4 Myerhoff/Simic LIFE'S CAREER-AGING
Volume 5 Hofstede CULTURE'S CONSEQUENCES
Volume 6 Williams/Best MEASURING SEX STEREOTYPES, Revised Edition
Volume 7 Pedersen/Sartorius/Marsella MENTAL HEALTH SERVICES
Volume 8 Lonner/Berry FIELD METHODS IN CROSS-CULTURAL RESEARCH
Volume 9 Brislin/Cushner/Cherrie/Yong INTERCULTURAL INTERACTIONS
Volume 10 Dasen/Berry/Sartorius HEALTH AND CROSS-CULTURAL PSYCHOLOGY
Volume 11 Bond THE CROSS-CULTURAL CHALLENGE TO SOCIAL PSYCHOLOGY
Volume 12 Ward ALTERED STATES OF CONSCIOUSNESS AND MENTAL HEALTH
Volume 13 Williams/Best SEX AND PSYCHE
Volume 14 Brislin APPLIED CROSS-CULTURAL PSYCHOLOGY

Sex and Psyche

Gender and Self Viewed Cross-Culturally

John E. Williams
Deborah L. Best

With the Assistance of:

Marja Ahokas, Finland
Ben Baarda, Netherlands
John Edwards, Canada
Howard Giles, England
Abdul Haque, Nigeria and Pakistan
Saburo Iwawaki, Japan
Heidi Keller and Hans-Georg Voss, Germany
Maritza Montero, Venezuela
Janak Pandey, India
Samir Tuma, Italy
Colleen Ward, Malaysia and Singapore

Cross-Cultural Research and Methodology Series
Volume 13

SAGE PUBLICATIONS
The International Professional Publishers
Newbury Park London New Delhi

For information address:

SAGE Publications, Inc.
2111 West Hillcrest Drive
Newbury Park, California 91320

SAGE Publications Ltd.
28 Banner Street
London EC1Y 8QE
England

SAGE Publications India Pvt. Ltd.
M-32 Market
Greater Kailash I
New Delhi 110 048 India

Printed in the United States of America

Library of Congress Cataloging-in-Publication Data

Main entry under title:

Williams, John E., 1928–
Sex and psyche : gender and self viewed cross-culturally / John E. Williams and Deborah L. Best.
p. cm. — (Cross-cultural research and methodology series : vol. 13)
Includes bibliographical references.
ISBN 0-8039-3769-5. — ISBN 0-8039-3770-9 (pbk.)
1. Sex role — Cross-cultural studies. 2. Sex differences (Psychology) — Cross-cultural studies. 3. Self-perception — Cross-cultural studies. I. Best, Deborah L. II. Title. III. Series: Cross-cultural research and methodology series : v. 13
HQ1075.W53 1990
305.3 — dc20 90-31839
CIP

FIRST PRINTING, 1990

Sage Production Editor: Susan McElroy

CONTENTS

To

Kathleen, James, Thomas, Kimberly, Jeannette, and Brock

and to

Mark and Eric

ABOUT THE SERIES

The Sage Series on Cross-Cultural Research and Methodology was created to present comparative studies on cross-cultural topics and interdisciplinary research. Inaugurated in 1975, the series is designed to satisfy a growing need to integrate research method and theory and to dissect issues from a comparative perspective; a truly international approach to the study of behavioral, social, and cultural variables can be done only within such a methodological framework.

Each volume in the series presents substantive cross-cultural studies and consideration of the strengths, interrelationships, and weaknesses of its various methodologies, drawing upon work done in anthropology, political science, psychology, and sociology. Both individual researchers knowledgeable in more than one discipline and teams of specialists with differing disciplinary backgrounds have contributed to the series. *While each individual volume may represent the integration of only a few disciplines, the cumulative totality of the series reflects an effort to bridge gaps of methodology and conceptualization across the various disciplines and many cultures.*

Volume 6 in the series (*Measuring Sex Stereotypes: A Thirty-Nation Study*) summarized much collaborative research looking into contemporary sex stereotypes. In that 1982 book, John E. Williams and Deborah L. Best explained how they tested adults and children in more than 30 nations by using multiple translations of the Adjective Check List. They couched their results in three theoretical perspectives: affective meanings, ego states, and psychological needs (after Henry Murray's system). That book presented many interesting findings, among which was the fact that sex stereotypes are remarkably similar across the diverse cultures in their sample. The similarities and few differences were interestingly discussed along various theoretical lines.

In the present volume, Williams and Best give us an extension of their research with the Adjective Check List. The main topics in this book are gender roles and perception of self, examined again from a multicultural perspective. The methodology was similar to that used in the earlier study, but this time they added the Sex-Role Ideology Scale. Both methods were employed in 14 countries using samples of university students. The present volume is clearly a sequel to Volume 6 as well as an extension and elaboration of methodology and theoretical viewpoints that the authors thoughtfully employed to help explain the results.

Volume 6 and the present volume are unique contributions to the substantive and methodological literature in cross-cultural psychological research. Cross-cultural research, especially that involving collaboration, is expensive and difficult to coordinate both conceptually and logistically. It is to Williams and Best's great and enduring credit that they have provided us with this interesting study. Its welcome thread of continuity, which is very rare in cross-cultural research, helps to weave the kind of nomological network that is often so painfully absent in all kinds of psychological research. We are very happy that this book appears in this series. We applaud the sensitivity, competence, tenacity, and patience of John Williams and Deborah Best.

Walter J. Lonner
John W. Berry

PREFACE

This book reports the findings of a study of perceptions of self and ideal self, and sex-role ideology, among women and men in 14 countries. This work may be viewed as the sequel to our earlier book *Measuring Sex Stereotypes: A Thirty-Nation Study*, a revised edition of which is being published concurrently with the present volume. The principal link between the two projects is that it is the earlier book's culture-specific definitions of sex stereotypes—the psychological characteristics differentially associated with women and men—which provide the basis for the culture-specific scoring of masculinity/feminity in the present volume. Readers interested in the subject matter of either of these volumes will want to familiarize themselves with that of the other.

In making this report on our second, large-scale, cross-cultural study, we continue to be impressed by the cooperative attitude and general good will that pervades the international community of psychological scientists. With grant funds to support large-scale cross-cultural projects being difficult to find, projects such as the present one are dependent on the voluntary assistance of the cooperating researchers in other countries. The successful completion of our projects is a tribute to their genuine interest in the advancement of knowledge about similarities and differences in the behavior of persons in different cultural settings.

ACKNOWLEDGMENTS

We are deeply indebted to our cooperating researchers, listed on the title page. Appreciation is extended, also, to the university students in the 14 countries whose generous contribution of time made this project possible.

We are grateful to Kelly Morton for her work on the data analyses and to Teresa Hill and Jane Reade for their invaluable assistance in producing the manuscript.

We wish to express our thanks to the administrative officers of Wake Forest University who have assisted us in our cross-cultural work over the years and, in particular, to the University Graduate Council for its support of this project through its Research and Publication Fund.

PART I

Background

1

ISSUES AND STRATEGIES IN CROSS-CULTURAL PSYCHOLOGY

Suppose that you have been fortunate enough to make a trip to a number of different countries in Europe, Asia, Africa, and the Americas. You take your responsibilities as a tourist seriously, and in each country you spend time walking the streets and visiting public places. In several countries, you are fortunate enough to meet people personally and to visit in their homes. Let's assume further that you are a dedicated "people watcher" and are particularly interested in the men and women whom you observe, the manner in which they behave, and how they interact with one another.

During your stay in Pakistan, you observe that men are highly visible and seem to be "in charge" in most situations. You do not see many women in public places and, when you do, they appear to be on specific errands and are often dressed in a manner that makes it difficult to tell much about them. You rarely see young men and women walking together as couples, enjoying what would be called a "date" in the United States. (On the other hand, if you are from the West, you may be a bit surprised at the number of young men you see holding hands.) During your stay in Finland, you notice that men and women seem to participate equally in many activities. Heterosexual couples are everywhere, with many young women and men dressed in a similar "unisex" style. From a distance, you might even have difficulty identifying the man and the woman in the couple—something that would never happen in Pakistan.

At the conclusion of your trip, you find yourself reflecting on the various experiences you had. It is obvious that there are important differences in the manner in which men and women behave in different countries, and it seems clear that there are differences from country to country in the customs governing appropriate relations between men and women. You find yourself wondering about possible differences in the way in which people of the same gender in different countries may view themselves. Are the "self-concepts" of men different in Pakistan and Finland? Do women in Pakistan view themselves as more "feminine" than women in Finland? Are the self-perceptions of men and women more similar in Finland than in Pakistan? If you are intrigued by such questions, you may find this book of interest.

Consider four general observations concerning the human condition. First, all human groups consist of men and women—if they did not, they would not long survive as functioning groups. The second point is that all human groups seem quite concerned with differences between women and men. Although this may originate in the obvious physical dissimilarities between the sexes, most groups tend to elaborate the differences and assert that there are important *psychological* differences between men and women (e.g., men are said to be more aggressive than women, and women are said to be more nurturant than men). These putative differences, which we call *sex stereotypes*, create models concerning the expected behavior of women and men across a great variety of situations. The third observation is that persons are expected generally to conform to the same sex model, that is, men are supposed to be manlike or masculine, whereas women are supposed to be womanlike or feminine. Persons whose behavior deviates noticeably from these norms are often the subject of social concern and disapproval. Our fourth point is that all human societies have customs prescribing the manner in which men and women are to interact with one another. For example, in one society there may be a norm of male dominance, in which men are seen as controlling the relations between the sexes, whereas in another society the interactions between men and women may be relatively egalitarian.

The present work is concerned with exploring, in a limited way, the variables just described: self-concepts and ideal self-concepts, masculinity/feminity, sex-role stereotypes, and sex-trait stereotypes. Our focus is a cross-cultural one because we wish to learn how these variables are related for men and women in different countries. We will be using data collected in 14 countries to examine the self-concepts of women and men, with reference to such general factors as their relative strength, activity, and favorability. Further, we will examine the self-concepts in terms of masculinity/femininity defined with reference to local (country-specific) sex stereotypes, as determined in an earlier study (Williams & Best, 1982). We will also investigate men's and women's sex-role ideologies (i.e., their beliefs about appropriate relations between the sexes, viewed along a continuum ranging from more traditional/male-dominant views to more modern/egalitarian views). As we study the foregoing, we will be attentive to possible pancultural similarities (findings that seem invariant in all of our countries), as well as possible cross-cultural differences (findings that appear to vary systematically with cultural variables). Before proceeding to a further examination of the question of self-concept differences in men and women, we will consider some issues concerning cross-cultural psychology in general.

CROSS-CULTURAL PSYCHOLOGY

In his recent *Annual Review of Psychology* article, Segall (1986, p. 524) noted that "while all behavior occurs in cultural contexts, only a small portion of behavioral research attends to this . . . the preponderance of contemporary psychological research is still designed, conducted, and interpreted as if culture did not matter." The field of cross-cultural psychology has evolved as a self-conscious effort to rectify this neglect of cultural variables by focusing on the degree to which psychological processes vary as a result of differing cultural influences; that is, to what degree does the manner in which people think and behave vary as a function of the culture in which they have been reared and currently live? In this sense, culture can be viewed as a "treatment," or independent variable in an experiment (Poortinga & Malpass, 1986; Strodtbeck, 1964).

As one must always begin somewhere, questions in cross-cultural psychology are often conceived in terms of whether psychological principles that appear to be valid in one culture can be successfully generalized to other cultures. For example, does the theory of general intelligence as it has developed in the West also apply to Eastern cultures? Can the "law of effect" be applied universally to all human beings or are there cultures in which the effects of rewards and punishments are substantially modified by other influences? To what degree is human visual perception conditioned by variations in physical environment at different places in the world? Do American theories of organizational behavior apply equally well in other countries? Is achievement motivation a pancultural universal?

In addressing such questions, cross-cultural psychology is concerned with the exploration of the generality of psychological theories and laws across a variety of human groups. As Jahoda (1980, p. 111) put it, "The question of the extent to which basic psychological processes are common to mankind is still perhaps *the* major one being pursued in cross-cultural psychology." If generality is found, fine! If not, attempts are then made to determine the variables that account for the lack of generality.

The Meaning of *Culture*

Before proceeding further, let us pause to consider the meaning of the term *culture*. Brislin (1983, p. 367), in his *Annual Review of Psychology* article, noted that "like a number of concepts long studied by psychologists, such as personality, intelligence, and abnormal behavior, there is no one definition of culture which is widely accepted." Triandis comments further in his Introduction to the *Handbook of Cross-Cultural Psychology* (Triandis, 1980, p. 1):

> Culture is one of those notions that are ever present in the work of social scientists, but one that has been defined in so many ways that no concensus has emerged . . . culture often refers to the total attainments and activities of any specific period and group of humans, including their implements, handicrafts, agriculture, economics, music, art, religious beliefs, traditions, and language. Different writers have emphasized different aspects of this construct.

We will not add to the confusion by attempting our own formal definition of culture, but we would like to share our frame of reference regarding the concept.

At a very general level of discourse, the term *culture* is often useful as a global term referring to the complex pattern (gestalt) of variables that distinguish various human societies. For example, to ask whether differences in the behavior of industrial workers in Japan and the United States may be related to differences in Japanese "culture" and American "culture" is useful in identifying an area of investigation. The question cannot, however, be answered at this level of generality; one must examine the two "cultures" analytically and attempt to determine the more *specific cultural variables* (e.g., family structure, attitudes toward authority, and so on) that may be related to the behavioral differences we wish to understand. In Whiting's (1976) phrase, we must learn to "unpackage" cultures.[1]

There is, to the authors, a general parallel between our use of *culture* and *cultural variables*, with reference to societies, and our use of the terms *personality* and *personality variables*, with reference to individual persons. The term *personality* is useful at a general descriptive level, but efforts to understand differences in the behavior of individuals require a consideration of specific personality variables (e.g., traits). Although the term *culture* may be useful for preliminary descriptive purposes, we share the views of Munroe and Munroe (1980) and Segall (1986) that it is usually necessary to work at the level of specific cultural variables in attempting to explain behavioral variations between human societies. Thus, it now appears that the classic efforts to study personality as a function of culture (which in the view of many was largely unsuccessful—see Draguns, 1979) may be usefully redefined as the study of personality variables as a function of cultural variables. The scope and design of the present project are consistent with this latter view.[2]

An Illustrative Study

An earlier project of ours can be used to illustrate the manner in which psychologists may be drawn into a cross-cultural approach. During the 1960s and 1970s, we conducted extensive studies concerned with race and color bias among children in the United States (Williams & Morland, 1976). A major finding was that preschool American children, from various racial groups, displayed an evaluative bias favoring light-skinned over dark-skinned persons and a similar bias favoring the color *white* over the color *black*. The question then arose as to how one is to account for this relatively consistent bias favoring light over dark among American children. Is the explanation to be sought in terms of factors peculiar to the United States, including the history and current patterns of race relations in this country? Or, could there be a general human tendency toward responding more favorably to light stimuli than dark stimuli? Data from three groups of cross-cultural studies were brought to bear on these questions.

First, there was the work of Adams and Osgood (1973) in which they studied the connotative or affective meanings (the associated "feelings") of seven color names in 23 different language-culture groups in Europe, Asia, and the Americas. These investigators found that the color name *white* was evaluated more positively than the color name *black* in all groups. A second line of evidence came from our own studies of the evaluative meanings of color names among Chinese, Philipino, Thai, East Indian, Danish, and German university students. In all of these groups, the color name *white* was evaluated more positively than the color name *black* (Williams & Morland, 1976). Finally, there were our own studies of preschool children in Japan, France, Italy, Germany, England, and Scotland, all of whom displayed a prolight/antidark bias (Best, Field, & Williams, 1976; Best, Naylor, & Williams, 1975; Iwawaki, Sonoo, Williams, & Best, 1978). Particularly impressive were the findings of an unpublished study conducted by Lorraine Scholfield in Zimbabwe in which native African children demonstrated a similar bias. In view of these cross-cultural similarities, it was clear that the biases observed among children in the United States should not be attributed solely to American influences and that some broader, pancultural influences were at work.

On the basis of these three lines of evidence, we speculated that the tendency for preschool children to respond more positively to light-colored than to dark-colored stimuli may be attributable to the generalization of a tendency to prefer the light of day to the dark of night, which is attributable, at least in part, to the diurnal nature of the young human (Williams & Morland, 1976). Looking at these studies via the cross-cultural method provided a strategy for determining whether our psychological findings should be attributed primarily to cultural variables or to pancultural variables.

Problems in Cross-Cultural Psychology

In view of the obvious utility of cross-cultural findings, one can question why the cross-cultural strategy is not more widely used. The answer lies, at least in part, in the difficulty of conducting good cross-cultural research. For example, there are the obvious logistical problems in arranging to gather data in a number of countries—an effortful and time-consuming task. In addition, there are a number of methodological problems that the aspiring cross-cultural researcher must address.

Cross-cultural research is often viewed as *quasi-experimental* in nature (Campbell & Stanley, 1966; Cook & Campbell, 1979; Malpass & Poortinga, 1986). In this type of research, one studies the behavior of groups of persons who have naturally experienced different "treatments"—in this case exposure to different levels of some cultural variable(s). The objective in using this method is to approximate, as closely as possible, the experimental method in which the groups to be compared are considered equivalent on all variables except the treatment variable(s). Researchers using the quasi-experimental method must attempt to achieve equivalence in: the characteristics of the subject groups (other than the treatment difference); the research instruments; and the circumstances under which the data are collected. Only when such equivalence is approximated can the researcher comfortably conclude that observed behavioral differences are attributable to the naturally occurring treatment differences.

Quasi-experimental research is difficult enough when conducted within a single cultural group; all of the equivalence issues become greatly magnified when the research involves persons from different cultural groups.[3] Consider only the question of equivalence in research instruments when the subjects speak different languages! In Chapter 3, we will consider some of these issues as they apply to the current project. Readers wishing to learn more about these methodological problems are referred to our discussion elsewhere (Williams & Best, 1982) and to the more comprehensive consideration of these matters in Volume 2 of the *Handbook of Cross-Cultural Psychology* (Triandis & Berry, 1980) and in *Field Methods in Cross-Cultural Research* (Lonner & Berry, 1986).

Emic Versus Etic Considerations

As we have seen, the use of a cross-cultural strategy presents the researcher not only with logistical problems; there are also a number of methodological and theoretical issues that should be dealt with before a study is begun. One such issue, the *emic-etic distinction*, applies both to theoretical constructs and to measurements. Brislin (1980, pp. 390-391) commented as follows:

> Briefly, the distinction relates to two goals of cross-cultural research. The first goal is to document valid principles that describe behavior in any one culture by using constructs that the people themselves conceive as meaningful and important; this is an emic analysis. The second goal of cross-cultural research is to make generalizations across cultures that take into account all human behavior. The goal, then is theory building; that would be an etic analysis.

From the foregoing, it can be seen that the emic view is concerned with questions of intracultural validity, a culture-specific approach; the etic view is concerned with intercultural or pancultural validity, a universal view. Berry (1980b, p. 12) elaborated these concepts further:

> The *etic* approach is characterized by the presence of universals in a system. When these variables are assumed, they have been termed *imposed etic* (Berry, 1969, p. 124) or *pseudo etic* (Triandis, Malpass, & Davidson, 1972, p. 6). In such cases, these etics are usually only Euro-American emics, imposed blindly and even ethnocentrically on a set of phenomena which occur in other cultural systems. . . . On the other hand, a true etic is one which emerges from the phenomena; it is empirically derived from the common features of the phenomena. Such an etic has been termed a *derived etic.*

The terms *emic* and *etic*, and their variants, provide a useful vocabulary for the discussion of cross-cultural concepts and methodologies in the context of the present investigation. We will return to these issues in Chapters 3 and 9.

Cross-Cultural Psychology and Cultural Anthropology

At this point, the reader may be wondering about the relationship of cross-cultural psychology to cross-cultural anthropology.[4] Both disciplines are concerned with the determinants of human behavior and they both wrestle with the contribution of culture to behavioral variability. There is, however, an important difference in their orientation to the matter of generalities and differences.

One way to attempt to capture these points of view is to note that the anthropologist basically is in the "difference business." Historically, cultural anthropology evolved from observation that human behavior showed important variations from one social group to another, and nothing pleases the anthropologist more than to find a group of people who behave differently from other groups. The cross-cultural psychologist, on the other hand, is primarily in the "similarity business." Although recognizing that behaviors of concern may in fact vary from culture to culture, nothing excites the psychologist more than to find out that there are general principles of human behavior that show little if any variation across cultures. Lonner (1980) provided a thoughtful examination of this difference in orientation.

This difference in perspective, on occasion, leads anthropologists and psychologists to a lack of appreciation of the work done in the other discipline. At the worst, the anthropologist may view the psychologist as dealing with superficial generalities, whereas the psychologist may view the anthropologist as being preoccupied with trivial differences. In our view, this occasional mutual lack of appreciation is unfortunate and counterproductive. Both disciplines have made and will continue to make important contributions to knowledge concerning human behavior, despite the differences in their general orientation toward the common subject matter.

Studies Comparing Small Versus Large Numbers of Cultural Groups

The ideal study in cross-cultural psychology would involve the intensive study of relevant behaviors in each of a large number of cultures. For practical reasons, this ideal is rarely achieved. Because the problems of data collection and analysis increase in direct proportion to the number of cultures studied, most cross-cultural studies tend to fall into one of two categories: the relatively intensive study of persons from small numbers of cultural groups (perhaps 2 or 3) or the relatively less intensive study of persons from large numbers of groups (perhaps 10 or more). The two approaches have different advantages and disadvantages associated with them.

Studies involving small numbers of cultures can be further subdivided into two categories, depending on whether the research is theory-guided or purely empirical. In studies of the first type, the small number of cultures have been selected, a priori, because they differ on some salient cultural variable that, theoretically, should lead to predictable differences in behavior. A study by Munroe, Shimmin, and Munroe (1984) exemplifies this approach. In this investigation, gender understanding (e.g., classification, identity, stability, consistency) and sex-role preference were measured in 3- to 9-year-olds from traditional communities in Belize, Kenya, Nepal, and

American Samoa. These groups were chosen for comparison because the socialization practices of the Kenyan and Nepalese samples strongly emphasize sex differences that should make gender classification more salient for these children than for those in the other two groups. Contrary to the predictions, the Kenyan children achieved gender understanding later than the other groups, but their lower performance was consistent with their highly restrictive socialization practices that inhibit linguistic development and their lack of complex sociocultural experiences (e.g., contact with the urban-industrial world). Because the four cultural groups were selected on an a priori basis, the findings were easily related to well-known cultural differences.

In contrast to theory-guided research, in the purely empirical type of study involving small numbers of cultures, the groups are not chosen on a systematic theoretical basis but are usually "targets of opportunity" or convenience that happen to be available to the researcher (see Lonner & Berry, 1986). The results of this type of study may or may not prove fruitful, depending on the nature of the findings. Studies of this sort are useful and easily interpreted when no important differences are found in the behavior of the subjects from the different cultural groups. Such findings, particularly when they are complex or patterned, merely provide evidence of the generality of the psychological principles involved (e.g., Bull & David, 1986; Runge, Frey, Gollwitzer, Helmreich, & Spence, 1981). Difficulties arise, however, when significant differences are found in the behaviors of interest between or among the cultural groups. In this situation, it is rarely possible to identify the salient aspects of the different cultures that account for the findings. If behavioral differences are found between subjects from Culture A and subjects from Culture B, and if the two groups differ in a variety of cultural aspects such as religion, economic development, educational level, then it is difficult to know to which one or more of these variables one should attribute the observed differences. In contrast, the merit in studies involving large numbers of cultures is that it is sometimes possible to determine which cultural variables may be associated with the behavioral differences observed. For example, if one has obtained data from 10 or 15 countries, then it may be possible to correlate differences in behavior separately with such variables as religion, economic development, and family structure and to determine which of these variables are associated with the behavioral variation.

Let us clarify the points we are making by noting some studies involving small or large numbers of cultures. Margalit and Mauger (1985) reported a comparative study of aggressiveness and assertiveness in Israel and the United States. From their study, the authors concluded that "Israelis generally respond more aggressively than Americans. Americans tend to have greater self-confidence, are more willing to accept or give praise, and are more likely to avoid conflicts. Israelis express anger more readily and more frequently disregard others' rights" (p. 497). These are intriguing findings but how are they to be explained in view of the many cultural differences between Israeli and American societies? In their discussion, the authors have little choice but to point out several possible explanations for their findings, without being able to identify the salient cultural variables that may underlie the observed effects.

A study by Spence and Helmreich (1978) also illustrates the problem of interpretation in empirical studies with small numbers of cultural groups. This study, which is examined from a methodological viewpoint in a later chapter, compared the self-descriptive responses of American men and Brazilian men to the Personal Attributes Questionnaire, which contains traits that are male-associated or female-associated in the United States. The results of the study indicated that American male university students showed a similar degree of endorsement of male-associated and female-associated traits in their self-descriptions. The Brazilian men, however, were found to differ from the American men in that they showed a greater endorsement of female-associated traits than male-associated traits. Taking these findings at face value, how are we to explain the "greater femininity" of Brazilian men relative to American men? If Brazil and the United States differed on only one cultural variable, for instance, religion, one might try to attribute the observed differences to this influence. However, because the United States and Brazil differ on a host of culturally related variables, it is difficult to speculate as to the cultural influences that might combine to produce the observed findings.

Cultural Comparison Variables

As noted before, if one employs a relatively large number of cultural groups in a study, then it may be possible to use various cultural indices as comparison variables in order to determine which cultural factors are associated with the variation in the behavior of concern. We can illustrate this point by mentioning some of the comparison variables that were chosen for use in the present project. One set of variables has to do with religion, as indexed by the percentage of the population in a particular country belonging to various major religious groups; a second group of variables has to do with economic-social development; a third set of variables has to do with the status of women in different countries. Although there are a number of other comparison variables that could have been examined, we selected variables that were objective and for which data were readily available for the countries being studied. Measures that are more subjective, such as closeness of kinship relations or degree of religious commitment, might have been more interesting, but such indices are usually not available for all cultures being studied, and they may be inappropriate for comparison among some cultures.

One problem in using cultural comparison variables is deciding at what level of analysis to proceed. For example, with regard to religion, should countries be classified in terms of the percentage of the population that is Christian, the percentage that is Muslim, etc. or should these variables be further subdivided in terms of the percentage Protestant, percentage Catholic, or percentage in each of the major Muslim subgroups? With regard to economic-social development, should one use an overall index based on the rank of the countries in terms of a composite measure of socioeconomic development? Or, should socioeconomic variables be treated in a more specific manner by dealing with such things as gross national product, the percentage of the population that is literate, and the average educational level in the population? Generally, our approach has been to use composite indices but also to examine certain component indices when available. Thus, for the religion variable, we will index the percentage of the population with a Christian affiliation but will also use percentage Protestant and percentage Catholic indices because the latter indices are statistically independent and, at times, show different relationships with the behaviors we are studying.

There is another problem in the use of cultural comparison variables of the type described. This arises from the fact that many of the cultural comparison variables, although operationally independent, are empirically related to one another. For example, if one picks a diverse group of countries and correlates the percentage of the population with a Protestant-Christian affiliation with an index of socioeconomic development, one will find a reasonably strong positive correlation between the two. In a cross-cultural study, if one finds that the behavior of interest covaries with both of these comparison variables then it is difficult, if not impossible, to tease out whether one or the other or both of the variables underlie the behavioral variation observed.

Many of the problems encountered with studies examining small numbers of cultures do not arise when a larger number of cultures are investigated. We will now describe, in some detail, two recent cross-cultural psychology studies in which relatively large numbers of countries were included. This discussion serves the dual purpose of illustrating the earlier point concerning the advantages of employing relatively large numbers of cultural samples and also of describing some substantive findings that are relevant to the current project.

Hofstede's Study of Work-Related Values

Hofstede (1980) compared work-related values in 40 countries by obtaining access to attitude survey data obtained from thousands of employees of subsidiaries of one large multinational business organization, coded as HERMES, which manufactures and sells high-technology products. The company had conducted a survey of its employees in order to gain information about a variety of topics. Included within the 150-item questionnaire were a number of items concerning work-related values, and it is these items that Hofstede extracted and used in his investigation.

Employing factor-analytic techniques, Hofstede derived four scales of work-related values. The first scale was called *Power Distance* and indicated the extent to which people within a society accept the idea that power in institutions and organizations is distributed unequally. The second scale was called *Uncertainty Avoidance*, indicating lack of tolerance for uncertainty and ambiguity. The third scale, *Individualism*, reflected the degree to which people are supposed to take care of themselves and their immediate families only, as opposed to situations in which persons can expect their relatives, clan, or organization to look after them. The final scale was named *Masculinity* and expresses the extent to which "masculine" values of assertiveness, money, and things prevail in a society rather than the "feminine" values of nurturance, quality of life, and people. Hofstede notes that across the 40 countries the Power Distance and Individualism scales were negatively correlated ($r = -.67$), but he felt that they were sufficiently distinct, conceptually, to use the scores separately in his analyses.

For each of the 40 countries in the study, Hofstede derived an index on each of the four work-related value variables. These scores were then correlated across countries with a variety of national comparison variables, including wealth (gross national product per capita), economic growth, latitude, population size, population growth, and population density. These analyses revealed a large number of intriguing relationships between the work-related values in different countries and the comparison variables. For example, countries with high Power Distance scores tended to be economically poorer countries, in the relatively low latitudes (close to the equator), and with relatively high population growth rates. An opposite set of findings was obtained for the Individualism scores: Countries with more individualistic values tended to be wealthier countries, in the higher latitudes (farther from the equator), and with relatively low population growth rates. On the other hand, economic growth rate in the different countries was unrelated either to Power Distance or to Individualism indices. Although this type of analysis does not point conclusively to the cultural factors responsible for variation in the psychological data, it can be used to narrow the range of possible explanations.

Williams and Best's Study of Sex Stereotypes

A second cross-cultural study involving a large sample of countries is our earlier cross-cultural sex-stereotype project (Williams & Best, 1982). This study was concerned with identifying the attributes differentially associated with women and men by young adults and young children in 30 countries. In 25 countries where adult data were collected (see Table 1.1), the 300 items of the Adjective Check List (ACL—Gough & Heilbrun, 1965, 1980b) were used as the basis of our method. These items, originally chosen as generally descriptive of differences in human behavior, are listed in Appendix A.

In each country, approximately 100 university students of both sexes were asked to serve as cultural reporters and to indicate for each item (or its translated equivalent) whether, in their culture, the item was more frequently associated with women, more frequently associated with men, or not differentially associated with the sexes. The responses of the subjects in each country were then tallied to determine for each item the frequency with which it was identified as male-associated and female-associated in a particular country. These two frequencies for each country were then employed to compute an *M% score* for each item according to the formula: M% = Male Frequency/(Male Frequency + Female Frequency) × 100.

If, for example, an item was reported by 90 subjects as male-associated and by 10 subjects as female-associated, the M% score would be 90%. On the other hand, if only 10 subjects said the item was male-associated and 90 said it was female-associated, the M% score would be 10%. Thus, it can be seen that highly male-associated items received high M% scores and highly female-associated items received low M% scores, that is, low M% scores could also be called *high F% scores*. In this manner, an M% score was computed for each of the 300 items so that each of the countries had its own array of 300 M% scores reflecting the relative association of each of the attributes with men and women. (The M% arrays for the 14 countries in the present project will be found in Appendix A.) Given the M% scores for all 300 items in a particular country, one can compute the mean and variance of any given subset of these items; for example, the items which an individual person might select as being descriptive of herself.

The M% scores obtained in each country provided the basis for our comparative study of sex stereotypes. Analyses were conducted first at the level of individual items and second by scoring the items in terms of three theoretical systems (Affective Meanings, Ego States, Psychological Needs). Working at the item level, we used the M% scores to compute correlation coefficients across the 300 items for all possible pairs of countries. All of the obtained coefficients were positive, indicating that there was some general agreement across countries in the attributes differentially ascribed to women and men. On the other hand, our analyses indicated that there were substantial differences in the degree of shared variation or common variance (r^2) between various pairs of countries, with some pairs being much more similar than others. For example, the common variance between England and the United States was 80%, whereas that between England and Pakistan was only 19%. These scores suggest that variations in M% scores have similar patterns in England and the United States, but rather different patterns in England and Pakistan.

We computed the mean and variance of the M% scores for all 300 items in each country with the results shown in Table 1.1. The mean M% scores indicate the degree to which the total item pool is viewed as more masculine or more feminine. Here it can be seen that there were some noticeable differences in the mean M% scores, suggesting that the total group of 300 items tended to be somewhat more male-associated in certain countries (e.g., Italy and India) and somewhat more female-associated in the other countries (e.g., Nigeria and Trinidad). The differences in the variances were even more dramatic, varying from 934 (SD = 30.6) in the Netherlands to 221 (SD = 14.9) in Venezuela. As large variances would be produced by having relatively large numbers of extreme M% scores, high (masculine) and low (feminine), whereas low variances would be produced by having small numbers of such extreme items, the differences among variances can be considered to reflect variation among countries in the degree to which men and women were viewed as being different in terms of their psychological makeup. In high variance countries, men and women were seen as relatively more different; in low variance countries, men and women were seen as relatively less different.

That the differences seen in Table 1.1 should not be dismissed as sampling errors was demonstrated by findings indicating that the distribution of means and the distribution of variances were each related to several cultural comparison variables. Across all 25 countries, the item-pool means tended to be higher (more masculine) in Catholic than in Protestant countries, higher in less-developed countries, and higher in countries where Hofstede's (1980) findings had indicated strong male work-related values emphasizing power and formal structure and deemphasizing individualism (Williams & Best, 1982, Appendix D). Although the reason for this effect is not clear, it may reflect a greater "salience" or "importance" assigned to men or male-associated characteristics in these countries. The item-pool variances tended

Table 1.1 Descending Orders of Means and Variances of 300 M% Scores in Each of 25 Countries[a]

Means		*Variances*	
Italy	63.5	Netherlands	934
India	59.4	Finland	831
Peru	58.8	Norway	760
Bolivia	57.0	Germany	756
Brazil	56.0	Malaysia	756
Israel	55.4	Nigeria	692
France	55.3	United States	670
Germany	53.9	Israel	654
England	53.4	Australia	652
Japan	52.5	Canada	631
Venezuela	52.5	Trinidad	629
United States	52.3	Japan	592
Pakistan	52.2	England	589
South Africa	52.2	South Africa	583
Netherlands	52.1	Peru	580
New Zealand	51.8	Italy	571
Norway	51.4	Pakistan	555
Scotland	51.4	Brazil	482
Finland	50.6	Ireland	456
Ireland	50.3	France	446
Canada	49.1	New Zealand	442
Malaysia	49.0	India	430
Australia	48.4	Scotland	296
Trinidad	46.7	Bolivia	261
Nigeria	46.3	Venezuela	221

a. The values for Singapore, where data were obtained subsequently, were: Mean, 48.6; Variance, 582.

to be higher (men and women seen as relatively more different) in Protestant than in Catholic countries, higher in more developed countries, and higher in countries where male work-related values placed less emphasis on power, assertiveness, money, and things and more emphasis on individualism (Williams & Best, 1982, Appendix D). It is interesting to note that in more developed countries with more individualistic value systems, the two sexes were viewed as more differentiated in terms of their psychological makeup than in less developed countries with more communal value systems.

On the basis of the foregoing findings, it appeared that the observed variations in means and variances were at least partially reflective of bona fide cultural differences, rather than merely reflective of sampling variation. These differences in means and variances will be seen to have important consequences in the present project when the M% scores for a given country are used as a basis for assessing the masculinity/femininity of the self-descriptions and ideal self-descriptions of persons from that country.

Table 1.2 Summary of Pancultural Similarities in Sex-Trait Stereotypes

	More Characteristic of Men	*More Characteristic of Women*	*Not Differentially Characteristic*
Affective Meanings			
	Active	Passive	Favorability
	Strong	Weak	
Ego States			
	Critical Parent	Nurturing Parent	Free Child
	Adult	Adapted Child	
Psychological Needs			
	Dominance	Abasement	Order
	Autonomy	Deference	Intraception
	Aggression	Succorance	Change
	Exhibition	Nurturance	
	Achievement	Affiliation	
	Endurance	Heterosexuality	

In addition to the item-level M% analyses, the cross-cultural sex-stereotype data were also analyzed by identifying the "focused" male and female stereotypes in each country and scoring these according to three different, theoretically based systems. In a given country, the focused male stereotype was defined as those adjectives that were associated at least twice as often with men as with women (i.e., M% scores of 67% and up). Similarly, the focused female stereotype was defined as those items that were associated at least twice as often with women as with men (i.e., M% scores of 33% and down). The three separate scoring systems were then applied to the groups of focused male and focused female stereotype items in each country.

The first scoring system (Best, Williams, & Briggs, 1980; Williams & Best, 1977) characterized each of the focused stereotypes in terms of three dimensions of affective meaning: favorability, strength, and activity. The second scoring system (Williams & Williams, 1980) summarized the stereotypes in terms of the five functional ego states of Transactional Analysis (Berne, 1961, 1966): Critical Parent, Nurturing Parent, Adult, Free Child, and Adapted Child. The third scoring system (Gough & Heilbrun, 1980b) characterized the stereotypes in terms of 15 psychological needs (Dominance, Abasement, Autonomy, etc.). Each of these analyses revealed substantial cross-cultural similarity in the psychological characteristics differentially ascribed to women and men. These findings, summarized in Table 1.2, were sufficient to support the proposal of a general pancultural model concerning the alleged psychological makeup of women and men, with cultural differences being viewed as variations around this model.

Let us illustrate. The Affective Meaning analysis indicated that, in all 25 countries, the male stereotype items were higher in Strength than were the female stereotype items. On the other hand, there was considerable variation in the magnitude of this effect, which was quite pronounced in countries such as Nigeria and Japan and much less pronounced in Italy and the United States. Similarly, in all countries the male stereotype items were higher than the female items in Activity but this effect was much larger in countries such as Nigeria and Pakistan than in countries such as India and Japan. Interestingly, there was no pancultural effect for Favorability, which was higher for the male stereotype in some countries (e.g., Japan, Nigeria, and Malaysia), higher for the female stereotype in other countries (e.g., Italy and India), and essentially equal in others (e.g., Finland and Trinidad).[5]

Although in all countries the male stereotype tended to be stronger and more active than the female stereotype, the variations in the *degree* of these effects were found to be related to cultural comparison variables (Williams & Best, 1982, Appendix D). For example, the magnitude of both the Strength and Activity differences between the male and female stereotypes was found to be greater in socioeconomically less developed countries than in more developed countries. Strength and Activity differences also tended to be greater in countries where the literacy percentage was low and the percentage of women attending the university was low. These findings suggested that economic and educational advancement may be accompanied by a reduction in the tendency to view men as stronger and more active than women.

The findings from the sex-stereotype study just described provide a major foundation for the current project. At a pancultural, etic level, we will inquire as to the degree to which the strength and activity differences found in the sex stereotypes also appear in the self-perceptions of men and women. At a culture-specific, emic level, we will observe the degree to which the stereotype items characteristic of a local culture are incorporated into the self-descriptions of men and women from that particular culture.

AN OVERVIEW OF THE BOOK

We will consider, in Chapter 2, general questions dealing with the self-perceptions of men and women, with particular attention to the topic of masculinity/femininity. We will also introduce the topic of sex-role ideology (i.e., beliefs concerning appropriate role-relations between the sexes).

The method involved in the current project is described in Chapter 3, followed by a critical evaluation of the method, noting its strengths and weaknesses from the perspective of the authors. In Chapters 4-7 we report the results of the project, the interpretations of which are, for the most part, reserved for Chapter 8. We will consider first, in Chapter 4, the findings related to sex-role ideology in the 14 countries. We chose to consider these findings first so that the subsequent results regarding self-concept may be related back to the sex-role ideology findings. The results related to the self-concepts of men and women are described in Chapters 5, 6, and 7 where we deal first with men's and women's self-concepts in terms of affective meaning, then consider the self-concepts in terms of masculinity/femininity, and finally examine the self-concepts in terms of diversity of masculinity/femininity.

The final chapters in the book provide a summary and interpretation of the findings. In Chapter 8 we provide a nontechnical review and interpretation of the principal findings in terms of cross-cultural similarities and differences in sex-role ideology and self-concept. In Chapter 9, we take a broader view of the project as we reexamine the study in terms of some of the basic issues in cross-cultural psychology and suggest directions for future research.

SUMMARY

In this chapter we have discussed some of the issues and strategies in cross-cultural research. The need to focus on cultural variables rather than culture, per se, was discussed and commonly encountered problems of "equivalence" in studies conducted in different cultural settings were noted. We commented on questions of intracultural (emic) and intercultural (etic) validity and the use of cultural comparison variables in multicountry studies. Because of their relevance to the present study, Hofstede's (1980) study of work-related values and Williams and Best's (1982) study of sex stereotypes were described in some detail. We ended the chapter with an overview of the remainder of the book.

NOTES

1. Berry (1979, 1980a) has designed carefully constructed models for the process of attempting to unpackage cultures.

2. Readers interested in differing views as to the importance of a well-defined, general concept of culture for work in cross-cultural psychology are referred to the debate involving Jahoda (1984), Rohner (1984), and Segall (1984) in the June 1984 issue of the *Journal of Cross-Cultural Psychology*.

3. Lonner (1979) noted four major types of equivalence which must be considered: functional, conceptual, linguistic, and metric.

4. Not all *cultural* anthropologists are *cross-cultural* anthropologists. Many cultural anthropologists advocate an "hermeneutic" approach in which an attempt is made to develop a

complete understanding of a single cultural system, in its own terms, without reference to any other cultural systems. This approach, with its lack of concern with generalizations about human behavior, often seems "antiscientific" to the cross-culturally oriented anthropologist and psychologist. Recently, Packer (1985) has advocated an hermeneutic approach to psychological research, in general.

5. In the United States, the female stereotype was noticeably more favorable than the male stereotype. Americans who feel that the male stereotype is somehow "better" than the female stereotype are probably responding to the greater strength and activity of the former.

2

GENDER, SELF-CONCEPT, AND SEX-ROLE IDEOLOGY

An important and perhaps distinctive human characteristic is the ability to view oneself as an object (Mead, 1934; Wylie, 1968). We observe our own behavior in a variety of situations, compare ourselves to other persons, and draw conclusions about the sort of people that we are and wish to become. In this and other ways we develop an overall perception of ourselves; once formed, this self-concept becomes an important determiner of our future behavior. Psychologists from William James to Carl Rogers have assigned considerable importance to the self-concept in their attempts to understand and explain human behavior. Further, it appears that psychologists' interest in self-concept has been increasing in recent years as seen, for example, in the expanded coverage given to this topic in more recent texts in social psychology.

Self-Concept: Generic = Actual + Ideal

Wylie (1968) has reviewed the work of psychologists who have placed heavy emphasis upon the self-concept in their theoretical work.[1] From this review, she identified a list of features of the generic or all-inclusive self-concept, which Liebert and Spiegler (1987, p. 278) have summarized as follows:

1. The person's experiencing himself or herself as a distinct entity which can be differentiated from others.
2. A sense of continuing to be the same person over time.
3. A person's physical characteristics *as experienced by the person.*
4. A person's past behaviors as experienced and remembered, especially those that are perceived as having been executed voluntarily or as having been under the control of the person.
5. The experiencing of a degree of organization or unity among the various aspects of the generic self-concept.
6. Evaluations, thoughts, and memories.
7. Varying degrees of consciousness or unconsciousness.

Wylie suggested that the enormous complexity and inclusiveness of the generic self-concept might become more manageable and useful by the

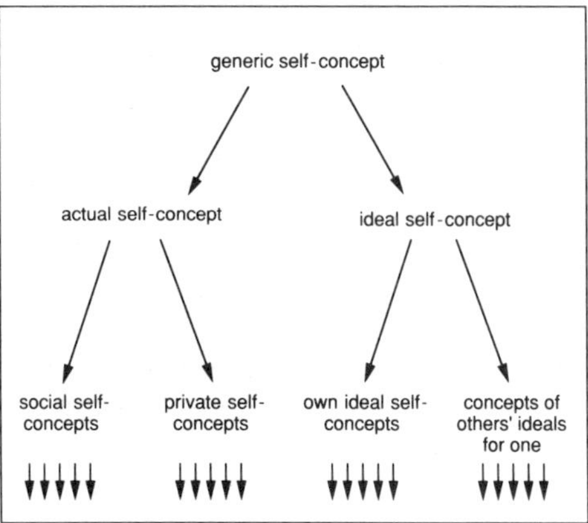

Figure 2.1. Wylie's Analysis of the Self-Concept
SOURCE: Adapted from Wylie(1968)

conceptual subdivisions suggested in Figure 2.1. First, the generic self-concept is divided into the *actual self-concept* (what I am) and the *ideal self-concept* (what I wish to become). The actual self-concept is then further divided into one's private self-concept (how I see myself) and one's social self-concept (the way I present myself to others). The ideal self-concept is also divided into *the way I want to be* and *the ideals that others have for me*.

The plan in the present project is congruent with Wylie's proposal that one should study both actual self-concepts and ideal self-concepts. Although we do not claim that our measures represent all features of the generic self-concept, our use of both actual self-measures and ideal self-measures certainly provides a better approximation than does the use of only actual self-measures, as is often done in studies of self-concept.

Self-Concepts of Men and Women

One can argue that there should be, on the average, some differences in the self-concepts of women and men. The pancultural sex stereotypes, discussed in the preceding chapter, assert that men and women are psychologically different along a number of dimensions and the models provided by the stereotypes would appear to encourage women and men to view themselves differently. This is particularly true as research indicates that children learn sex stereotypes at an early age. Our own research with young children in 24 countries (Williams & Best, 1982) indicates that most 5-year-old children have learned some of the principal components of the sex stereotypes. This knowledge increases during the early school years so that by age 11 most children are aware of most components of the adult-defined stereotypes. Thus, children grow up in societies that believe that men and women are psychologically different, and this would appear to encourage the children to perceive themselves in ways that are congruent with their own gender models.

This is not, however, a purely cognitive matter. Most societies engage in differential socialization practices, with boys being treated differently (Block, 1979; Lewis & Weinraub, 1979; Moss, 1974) and being encouraged to engage in certain types of activities whereas girls are encouraged to participate in different activities (Barry, Bacon, & Child, 1957; Ember, 1981). Participation in these activities and the associated rewards provide another reason for expecting women to perceive themselves somewhat differently than do men. Similar reasoning leads to the expectation of differences in the ideal selves of men and women.

There have been a host of studies concerned with the question of differences in the self-concepts of women and men. Space limitations prevent even a brief attempt to summarize the findings of these studies here. The interested reader is referred to Wylie's reviews of this literature (Wylie, 1974, 1979). We will content ourselves with two general observations. First, we note that in most investigations comparing the self-concepts of men and women, some differences are found and these are most often congruent with the sex stereotypes (Bem, 1974; Spence, Helmreich, & Stapp, 1974, 1975; Williams & Best, 1982). The second point is that the differences observed are usually relatively small in magnitude; that is, the modal self-perceptions of men and women are not dramatically different (Deaux, 1984; Spence, Deaux, & Helmreich, 1985; Williams & Best, 1982). Another way to put this is that the self-concept differences *within* each of the two gender groups are usually much greater than the average differences *between* the gender groups. The personality differences among men and among women are much greater than the average differences between men and women.

As an illustration of the foregoing, we can note the standard psychological needs scoring system for self-descriptions obtained via the Adjective Check List (Gough & Heilbrun, 1980b). If one examines the ACL manual, one observes that separate norms are provided for women and men, reflecting the authors' judgment that men's and women's self-descriptive responses to the Adjective Check List were sufficiently different to require separate gender comparison groups. On the other hand, an examination of the normative tables for men and women indicates that in most instances the gender differences are relatively small in relation to the wide differences found among persons within each of the two gender groups. On the basis of evidence such as this, we conclude that although there are average self-concept differences between women and men, these differences are not as dramatic as many people would perhaps expect. In other words, most of the variability among people in self-concepts is *not* related to gender.

Choice of Assessment Instrument

There are a large number of personality assessment methods that might be considered for use in a cross-cultural study of self-concept and, if one were designing such a study, de novo, it would be a major task to determine what instruments should be used. We did not face this problem because our self-concept study was an outgrowth of our earlier sex-stereotype project (Williams & Best, 1982). It was obvious that we should use the Adjective Check List as our personality assessment procedure because we had employed the ACL items in our sex-stereotype project, and because we wanted to relate the findings of the two studies. It should be noted that the ACL is in wide use as a self-descriptive personality assessment procedure in the United States and other countries, particularly in Italy and France.

Another advantage in using the ACL is the ease with which it can be adapted to the assessment of the ideal self-concept. Few persons are fully content with themselves as they are and their aspirations for change may be psychologically significant. For this reason, we wished to study not only the perceived self (what I am) but also the ideal self (what I would like to be) of our women and men subjects. The assessment of both actual and ideal self-concepts provided the opportunity to make analyses of the total or generic self-concept, viewed as the sum of the two components.

Having decided to use the ACL for the description of self and ideal self, there was the question of which of the alternative scoring systems to use in the analyses of the findings: the 3-factor Affective Meaning scoring system (Best et al., 1980; Williams & Best, 1977); the 5-factor Ego State scoring system (Williams & Williams, 1980); or the 15-factor Psychological Needs scoring system[2] (Gough & Heilbrun, 1980b). We chose to use the Affective Meaning scoring system for two reasons: First, the work of Osgood and his associates (Osgood, May, & Miron, 1975) suggested that the Affective Meaning system might have greater pancultural validity than the other two systems, which may be more subject to American bias; and second, the practical matter that it is easier to deal with self-concept scored in terms of 3 scores, rather than 5 or 15. (In a study involving 1,563 subjects from 14 countries, we were looking for any legitimate way to simplify our task!) For these reasons, we chose to examine the self-concepts of men and women in terms of affective meanings, that is, in terms of their relative strength, activity, and favorability.

As noted in the preceding chapter, the sex-stereotype project revealed that in all countries studied, men were viewed as being stronger and more active than women. We wished to explore the question of whether these general differences in the sex stereotypes would also be reflected in the self-perceptions and ideal self-perceptions of men and women in different countries. Further, we wished to determine whether the degree to which the stereotypes were incorporated into the self-perceptions would be found to differ systematically in relationship to various cultural comparison variables such as socioeconomic development, religion, and the status of women.

Our second approach to the examination of men's and women's self-concepts was in terms of masculinity/femininity, defined as the degree to which persons in a particular culture incorporate male-associated and female-associated characteristics from that culture into their own self-descriptions. The concepts of masculinity and femininity have a long and checkered history. We will now examine these concepts and review the different approaches that researchers have used in studying the self-concepts of men and women from this perspective.

MASCULINITY/FEMININITY

The twin concepts of masculinity and femininity appear in most, if not all, cultures; a concern for what is manlike and womanlike seems an intrinsic component of the folk psychology of human societies. Phrases such as "She is quite feminine" or "He is very masculine" are usually used in an approving way, whereas phrases such as "She is somewhat masculine" or "He is a bit feminine" usually carry perjorative undertones. There seems to be a clear expectation that men are expected to be manlike and women are expected to be womanlike, and that significant departures from these expectations result in negative social concern or disapproval. The widespread popular use of the concepts of masculinity and femininity, and the social importance ascribed to them, have led psychologists and other scientists to consider these concepts worthy of systematic study. Some psychologists have attempted to incorporate these concepts into their theories because of the social significance attached to the concepts by ordinary persons. We must remind ourselves that psychologists did not invent masculinity and femininity.

An examination of the popular conception of masculinity and femininity (M/F) suggests that it is predicated on two general facts. First, there is the observation that certain attributes or characteristics are, or are believed to be, found more frequently in one gender or the other. Let us illustrate this point by describing two hypothetical Americans. The first person is tall and heavily muscled with abundant body hair and a low-pitched voice, is aggressive and independent in personality style, and wears relatively plain clothing. The second person is short and lightly muscled, with little body hair and a high-pitched voice, is unassertive and dependent in personality style, and wears highly ornamented clothing. Although it is possible that the first person might prove to be a woman and the second person a man, we believe that the reader will agree that the reverse is much more likely to be true. This is because the first group of attributes are more frequently found in American men and the second group in American women and, thus, it is uncommon to find a woman possessing the first group and a man possessing the second.

The second idea underlying the concept of M/F has already been anticipated in the foregoing illustration; namely, the observation that within each gender group there is substantial variation in attributes among individual persons. All women are not alike; neither are all men. With few exceptions, the characteristics considered to be more manlike and more womanlike also vary among members within each gender group. Thus, the attributes of one woman may be almost entirely womanlike, the attributes of a second woman may be a mixture of manlike and womanlike, and the attributes of a third woman may be almost entirely manlike—although the latter would be unusual. Following conventional definitions (Bem, 1974; Spence et al., 1974), the first woman would be described as feminine, the second woman as androgynous (having characteristics of both sexes), and the third woman as masculine. Thus, we see that the M/F concept is based first on the establishment of what is manlike and womanlike and second on the assessment of the individual person's attributes with regard to this classification. To put this more formally, the scientific study of M/F requires: (1) a method for the empirical definition of sex stereotypes, the characteristics believed to be differentially distributed in women and men; (2) a method for assessing the attributes of the individual person; and (3) a system for comparing the individual's attributes to the sex stereotypes. Thus, it can be seen that the sex stereotypes serve as the criterion, or "yardstick," against which the masculinity/femininity of the individual person is assessed. In passing, we note that the term *stereotype* is used here in its contemporary, cognitive sense to indicate beliefs about the differing characteristics of social groups (Insko & Schopler, 1972; McCauley, Stitt, & Segal, 1980; Tajfel, 1969) and not in the earlier sense in which stereotypes referred to belief systems linked to prejudice toward social groups and were assumed to reflect a defective or distorted type of thinking.

A comprehensive, multidimensional assessment (Spence et al., 1985) of sex stereotypes and, subsequently of M/F, would be an enormous task, involving the consideration of psychological traits, physical characteristics, and social roles and conventions (e.g., dress). Furthermore, it is not clear what relationships may, or may not, exist among these different "types" of M/F. The fact that the study of M/F in terms of psychological traits has received more attention than the other types should not be taken to indicate that psychological M/F is more important than the others. Myers and Gonda (1982), in a study in which persons were asked to define the terms *masculine* and *feminine* using an open-ended format, found that physical attributes were mentioned more frequently than psychological attributes.

Studies focusing on physical attributes have shown that young adults make reliable judgments of masculinity and femininity based on head-and-shoulder photographs. Furthermore, strong links have been found between the M/F of persons judged from their photographs and their physical attractiveness (PA) judged from the same photos. Lucker, Beane, and Helmreich (1981) found a .53 correlation between university students' judgments of the masculinity and the physical attractiveness of male targets, whereas the correlation for female targets was .85. In an unpublished 1986 study from our own laboratory, Lisa Siebert found that ratings by university student subjects revealed a .64 correlation between male targets' PA and masculinity and a .85 correlation between female targets' PA and femininity. The similar findings of the two studies indicate that the type of masculinity and femininity judged from photos is predictably related to physical attractiveness, with the relationship being particularly strong for women targets. In the latter case, it seems likely that women judged as feminine from photographs would be the beneficiaries of many of the positive attributions made to women judged to be physically attractive (e.g., Dermer & Thiel, 1975; Dion, Berscheid, & Walster, 1972; Gillen, 1981; Jackson, 1983); positive attributions to physically masculine men would also be expected but not to the same degree as with women. There has been, unfortunately, little systematic study of the relationship between M/F based on physical features and M/F judged from psychological characteristics. The exploration of this question is important in determining whether M/F, assessed in different ways, is a unitary or multidimensional concept.

Because there is no basis for claiming that M/F based on psychological traits is more important than M/F judged in other ways, one may inquire as to why, in the current project, we have chosen to restrict ourselves to psychological stereotypes and psychological M/F. The reason is that we have the most to contribute in this realm. Our previous cross-cultural studies in which we defined the psychological sex stereotypes in a large number of countries can serve as the criteria for a cross-cultural study of psychological

M/F. Our subsequent discussion of sex stereotypes and M/F will be confined to the psychological domain.

Considerations in the Measurement of Sex Stereotypes

In principle, the determination of psychological sex stereotypes would involve a consideration of all possible psychological traits with regard to whether they were differentially distributed by gender. Practically speaking, this would be an impossible task. In the English language, for example, Allport and Odbert (1936) identified 17,953 words referring to psychological or personality characteristics. Even after the elimination of synonymic words, the number of traits to be included in an exhaustive study of sex stereotypes would be overwhelming. But, if we cannot be exhaustive at least we should be comprehensive, using a list of traits that seem to sample much of the variability in human personality.

Our point can be illustrated by noting the practice among some researchers (e.g., Bem, 1974; Berzins, Welling, & Wetter, 1978; Spence & Helmreich, 1978) of including only positively valued (good) traits in their measures of M/F. This limitation precludes the study of the negative side of sex stereotypes, which is very real: for example, men are said to be more cruel and coarse, women are said to be more fickle and frivolous (Williams & Best, 1982). Studying only positively valued traits leads to an overly benign view of sex stereotypes and of related concepts such as androgyny.

Another desirable feature in a sex-stereotype assessment method is that it should lead to some type of scaling of the *degree* to which given traits are associated with one sex or the other so that this may be taken into account in the subsequent assessment of M/F. For example, the traits *aggressive*, *adventuresome*, *alert*, and *awkward* are all generally associated with men in the United States but the first two traits are more highly associated than the last two. Similarly, *affectionate*, *emotional*, *loyal*, and *resentful* are all female-associated traits but the former two are more highly associated than the latter two (Williams & Best, 1982). It seems consistent with our general rationale for the assessment of masculinity and femininity that traits highly associated with a given gender should be given more weight in determining overall masculinity/femininity scores than traits that are only moderately associated. Other researchers (e.g., Bem, 1974; Berzins et al., 1978; Spence & Helmreich, 1978), not sharing this view, have been content to use a categorical classification of items as simply masculine or feminine (or neutral), without attempting to represent the variability in degree of association within these categories. In our earlier study of sex stereotypes (Williams & Best, 1982), we represented degree of association by an M% score, which reflected the relative frequency with which a trait was associated with men relative to its association with women. Thus, the higher the M% score the more highly the trait was associated with men, and the lower the M% score the more highly it was associated with women. M% scores near 50% indicated items that were equally associated with both sexes.

Considerations in the Assessment of the Individual

There are at least three approaches to the assessment of attributes of individual persons: ratings by others based on direct observation of a person's behavior; ratings by others presumed to be familiar with an individual's typical behavior; and ratings made by the individuals themselves. Although M/F researchers have shown a strong preference for the self-report method, a wider perspective is gained by a brief consideration of all three.

Direct Observation. The attributes of an individual person can be assessed by a concensus among trained persons who have observed his or her behavior across a variety of situations. This method has evolved from social learning theory and is often employed in executive assessment programs where several judges watch participants interact with one another as they work on a variety of tasks across a period of several days. Historically, the 300-item Adjective Check List, which we use for stereotype assessment and for self-description, was first developed by Harrison Gough and his associates to enable staff members to record their impressions of participants at the Institute of Personality Assessment and Research at the University of California, Berkeley. Applying this rationale to the study of M/F, descriptions of individuals obtained by direct observation could be scored in terms of previously established sex stereotypes to obtain a measure of M/F.

Ratings by Familiar Others. In this method, persons presumed to have observed the individual's behavior in many real life situations provide the ratings. The raters may be family members, friends, or work associates. An illustration of this method is provided in an exercise which has been employed at the Center for Creative Leadership in Greensboro, North Carolina. Before arriving for a week-long executive assessment program, the participants ask several of their associates to describe them employing a 48-item ACL. If one were using this approach in studying M/F, the consensus among several assessors could be used to obtain a list of attributes which could then be scored for M/F by reference to sex stereotype data.

Self-Descriptions. Self-descriptions, the most popular method for the assessment of M/F, provide a rich but somewhat troublesome approach to the assessment of M/F (Wylie, 1974). The richness is due to the fact that the individuals themselves have had innumerable opportunities to observe their own behavior and, in principle, should know themselves better than any other person could. The troublesome part of a self-description is that it may be distorted by the individual's personal motives. When the observer and the observed are the same person, the resulting description may be something less than totally objective!

Self-descriptions are least accurate when there are external incentives to be other than frank, for example, when one is completing a personality inventory as part of a job application. Even when one endeavors to give the most honest self-appraisal, there is the ever present motive of self-esteem or positive self-presentation (Jones & Pittman, 1982) which leads to the tendency to emphasize positive traits and deemphasize negative ones. Everyone has known someone who seemed oblivious of some negative trait that was all too obvious to the persons around him or her.

A unique aspect of the self-descriptive approach is the opportunity to inquire not only about the perceived self (as I am) but also about the ideal self (as I would like to be). The examination of both of these concepts adds another dimension to the study of M/F, one which has received little attention in previous research.

We noted earlier in our discussion of sex-stereotype definition that it seemed desirable to assess the *degree* to which particular traits are associated with a given gender. When this is done, there are two principal consequences for the scoring of self-descriptions for M/F. First, it is possible to obtain a weighted mean based on all the items that are indicated as self-descriptive rather than simply counting the number of masculine, feminine, and neutral items endorsed, as is done in some other M/F assessment procedures (e.g., Heilbrun, 1981). Thus, a man who describes himself using *highly* male-associated items (such as aggressive and adventuresome) will obtain a higher mean score than a man who describes himself with *moderately* male-associated items (such as alert and awkward).

In our previous cross-cultural study of sex stereotypes, we computed an M% score for each of the 300 items in a particular country; the higher the M% score the greater the degree of male-association, and the lower the M% score the greater the degree of female-association. This enabled us, in the present investigation, to score a given self-description by computing the mean M% score for the subset of items which the individual had indicated as his or her characteristics. Thus, a mean self-description M% score of 60% would indicate relative masculinity, and a mean score of 40% would indicate relative femininity. The mean M% score of the individual's ideal self-description can be computed in a similar manner, enabling one to determine whether the M/F of the ideal self differs from that of the perceived self.

The second advantage in using weighted stereotype items is that it is possible to index the variability of the subset of items that an individual checks as self-descriptive. A basic principle of descriptive statistics is that, in comparing two score distributions, an examination of the means is not sufficient; one must also examine the variability around the means. Consequently, although two persons might produce self-descriptions that yielded identical mean M% scores (say 50%), the variability around the mean might be appreciably different because one person tended to select items with very high and very low M% scores, whereas the other used items with less extreme M% values. Therefore, the scoring of a self-description for both the mean and the variance of the items checked provides a more complete summary than does the use of the mean alone.

Psychological Androgyny. This seems an appropriate place to consider the important issue of the definition and measurement of *psychological androgyny*, which has been addressed by such investigators as Bem (1974), Berzins et al. (1978), and Spence and Helmreich (1978). Each of these investigators first obtained separate Masculinity (M) and Femininity (F) scores for each subject. Using a median-split technique, subjects were then classified into a fourfold typology: masculine (high M, low F); feminine (high F, low M); androgynous (high on both M and F); and undifferentiated (low on both M and F).[3]

The last two categories are of interest here. Both represent "balanced" self-descriptions with similar frequencies of endorsement of male-associated and female-associated items. This is analogous in our method to obtaining a weighted M% mean near 50%. It can be argued that the difference between the androgynous and the undifferentiated descriptions is that, from the point of view of M/F, the former represents a more diverse self-description and the latter a less diverse self-description. This seems akin to the variance of M% scores noted above. Therefore, in terms of our method, persons with mean M% scores near 50% and large variances might be called *androgynous*, whereas those with similar mean scores and small variances might be called *undifferentiated*. Viewed in this way, the androgyny/undifferentiated classification might be seen as a special case of the more general concept of intrasubject variance in M/F. Consistent with this view are LeVerrier's (1987) findings that persons classified as androgynous by a variety of median-split method tend to have larger individual M% variance scores than persons classified as undifferentiated. An important difference in our procedure is that the variance scores we employ can be computed not just for persons with balanced self-descriptions, but for all subjects.

Another issue related to the assessment of psychological androgyny is the question of the role of individual differences in self-esteem in generating androgynous scores. The instruments most often used in androgyny research in the United States have been the Bem Sex Role Inventory (Bem, 1974), the Personal Attributes Questionnaire (Spence & Helmreich, 1978), and the PRF Andro Scale (Berzins et al., 1978). For each of these measures, the items consist of favorable attributes which are differentially associated with men and women. Heilbrun (1981) has noted that the use of items, all of which are socially desirable, may confound the measurement of androgyny with self-esteem. Persons with high self-esteem tend to endorse large numbers of positive attributes as self-descriptive. Faced with the exclusively positive attributes on these M/F measures, the person with high self-esteem may tend to select rather large numbers of both male-associated and female-associated attributes and, thus, be classified as *androgynous*. In a similar manner, the person with low self-esteem might choose few of the positive items, masculine or feminine, and as a result be classified as *undifferentiated*. This may contribute to the usual finding of higher self-esteem for androgynous individuals when compared with undifferentiated or sex-differentiated, especially feminine-typed persons (e.g., Bem, 1977; Kelly & Worell, 1977; Spence et al., 1975). The problem of the potential confounding of self-esteem in the assessment of androgyny appears to be lessened when the subject is presented with male- and female-associated items that are both positive and negative in value (Kelly, Caudill, Hathorn, & O'Brien, 1977), as is true in the Heilbrun ACL scale and also in the procedure used in the present project.

Earlier in this chapter we limited our concern to psychological M/F. We will now focus our attention further by restricting ourselves to self-descriptive methods. Thus, we are confining our attention to one domain of sex stereotypes and to one method for the assessment of individual persons. These restrictions must be kept in mind both in the following review of previous research and in our cross-cultural study reported in later chapters.

Methods for the Assessment of Psychological Masculinity/Femininity Via Self-Descriptions

The modern era in the assessment of masculinity/femininity in the United States can be dated from the publication of Constantinople's review paper in 1973. In this paper, the author summarized previous efforts in the assessment of M/F and offered several cogent criticisms. One concerned the issue of *bipolarity* in the assessment of M/F. Some of the early scales were constructed on the assumption that masculinity and femininity were mutually exclusive and represented different poles of a single dimension. Under these conditions, it was impossible for a subject to provide a self-description that was both highly masculine and highly feminine. More recent researchers have responded to this criticism by devising scales in which masculinity and femininity are assessed independently, thus, making it possible for a person to score high (or low) on either or both factors (Bem, 1974; Heilbrun, 1976; Spence et al., 1974).

Another issue raised by Constantinople is the question of whether masculinity is to be considered as a unidimensional or multidimensional concept, with the same question being raised for the concept of femininity. Constantinople and subsequent writers have been troubled by the fact that masculinity scales and femininity scales are usually found to be multifactorial and, thus, all the items on a particular scale do not seem to be measuring the "same thing." In our view, this is largely a pseudo issue. If masculinity means *manlike*, then there are many ways in which an individual might indicate that he or she is manlike, and there is no necessity that these various indicators must be related to one another (Brannon, 1978; Spence & Helmreich, 1980, 1981). Only if one assumes that masculinity is a unitary concept, would one be embarrassed by findings of multidimensionality. In our view, this is an unnecessary, and false, assumption.

Having recognized the usefulness of assessing masculinity and femininity separately from one another, there remains the question of whether the independently derived masculinity and femininity scores can be meaningfully combined into a single score which would reflect whether, overall, the self-description was more manlike or womanlike. It is our impression that recent researchers have shied away from this, perhaps believing that combining separate M and F scores re-evoked the bipolarity issue (Bem, 1979; Spence & Helmreich, 1981). It is our view that the question of combining M and F scores into a single index is quite separate from bipolarity and is simply an empirical question of utility. Spence (1984, pp. 54-55), who considers masculinity and femininity to be *dualistic*, concurs with this view:

> Given a set of data from one or more criterion measures, what is the combination rule that provides the best fit in describing the joint contribution of M and F to each of the criterion variables? A subsidiary question is whether consideration of the joint contribution of M and F provides more or different information than could be inferred from the separate relationships of M and F with the criterion . . .

The method used in the present project involves the combination of masculinity responses and femininity responses into a single score, as represented by the mean M% scores described earlier. In our procedure, individuals are free to endorse as many male-associated and female-associated items as they choose, thus avoiding the bipolarity problem. On the other hand, we have chosen not to obtain separate M and F scores but to employ a composite score that indicates whether an individual's total self-description tended to be more manlike, more womanlike, or balanced between the two.

Another of Constantinople's criticisms of M/F research, which is still largely valid, is the highly empirical, as opposed to theoretical, basis for the development of M/F scales. The definitions of what is manlike and womanlike employed in most M/F measures are derived on empirical bases and then, after the fact, there is an attempt to rationalize the findings by relating them to some previous conceptual formulation. One such theoretical scheme is that of Parsons and Bales (1955) who suggested that masculinity is defined by cognitive instrumentality and goal directedness whereas femininity is defined by expressive, supportive, and affective responses. A second theoretical formulation to which empirical researchers often relate their findings is that of Bakan (1966) who distinguished between the *agentic* concerns underlying masculinity (i.e., a concern for one's self and one's own goals) and the *communal* concerns underlying femininity (i.e., a concern for self only in relation to others). Although these theoretical formulations and others are often introduced in relation to the findings of M/F studies involving various scales (Bem, 1974; Spence & Helmreich, 1981), it should be noted that most of the scales we will discuss have not been devised in an effort to measure such theoretical concepts directly. A partial exception to this is the development of the PRF Andro scale to be discussed below.

We will now summarize several of the major M/F scales that have been developed and employed in recent years in the United States. We have expressed our view that, ideally, the assessment of M/F requires three steps: (1) the establishment of an independent sex-stereotype criterion by consideration of a comprehensive list of traits in order to determine which are male-associated and which are female-associated; (2) the description of an individual's traits; and (3) an examination of the individual's traits in relation to the sex-stereotype criterion. We will see in the studies reviewed here that few previous investigations have fully conformed to this rationale.

One major approach to the study of M/F has avoided the independent specification of sex stereotypes by defining M/F solely in terms of differences in the self-descriptive responses of women and men. The rationale for this method seems to be that masculinity is something possessed primarily by men, and femininity by women, and that any personality test item to which women and men respond differently can be used as an indicator of M/F.[4] In building an M/F scale by this method, one administers a large pool of test items to groups of men and women and determines those items to which the sexes respond differently, to an appreciable degree. This subset of items is then used to compose a M/F scale with certain items keyed as masculine and others as feminine. Subsequently, this key is applied to a person's self-description, and M/F scores are obtained. Obviously, by this method, one is masculine if one describes oneself as men do and one is feminine if one describes oneself as women do. Among the better known scales of this sort are those developed by Gough (1952, 1966), Hathaway and McKinley (1943), Heilbrun (1981), Strong (1936), and Terman and Miles (1936).

Heilbrun's ACL Scale. We will discuss the work of Heilbrun (1981) as a general illustration of this method. Heilbrun's work is of particular interest in the present context because of his use of the Adjective Check List – the same set of 300 items we employed to define sex stereotypes in our earlier cross-cultural study (Williams & Best, 1982) and also used for the self-descriptions and ideal self-descriptions in the present investigation.

Heilbrun's approach was to compare the responses of American male and female university students with an additional restriction: The men who served as subjects had made a primary identification with masculine, instrumental fathers whereas the women had made a primary identification with feminine, expressive mothers. These men and women responded to the 300 items of the ACL indicating those adjectives that were self-descriptive. From this, Heilbrun identified 28 items that were used significantly more often by the men and 25 items used significantly more often by the women. These groups of items were used to compose his masculinity and femininity scales, respectively.

As the same set of 300 adjectives were used in Heilbrun's M/F studies and in our sex-stereotype studies (Williams & Best, 1982), we can inquire about the relationship between his findings and the sex stereotypes in the United States. In one sense, the results are quite consistent. All of Heilbrun's 28 masculine items had M% scores above 50% on our sex-stereotype measure, with a mean M% score of 81.54%. Similarly, all of his 25 feminine items had M% scores below 50%, with a mean of 18.16%.[5] Thus, it is clear that the items to which Heilbrun's women and men responded differently were sex-stereotype items as defined in our study. In another sense, the correspondence between Heilbrun's findings and ours was rather poor. In our sex-stereotype study, 100 items were found to have M% scores of 67% or more (i.e., were associated with men at least twice as often as with women), and 85 items had M% scores of 33% or less (i.e., were associated with women at least twice as often as men). Of the 100 male-stereotype items, only 24 appear on Heilbrun's masculinity scale. Similarly, of the 85 female-associated items, only 22 appear on his femininity scale. Thus, only about one quarter of the traits stereotypically said to differentiate between men and women are identified using Heilbrun's method.

Heilbrun (1981, p. 9) reported findings from a similar ACL study by Harrison Gough involving the analysis of approximately 10,000 self-descriptions by women and men. Gough identified 20 items that were more frequently employed by men and 26 that were more frequently employed by women, although we are told that some items were eliminated because they were infrequently checked by either sex, even though they were endorsed to different degrees by women and men. How are Gough's 20 masculine and 26 feminine items related to the sex stereotypes? As before, all of the masculine items had M% scores above 50% with a mean of 78.80. All but two of Gough's feminine items had M% scores below 50% with a mean M% of 26.46% for the 26-item set. Thus, the great majority of Gough's items are also sex-stereotypic items. When the question is asked the other way, the correspondence again is much less: Gough's masculine-item group contains only 15 of the 100 male sex-stereotype items and 16 of the 85 female sex-stereotype items identified by our research method.

The findings of Heilbrun and Gough indicate that virtually all items to which men and women respond differently are sex-stereotype items, but that a majority of sex-stereotype items are not responded to differently by men and women. This leads to an intriguing question: Are the items to which men and women respond differentially a random subset of the sex-stereotype items or are the differential items qualitatively different from the other sex-stereotype items? We made a preliminary examination of this question by performing the following analysis. Twenty-four of Heilbrun's M scale items have stereotype M% scores of 67% and up (mean M% = 85.0%) and 22 of his F scale items have stereotype M% scores of 33% and down (mean M% = 15.6%). For comparative purposes, we selected two sets of stereotyped items that were not on the Heilbrun scales; a set of 24 male-stereotyped items (mean M% = 85.2%) and a set of 22 female-associated items (mean M% = 15.7%). Thus, each of the selected item sets was closely matched to the corresponding Heilbrun set in terms of the degree of sex stereotyping as indicated by the mean M% scores.

In order to make qualitative comparisons between the Heilbrun item sets and the respective matched sets, each item set was scored in terms of three factors of affective meaning (favorability, strength, and activity) using our previously developed scoring system (Best et al., 1980; Williams & Best, 1977). In comparison with the matched set of male-associated items, the Heilbrun M scale items were found to be appreciably more favorable, stronger, and more active. In comparison with the matched set of female-associated items of the Heilbrun F scale, items were more favorable, stronger, and much less active. These findings provide a strong suggestion that the sex-stereotype items that are differentially endorsed by men and women are not a random set from the total sex-stereotype pool but a "selected" set that differs qualitatively from "unselected" items. Both men and women select stronger, more favorable items to describe themselves than to describe the typical man or typical woman. The question of why certain stereotype characteristics are differentially incorporated into the self-descriptions of men and women, whereas other stereotype characteristics are not, provides an interesting line for future research.

The consistent findings of the Heilbrun and Gough studies suggest the following conclusions concerning masculinity and femininity scales derived from differences in the self-descriptions of women and men: First, these scales are generally congruent with the stereotypes; second, these scales appear to reflect only a portion of the total stereotypes. For example, an individual whose self-description includes the adjectives *active*, *adventurous*, and *independent* receives no "credit" toward masculinity on the Heilbrun and Gough scales, even though these items have M% scores of 83%, 98%, and 94%, respectively. Likewise, a person whose self-description includes *changeable*, *imaginative*, and *sophisticated* receives no "credit" toward femininity, despite the respective M% scores of 18%, 18%, and 14%. These findings suggest that M/F scales derived solely from self-descriptive differences between men and women cannot be considered equivalent to measures that are based on an independent sex-stereotype criterion.

The Bem Sex-Role Inventory. A different approach to the assessment of psychological masculinity/femininity was taken in the development of the Bem Sex Role Inventory (BSRI) (Bem, 1974). The emphasis in this procedure is on characteristics that are viewed more favorably when associated with one sex or the other. As a first step, Bem and several of her students constructed a list of 200 items, all of which seemed positive (favorable) in value and either masculine or feminine in tone. In addition, they also selected 200 items that seemed not to be masculine or feminine in tone but that were either favorable or unfavorable in value. A group of undergraduate students then rated each of the 400 items as to how desirable it would be for men to possess this particular characteristic. A second group of subjects rated the desirability of each of the items for women. The foregoing data were then used to select items for the final scale, which consisted of 20 items that were judged significantly more desirable for men than for women (the masculine items), 20 items that were judged significantly more desirable for women than for men (the feminine items), and 20 items that were judged equally desirable for both men and women. The 60 items, so selected, are presented to the subjects who use a 7-point scale to indicate how well each of the 60 items describes themselves. From each subject's responses, a masculinity score is derived by obtaining the mean rating for the 20 masculine items and a femininity score is computed by obtaining the mean score for the 20 feminine items.

It can be noted that the procedure used in developing the BSRI differed in several respects from the method used by Heilbrun and Gough and the method we employed in the present project. First, the initial item pool for item selection was based on the expert judgment of Bem and her students. A second point is that all of the items judged to be masculine and feminine in the initial pool were favorable in nature and, thus, there was no opportunity to use unfavorable attributes in the assessment of masculinity and femininity. Finally, we note that the instructions to the undergraduate raters were to indicate whether a given characteristic was more favorable when associated with one sex or the other; they were not asked whether, in fact, the characteristic of interest occurred more or less frequently with one sex or the other.

The differences just noted lead to a conceptually different type of psychological masculinity/femininity. A person obtains a high score on masculinity when he or she endorses as highly self-descriptive a number of characteristics that are viewed more favorably in men than in women. A high score on femininity is obtained by endorsing as self-descriptive items that are viewed as more favorable when associated with women than with men. In sum, the BSRI indexes the degree to which individuals consider themselves to be like an ideal man or ideal woman. This is quite different from the procedure used by Heilbrun and Gough or from that we employ in this study. In our investigation, masculinity/femininity is based on the degree to which the individual is similar to the characteristics of men and women as reflected in the independently specified sex stereotypes.

The Spence and Helmreich Personal Attributes Questionnaire. Still another approach to the assessment of M/F was taken by Spence and Helmreich (1978) who chose items for their Personal Attributes Questionnaire (PAQ) in the following manner. They began with a list of over 130 items, most of which had been assembled by Rosenkrantz, Vogel, Bee, Broverman, and Broverman (1968) from nominations by students of characteristics differentiating men and women. Spence and Helmreich then administered this item pool to large groups of university students with instructions to rate, for each item, either the typical adult male and typical adult female, the typical college student of each sex, or the ideal individual of each sex. Using these data, the investigators identified 23 socially desirable items that were more highly associated with men and were assigned to the Masculinity scale. The 18 socially desirable items more highly associated with women were assigned to the Femininity scale. In addition, they identified a group of 13 items that appeared to be socially desirable in one sex but not in the other, and these items were assigned to a Sex-Specific (Masculinity/Femininity) scale. One item could not be classified. In a later revision of this method (Spence, Helmreich, & Holahan, 1979), socially undesirable items associated with each gender were added.

Recall that when assessing M/F in individual persons, Bem presents the person with the 60 items from the combined Masculinity, Femininity, and Neutral scales. In a similar way, Spence and Helmreich present 55 items embracing the Masculinity, Femininity, and Sex-Specific (Masculinity/

Femininity) scales. Thus, all of the items presented to the subject are scored items. Note that this differs from Heilbrun's procedure where the full 300-item ACL is used for self-description with only certain items being scored for M/F.

The Berzins, Welling, and Wetter PRF Andro Scale. The final M/F measure to be discussed is the PRF Andro scale (Berzins et al., 1978). The items for this scale were taken from the Personality Research Form (PRF) (Jackson, 1967), which contains 400 items that are usually scored in terms of 20 content scales (abasement, achievement, and so forth). Thus, the PRF Andro measure was based on the items from a general personality assessment procedure rather than having been selected specifically for the assessment of M/F.

To select potential M and F items from the PRF item pool, the original PRF scale placement of the items was disregarded and the items' content was evaluated for consistency with Bem's rationale and consistency with "rationally derived abstract definitions of the main content themes of Bem's Masculinity and Femininity scale" (Berzins et al., 1978, p. 128). The former criterion refers to the authors' attempt to select items that appeared to be more desirable in men than in women or vice versa. The second criterion refers to the authors' judgment that the BSRI M scale reflected primarily a dominant/instrumental theme and the BSRI F scale reflected primarily a nurturant/expressive theme. Subsequently, the authors had introductory psychology students rate the selected items in terms of sex-typed desirability to obtain consensual validation of the authors' judgments. The final form of the PRF Andro scale consists of 29 masculinity and 27 femininity items, which are responded to in a true/false format.

We can note some similarities and differences between the PRF Andro scale and the scales discussed previously. The PRF Andro scale is similar to M/F scales based on the Adjective Check List in that, in both cases, the initial item pool was one that was intended to be generally descriptive of human personality rather than being specifically selected as being related to M/F. In such cases, the M/F score can be derived from the general personality description provided by the subject or it can be administered as a separate scale. As noted above, the PRF Andro scale shares the rationale of Bem's BSRI scale in that items were selected only if they were considered to be more desirable in one gender or the other. There was, however, an additional restriction placed in the selection of the PRF Andro items. This was the stipulation that masculine items should reflect a dominant/instrumental theme and the feminine items should reflect a nurturant/expressive theme. Whenever such a rationale is employed, it leads to the expectation that the items on each of the two scales will tend to correlate with one another and provide evidence of a "unidimensional" factor. Subsequent factor analytic studies involving the PRF Andro scale have not supported this expectation; rather, both the M scale and the F scale items have been shown to be factorially complex (Berzins et al., 1978; Ramanaiah & Martin, 1984).

Convergent Validity. To what degree do the masculinity scales from the different measures we have discussed measure "the same thing"? What about the femininity scales? There have been a large number of studies exploring these relationships. Here we will summarize the findings from two studies in which M and F scores for four instruments were compared; the Heilbrun ACL scale, the BSRI scale, the PAQ scale, and the PRF Andro scale.

Kelly, Furman, and Young (1978) found the common variance (r^2) between the various pairs of the four masculinity scales to range from 37%, for the Heilbrun and PRF Andro scales, to 72% for the BSRI and PAQ scales. The estimated common variance among the pairs of the four femininity scores ranged from 26%, for the PAQ and Heilbrun scales, to 53% for the BSRI and PAQ scales. In a similar study, Wilson and Cook (1984) found that the common variance among the M scales ranged from 32%, for the PAQ and PRF Andro comparison, to 44% between the PAQ and the BSRI. The common variance among the F scales ranged from 18%, between the PRF Andro and the PAQ scales, to 48% between the PAQ and BSRI scales.

Two observations can be made on the basis of these findings. First it is clear that, despite the differences in scale construction, all of the M scales have "something in common" as do all of the F scales. The second observation is that, with few exceptions, the correlations between the scores from different scales are appreciably less than the reliabilities of the individual scales and thus it is clear that the scales should not be considered as completely equivalent in nature.

LeVerrier (1987) conducted a study comparing M and F scales based solely on sex stereotypes with the Heilbrun and Bem measures. Subjects were 180 American university students, evenly divided by sex, who had taken both the BSRI and a self-descriptive ACL. LeVerrier scored each BSRI in standard fashion to obtain an M and an F score. The ACLs were scored to obtain Heilbrun's M and F scores. The ACLs were then scored a second time to obtain M and F scores based on the sex-stereotype values of the individual items. This was done by using Williams and Best's (1982) United States M% values to identify as M scale items the 51 items with M% values of 80% or higher and as F scale items the 42 items with M% values of 20% or lower. M and F scores were the frequency counts of endorsed items out of the two subsets. LeVerrier then intercorrelated the M and F scores from each of the three scales obtaining the results seen in Table 2.1.

An examination of the tabled values indicates that the Sex Stereotype M (SSM) scale correlates substantially with both the Bem M scale and the

Table 2.1 Correlation Coefficients Between Individual Masculinity (M) and Femininity (F) Scores for the Bem (BSRI), the Heilbrun (H), and the Sex-Stereotype (SS) Scales

	BSRIF	SSM	SSF	HM	HF
BSRIM	–.16*	.60***	–.12*	.63***	–.11
BSRIF		–.12	.43***	–.21**	.51***
SSM			.31***	.86***	.29***
SSF				.25***	.82***
HM					.16*
HF					

* $p < .05$, ** $p < .01$, *** $p < .001$

Heilbrun M scale, whereas the Sex Stereotype F (SSF) scale correlates substantially with both the Bem F scale and the Heilbrun F scale. From this, we conclude that M and F scales based solely on sex stereotypes show substantial convergent validity with other well-known M/F scales developed following other rationales.

LeVerrier (1987) was also concerned with the question of convergent validity among "combination" M/F scores in which the individual M and F scores are combined, to provide an index that reflects whether, overall, the self-description is "more manlike" or "more womanlike." Combination scores were computed for the Bem, Heilbrun, and Sex Stereotype measures by subtracting the F score from the M score. In addition, the mean American M% score for all endorsed items was added as a fourth combination M/F score.

The intercorrelations among the four combination M/F scores are displayed in Table 2.2 where the values range from .73 to .87 indicating a high degree of convergent validity. In the context of the current project, the findings concerning the mean M% scores are of particular interest since we have chosen to use this score as our principal measure of M/F. LeVerrier's findings indicate that the use of this combination score should yield results that are quite similar to those that might have been obtained using other combination scores based on more established M/F scales such as those of Bem and Heilbrun.

Earlier Studies by the Authors. We will now describe findings from a series of our earlier studies conducted in the United States, which illustrate our approach to the study of M/F and, hence, serve as the forerunners of the project described in this book. Initially, we conducted two studies concerned with the definition of sex stereotypes. These definitions focused upon prototypes or characteristics that define women and men as separate categories of individuals (Ruble & Ruble, 1982). Our first study (Williams & Bennett, 1975) employed our standard ("relative") stereotype method in which university students responded to each of the 300 items of the ACL by indicating

Table 2.2 Correlation Coefficients Between M/F Combination Scores for the Bem (BSRIC), Heilbrun (HC), Sex Stereotype (SSC), and Mean M% Procedures

	SSC	HC	M%
BSRIC	.73***	.74***	.73***
SSC		.76***	.87***
HC			.79***

*** $p < .001$

whether the attribute was *more* frequently associated with men, or *more* frequently associated with women, or not differentially associated with the sexes. Our second study (Williams & Best, 1977) employed a different ("absolute") method in which one group of subjects used the ACL items to describe "men in general," and a second group of subjects described "women in general." After determining that there was a high degree of congruence in the findings of the two studies, the results were merged, via standard scores, to provide a Sex-Stereotype Index (SSI) score for each of the 300 items (Williams & Best, 1977).[6]

An SSI score of 500 indicated that the trait was equally associated with women and men; scores above 500 indicated degrees of male-association—the higher the score the higher the association; scores below 500 indicated degrees of female-association—the lower the score the higher the association. Thus, for example, the highly male-associated attribute *aggressive* had an SSI score of 761, the highly female-associated attribute *emotional* had a score of 254, and the stereotypically neutral attribute *intelligent* had a score of 501.

The SSI scores were then employed to score the self-descriptions and ideal self-descriptions of university students by obtaining a mean SSI score for the subset of the 300 items chosen as descriptive of self, and for those chosen as descriptive of ideal self. The findings of these studies, reported in detail elsewhere (Williams & Best, 1982, p. 279), revealed that the mean SSI score for self-description of the typical female student was about 480, which might be described as "moderately feminine," whereas that of the typical man was about 495, which seems best described as "balanced." This asymmetrical pattern for men and women has also been reported by Heilbrun (1981, pp. 23f) both for American men and women university students and for older and more diverse groups of American men and women. Likewise, Spence and Helmreich (1978, p. 50) reported that the typical American male university and high school student endorses similar numbers of masculine and feminine traits, whereas the typical female student endorses more feminine than masculine traits.[7] Thus, although the relative difference between the men's and women's self-descriptions was in the expected direction in all these studies, the tacit assumption that the men would be found to be "moderately masculine" was not supported. It is also noteworthy that the difference of 15 points between the typical men's and the typical women's self-description is not a large one when viewed against the variability in SSI scores within each group, which ranged from 431 to 520 for the women and from 446 to 540 for the men. Thus, there appeared to be much greater variability in M/F *within* each of the gender groups than between them.

What about the mean SSI scores for the ideal self-descriptions of female and male university students? These were found to fall in a symmetrical manner around the scale midpoint with the typical man scoring 506 and the typical woman 492. Although the difference between these ideal scores again is not great, each shows a "tilt" toward the same-sex stereotype. It is also interesting to note that, in moving from self to ideal self, both men and women shifted toward higher scores. It appears that, generally, the university students in these studies wish to be less feminine or more masculine than they consider themselves to be.

From the foregoing review of these various methods for assessing M/F from self-descriptions, we conclude that there is a substantial degree of qualitative similarity among the methods and, hence, that they may all, to one degree or another, be considered measures of psychological M/F. Even the restriction of the items on several measures to positively valued traits may not be a great limitation because the self-descriptions of most persons include more positive than negative attributes.[8] If one intends to use M/F scores only to identify individual differences in M/F among American women and men, the scales may be equally useful. If, on the other hand, one wishes to compare the relative differences in M/F between persons in different cultures, it seems to us that a method based on a comprehensive assessment of culture-specific sex stereotypes is essential.

SEX-ROLE IDEOLOGY

Normative or prescriptive beliefs concerning the nature of appropriate role relationships between women and men have been called *sex-role ideology*. In more traditional societies, men have usually been viewed as more dominant and/or important than women, whereas in more modern societies, one sees movement toward more egalitarian relationships. Thus, one might expect variations across countries in the general or typical beliefs about the appropriateness of various social practices involving women and men, such as responsibilities in child rearing or work outside the home, evaluated along a traditional/modern scale. In addition, it seems reasonable to expect that there will be sizable variations in sex-role ideology among individuals in a given country and that these variations might be systematically related to the self-concepts of individual persons. A reasonable a priori hypothesis might be that more masculine men and more feminine women would hold relatively traditional sex-role beliefs, whereas more androgynous persons, of both sexes, might be relatively more egalitarian.

Several instruments have been developed in an effort to assess sex-role ideology. Prominent among these has been the Attitudes Toward Women (ATW) scale developed by Spence and Helmreich (1972, 1973). In its short version, the ATW presents a series of 15 statements (e.g., A woman should be as free as a man to propose marriage; the intellectual leadership of a community should be largely in the hands of men; and so forth) and asks the respondent to indicate degree of agreement with each statement. From these responses, a total score is obtained with high scores indicating relatively modern or liberal views and low scores indicating relatively traditional or conservative views.

In a cross-cultural investigation employing the ATW, Spence and Helmreich (1978) found that Lebanese university students have more liberal views than American students, who, in turn, have more liberal views than Brazilian students. Also noteworthy was the finding that, within each country, the women had more liberal views than the men. In further analyses, the investigators studied the relationship of individual differences in ATW scores and individual differences in masculinity/femininity in each country. Contrary to what might be expected, in no case was any substantial relationship found.

Another measure of beliefs concerning proper role relations between women and men is the Sex-Role Ideology (SRI) scale developed in Canada by Kalin and Tilby (1978). The SRI scale consists of 30 declarative statements (see Table 4.1) about relations between men and women with which the subject expresses degrees of agreement or disagreement along a 7-point scale. According to the authors, the 30 items can be divided into five broad content areas: (1) work roles of men and women, 6 items; (2) parental responsibilities of men and women, 5 items; (3) personal relationships between men and women; friendship, courtship, and sexual, 7 items; (4) special role of women, and "pedestal" concept, 8 items; (5) motherhood, abortion, and homosexuality, 4 items. Half of the items are phrased in a traditional or male dominant manner (e.g., "A woman should be more concerned with helping her husband's career than having a career herself") and half of the items are phrased in a modern or egalitarian manner (e.g., "A woman should have exactly the same freedom of action as a man"). In scoring, the traditional items are reversed so that the high total scores are always indicative of modern views.

The Kalin scale was validated employing the "known groups" method with feminist and traditional groups (Kalin & Tilby, 1978). The women in the feminist group were members of women's liberation groups who were openly identified as profeminist. The women in the traditional group met at least one of the following criteria: they belonged to a group which stressed the traditional values of home and family; they belonged to women's groups in conservative churches; or they were elderly. All test items were found to discriminate between the two groups, with the highest item mean of the traditional group falling considerably below the lowest item mean in the feminist group.

In subsequent research, Kalin, Heusser, and Edwards (1982) compared SRI data obtained in England and Ireland with those obtained in Canada and concluded that the psychometric characteristic of the scale made it appropriate for use in all three countries. An important finding from this study was that, in all three countries, female students were significantly more modern or egalitarian in their views than were male students.

Milo, Badger, and Coggins (1983) factor analyzed the SRI scale and identified two principal factors, the first of which was interpreted as measuring agreement with the overall goals and values of feminist ideology, and the second represented agreement with the norms of a traditional family-oriented sex-role division. Despite this evidence of factorial heterogeneity, the reported item-analysis data indicate that all items correlate significantly with total score and that, hence, the total score may be viewed as an overall index of sex-role ideology along a traditional to modern dimension.

Sex-role ideology, as assessed by the Kalin measure, was included in the current project for several reasons. First, it was considered of interest to determine whether the typical sex-role ideology would be found to vary substantially from country to country. If so, we could then explore the question of whether this variation was systematically related to various cultural comparison indices (e.g., status of women variables, religion, socioeconomic development). A second purpose was to test the hypothesis that women tend to be more modern in sex-role ideology than men, as had been suggested in several earlier studies. Finally, we wished to explore the question of possible relationships between individual differences in sex-role ideology scores and individual differences in the self-concepts of women and men, scored in terms of affective meaning and in terms of masculinity/feminity.

SUMMARY

In this chapter, it was proposed that the study of self-concepts should involve a consideration of both perceived and ideal self. The general concept of masculinity/femininity (M/F) was discussed with the observation that the usual study of psychological M/F via self-report involves the study of *one* type of M/F via *one* method. The concept of psychological androgyny was introduced and a new assessment strategy proposed. Popular methods for the assessment of psychological M/F were described and their interrelationships reviewed. The concept of sex-role ideology was introduced and methods for its assessment discussed.

NOTES

1. See also Baumeister's (1987) excellent historical review of the concept of self.

2. Best and Williams (1984) used Transactional Analysis Ego State scales to examine self-descriptions and ideal self-descriptions in the present project from Canada, England, Finland, Malaysia, the Netherlands, the United States, and Venezuela.

3. Several writers (e.g., Myers & Gonda, 1982; Sedney, 1981) have pointed out problems in this typological approach. Heilbrun (1981) has argued for the assessment of androgyny as a continuous variable, which is consistent with the approach in the current project.

4. See Constantinople's (1973) criticism of this "strictly empirical" approach.

5. When LeVerrier (1987) replicated Heilbrun's item analysis approach using *unselected* men and women students, her 30 M scale items had a mean M% score of 72.0% and her 32 F scale items had a mean M% score of 28.0%. Apparently, the items to which Heilbrun's selected men and women responded differently were more highly sex stereotyped than the items to which LeVerrier's unselected men and women responded differently. On the other hand, the convergent validity between the respective scales was quite high: M scales, $r = .86$; F scales, $r = .79$.

6. The merging of the data from the first and second studies was justified by the similarity of two difference scores for each item. For study one, the difference was between the frequency with which an item was endorsed as being more characteristic of men than women and the frequency with which it was endorsed as being more characteristic of women than men. For study two, the difference was between the frequency with which the item was endorsed as characteristic of men in general and the frequency with which it was endorsed as characteristic of women in general. Across the 300 items, the two sets of difference scores correlated +.78. Basow (1980) has suggested that because most researchers ask questions about males relative to females, and vice versa, the differences between the sexes are emphasized. She suggested that questionnaires that use absolute rather than relative questions would result in showing more similarities between the sexes. Although we agree that, in principle, relative methods are designed to "tease out" differences, we found a high degree of correspondence in the results of the two methods and chose to use the relative method in our cross-cultural research.

7. Davis, Williams, and Best (1982) reported parallel findings regarding the self-descriptions of elementary school children.

8. LeVerrier (1987) has demonstrated that the likelihood of ACL items being endorsed as self-descriptive is an increasing linear function of their favorability scores.

PART II

Tactics

3

RESEARCH PLAN AND METHODS

GENERAL PLAN OF THE PROJECT

The overall plan for the present project was to obtain descriptions of perceived self and ideal self, and a measure of sex-role ideology, from young women and men in a number of culturally diverse countries. The two self-descriptions would be evaluated in terms of: (1) three general affective meaning components – strength, activity, and favorability; and (2) masculinity/femininity, scored on a culture-specific basis. Relations among these measures would be examined within each country and compared, across countries, with a variety of cultural indicators.

In implementing the project, we contacted the researchers in different countries who had participated in our earlier sex-stereotype study, explained the general plan of the new project, and asked if they would like to become involved. Following our usual practice, we proposed that the data collected by participating researchers in particular countries would be considered their own to use in whatever manner they chose, for example, reading papers at professional meetings or publishing papers in professional journals.[1] We asked, only, that the data be shared with us for purposes of cross-cultural analyses.

Persons from 11 countries responded to our request. Subsequently, two persons, after collecting data in one country, moved to a second country and collected data there also. In this way, we obtained data from 13 foreign countries which, with our own data from the United States, enabled us to compare findings in 14 countries. The voluntary manner in which the participating researchers were obtained might have led to a rather narrow or atypical sample of countries. Fortunately, this did not occur.

The 14 countries in the project are listed, by continent, in Table 3.1. The sample of countries cannot be considered a representative one on a holocultural or worldwide basis; European countries are overrepresented and there are some obvious "gaps" (e.g., Eastern Europe and the Middle East). The sample of countries is also biased toward major countries and toward relatively developed countries. On the other hand, the countries are geographically dispersed and culturally diverse. If one includes the countries of North and South America within the European tradition, then the sample includes eight "European" and six "non-European" countries. Serendipitously, the 14 countries also constituted a reasonably representative

Table 3.1 The 14 Countries in the Study

Asia	*Europe*	*Africa*	*South America*	*North America*
India	England	Nigeria	Venezuela	Canada
Japan	Finland			United States
Malaysia	Germany			
Pakistan	Italy			
Singapore	Netherlands			

sample of the total group of countries involved in the earlier study of sex stereotypes, as will be seen later in this chapter. Overall, it appears that the sample of countries is sufficiently diverse to permit a meaningful study of cross-cultural similarities and differences in self-concepts and sex-role ideology.

We will now proceed to a description of the details of the method. Following this, we offer a critique of the method in which we indicate what we consider to be its relative strengths and weaknesses.

DESCRIPTION OF THE METHOD

Subjects

The plan was to obtain as subjects a group of approximately 100 university students, evenly divided by sex, in each of the 14 countries. Each cooperating researcher was asked to identify a group as representative as possible of the student population. Other than this, the manner in which the subjects were selected and their cooperation enlisted was left to the discretion of the local cooperating researcher. Data were gathered during the years 1982-1985.

The actual numbers of subjects, together with their universities, the languages employed in the research procedures, and the symbols used to identify the samples are shown in Table 3.2. Also summarized in the table are other characteristics of each subject group: percentage indicating various religious affiliations (in Japan[2] and Germany this information was not obtained); percentage whose mothers were employed outside the home during their childhood; mean number of siblings; and percentage who lived in an urban area during childhood.

Although it would have been possible to use the individual subject demographics in the analyses of self, ideal self, and sex-role ideology, we were more interested in general cultural comparison variables. First, our individual subject-level descriptive data are incomplete, and second, the

Table 3.2 Characteristics of the University Student Samples

				Religion								
Country	*Institution*	*No. of Subjects Men/Women*	*Language*	*% Cath.*	*% Hin.*	*% Mus.*	*% Prot.*	*% Budd.*	*% Other and None*	*% Mother Emp.*	*Mean no. Sibs*	*% Urban*
Canada (CAN)	St. Francis Xavier Univ.	50/50	Eng.	70	1	2	22	1	4	49	4.4	51
England (ENG)	Univ. of Bristol	50/50	Eng.	10	0	0	46	0	43	42	1.9	71
Finland (FIN)	Univ. of Helsinki	48/49	Fin.	—	—	—	64	—	36	81	1.9	65
Germany (GER)	Technische Hochschule Darmstadt	49/49	Ger.	—	—	—	—	—	—	29	1.8	51
India (IND)	Univ. of Allahabad	43/49	Eng.	0	95	3	0	0	3	10	4.1	67
Italy (ITA)	Univ. of Venice	74/69	Ita.	89	0	0	0	0	12	13	1.6	74
Japan (JAP)	Hyogo Univ. and Gifu Univ.	132/153	Jap.	—	—	—	—	—	—	—	1.9	42
Malaysia (MAL)	Univ. Sains Malaysia (Minden)	40/50	Bahasa Malay. and Eng.	0	12	30	29	18	11	14	5.3	61
Netherlands (NET)	Univ. of Utrecht	47/50	Dutch	17	1	0	26	0	56	39	2.8	57
Nigeria (NIG)	Univ. of Jos	66/25	Eng.	33	0	22	37	0	8	21	7.1	41
Pakistan (PAK)	Univ. of Sind (Jamshoro)	34/36	Urdu	0	1	99	0	0	0	7	6.5	57
Singapore (SIN)	National Univ.	50/50	Eng.	7	1	4	48	8	30	18	4.2	66
United States (USA)	Wake Forest Univ. Winston-Salem, NC	50/50	Eng.	11	0	0	85	0	4	39	1.9	58
Venezuela (VEN)	Univ. Central de Venezuela (Caracas)	50/50	Span.	61	0	0	6	0	33	32	4.3	83

cultural comparison variables are more reflective of our concerns with the cultures as a whole, rather than with specific subject characteristics. Although the cultural comparison and individual subject scores may differ for several countries, correlations were relatively high across all 14 countries.[3]

Questionnaire Materials and Administration

Each subject completed four questionnaires dealing, respectively, with self-description, ideal self-description, sex-role ideology, and personal characteristics (age, education, etc.). The questionnaires were presented in English, when appropriate, or in another language, as indicated in Table 3.2. Overall, nine different languages were employed. In Malaysia, each ACL item was presented in English and, side by side, in Bahai Malaysian. In India, where the items were presented in English, a glossary was used providing dictionary definitions for 38 of the less familiar English words (e.g., high-strung, spendthrift, zany).

The translated versions of the ACL items were those used in the earlier sex-stereotype study (Williams & Best, 1982). The translated versions of the instructions for the self-descriptions and ideal self-descriptions, the sex-role ideology items and instructions, and the personal characteristics questionnaire, were arranged by the local cooperating researchers using variations of the "committee" and "back-translation" methods described by Brislin (1980, p. 431). We will return to the matter of the translation of materials later in this chapter.

The questionnaires were administered to groups of students by the local cooperating researcher, or by an advanced student working under his or her supervision, at a time and place chosen by the local researcher.

The following general instructions were employed to introduce the subjects to the nature of the task:

> The purpose of this study is to learn more about the manner in which university students view themselves and their ideal selves, and the relationship of these views to their opinions about women and men and certain other background variables.
>
> Our purpose is to gain a general picture of university students. We are not interested in you as an individual person but as a member of the university student group. Because of this, we have *not* asked you to indicate your name.
>
> There are four tasks to be completed. First, you will be asked to consider a large group of adjectives and to pick those which are descriptive of yourself as you really are. Then, you will be asked to consider the same group of adjectives and pick those that are descriptive of the person you would like to be, i.e., your ideal self.

> Following this, you will be asked your opinion about a number of questions relating to women and men. Finally, you will be asked to provide some information concerning your current status in the university and about your background.
>
> When I give the signal, please open the booklet to the first page, read the instructions, and begin work. You may work through the booklet at your own rate. When you are finished, please close your booklet and remain seated.
>
> Please turn to the next page and begin work.

Following the general instructions, the subject was presented with the 300 items of the ACL (see Appendix A), or their translated equivalents. The subjects then proceeded to indicate those adjectives which he or she considered to be descriptive of *self*, according to the following instructions:

> On the following page you will find 300 adjectives which are sometimes used to describe people. You are asked to describe yourself by selecting adjectives which you consider to be *descriptive of you as you really are*, not as you would like to be.
>
> Please read each adjective quickly and check those which you consider to be self-descriptive. Do not worry about duplications, contradictions, and so forth. Work quickly and do not spend too much time on any one adjective.

After completing the self-descriptive task, the subject was presented with another page on which were listed the same 300 adjectives and was asked to describe his or her *ideal self*, according to the following instructions:

> On the following page you will find 300 adjectives which are sometimes used to describe people. You are asked to describe your ideal self by selecting adjectives that you consider to be *descriptive of the person you would like to be*, not the person you really are.
>
> Please read each adjective quickly and indicate those that you consider to be descriptive of your ideal self. Do not worry about duplications, contradictions, and so forth. Work quickly and do not spend too much time on any one adjective. Do not be concerned as to whether the adjectives which you check to describe your ideal self are the same or different from the adjectives which you used earlier to describe yourself.

The third questionnaire was the Kalin Sex Role Ideology measure (SRI) (Kalin & Tilby, 1978). The instructions presented to the subject were as follows:

> A number of statements are listed on the next two pages. Each represents a commonly held opinion and there are no right or wrong answers. We are

interested in the extent to which you agree or disagree with such matters of opinion.

Read each statement carefully. Then, using the answer sheet on the third page, indicate the extent to which you agree or disagree by circling the response alternative that best expresses your opinion. The response alternatives and their meanings are indicated below:

If you disagree *strongly*	circle 1
If you *disagree*	circle 2
If you disagree *slightly*	circle 3
If you are *undecided* or *have no opinion*	circle 4
If you agree *slightly*	circle 5
If you *agree*	circle 6
If you agree *strongly*	circle 7

First impressions are usually the best in such matters. Read each statement, decide if you agree or disagree and the strength of your opinion, and then mark the appropriate alternative on your answer sheet. Read the items carefully, but work as rapidly as you can. *Give your opinion on every statement.*

If you find that the response alternatives given do not adequately indicate your opinion, use the one which is *closest* to the way you feel.

The subject then responded to each of the SRI items, which are reproduced in the next chapter in Table 4.1. In an effort to make the sex-role ideology measure culturally appropriate, the cooperating researcher in each country had been asked to consider adding additional items and/or deleting certain items. Although no items were added, items were deleted in three countries. In Malaysia and Singapore, two items (11 and 30) were considered culturally inappropriate and were not included in the questionnaire. Similarly, items 16, 21, and 23 were not used in Pakistan. In addition, item 9 was omitted from the Italian version because of a printing error.

Following completion of the SRI, the subject was asked to provide information relating to: sex, age, course of university study and year, approximate class standing, planned occupation, religious affiliation, parents' occupations, number of siblings and birth order, and whether principal residence during childhood was urban or rural.

Cultural Comparison Variables

A principal strategy in the present project was to obtain, in each country, typical (mean) scores related to self-concepts and sex-role ideology and to correlate these scores, across countries, with a variety of indices related to cultural variation. Although we recognized that in some cases our variables could oversimplify a very complex issue (e.g., percentage of women employed outside the home does not reflect the status of these jobs nor the economic necessity or choice involved in working), we tried to select variables that would be indicative of cultural differences that may influence men's and women's perceptions of themselves and their ideals.

The particular indices employed were chosen with two considerations in mind: they reflected a diversity of cultural variables (e.g., economic-social development, religion, status of women); and there were reliable data available for our particular set of countries. Following Davidson's and Thomson's (1980) distinction, we note that most of our comparison variables are of their "aggregate" type, that is, averages of measures which vary across individuals within a cultural group (e.g., religious affiliation). Only our latitude index seems clearly of their "global" type, that is, constant for all persons in the cultural group. The comparison variables employed are listed in Table 3.3 where the numbers in parentheses indicate the reference sources from which the data were obtained.[4]

Economic-Social Development (C1). In order to have an overall indicator of development, we employed Sivard's composite index in which countries are ranked in terms of overall economic-social development based on the following three equally weighted factors: GNP per capita, education, and health. For education and health a summary rank is first obtained for five indicators in each category. The education composite consists of public expenditures per capita on education, school age population per teacher, percentage of school age population in school, percentage of women in total university enrollment, and the literacy rate; the health composite consists of public expenditures per capita on health, population per physician, population per hospital bed, infant mortality rate, and life expectancy.[5] Sivard's index is derived in a manner similar to other composite indices used to describe or rank the quality of life in various countries, e.g., Physical Quality of Life Index[6] (Morris, 1979; Sewell, 1980), but it is a more comprehensive index. Certainly other measures representing the quality of life and level of development could be used, such as strength of family ties or informal community social support systems, but cross-cultural indices of such measures are not readily available and, if they were, they would probably be highly subjective.

An overall ranking of these development variables was considered more useful than individual indices for examining relationships among development, self-concept, and sex-role ideology. As the economic-social development index is computed in *rank* form, low numbers indicate high economic-social development, that is, the most favorable rank was 7, in the United States, and the least favorable rank was 118, in Pakistan. For ease in exposition, we have inverted each index value by subtracting it from 120 so

Table 3.3 Individual Country Values for Each of the 10 Cultural Comparison Variables

	CAN	*ENG*	*FIN*	*GER*	*IND*	*ITA*	*JAP*	*MAL*	*NET*	*NIG*	*PAK*	*SIN*	*USA*	*VEN*
C1: Economic-Social Development see text (1)	112	104	109	111	5	99	100	60	107	19	2	79	113	73
C2: Catholic % of population with Roman Catholic affiliation (2)	46.6	13.1	0.1	43.8	1.3	83.2	0.9	2.8	42.6	12.1	0.5	4.7	30.0	94.8
C3: Protestant % of population with Protestant affiliation (2)	28.0	15.0	92.5	46.7	1.1	0.4	1.1	1.4	41.8	15.2	0.8	2.6	40.0	1.0
C4: Total Christian % of population with Christian affiliation (2)	91.0	86.9	94.4	92.8	3.9	83.6	4.0	6.2	85.7	49.0	1.8	8.6	88.0	96.2
C5: Muslim % of population with Muslim affiliation (2)	0.6	1.4	0.0	2.4	11.6	0.1	0.0	49.4	1.0	45.0	96.8	17.4	0.8	0.0
C6: Women Employed % of women employed outside of home (3)	28.4	32.9	43.3	30.9	11.9	19.6	35.2	22.0	19.0	16.0	5.4	18.5	33.9	17.3
C7: Women in University % of women in university enrollment (1)	48	35	49	35	27	41	23	32	28	15	27	43	47	40
C8: Urban urban % of total population (1)	76	78	59	92	21	67	76	27	88	20	26	100	74	75
C9: Latitude latitude of capital city (4)	46	52	60	51	29	42	36	4	52	10	25	1	41	10
C10: Work-Related Values see text (5)	70.5	77.0	65.0	66.0	35.5	63.0	46.0	—	71.0	—	29.5	23.0	75.5	15.5

that high numbers indicate high economic-social development (i.e., the United States value becomes 113 and the Pakistan value becomes 2). Looking at the economic-social development scores, the countries with the higher scores are primarily North American and northern European, whereas the lower scoring countries are primarily Asian. These groupings reflect many of the usual differences between more developed and less developed countries.

Religion. We employed indices of the percentage of the population with the following major religious affiliations: Catholic (C2), Protestant (C3), total Christian (C4), and Muslim (C5). These represented the major religious groups in the countries studied. Indices of religion were included because our earlier research (Williams & Best, 1982) revealed cross-national variations in sex stereotypes that were related to religious differences between countries. Furthermore, religious beliefs of the majority group in a particular country would certainly influence other aspects of the local culture, even perhaps the values and experiences of members of the various minority religious groups.

Status of Women. We indexed the percentage of women employed outside the home (C6) and the percentage of women in the total university enrollment (C7). These indices seemed particularly relevant in a study concerned with gender differences in self-concept and sex-role ideology because they seemed to quantify at least two ways that opportunities afforded women in various cultures could differ.

General Demographics. We employed the percentage of the population classified as urban (C8) and the latitude (i.e., distance from the equator) of the capital city of the country (C9). Although urbanization is generally considered to be an indicator of development, in some countries, particularly in some third world nations, urbanization may be more indicative of crowded, slum-level living conditions. Note, also, that because all of our countries are from the northern hemisphere, the latter measure represents degrees of *northern* latitude. Latitude serves as a rough global indicator of climate.

Work-Related Values. In Chapter 1, we reviewed Hofstede's (1980) study of work-related values in 40 countries. Twelve of the 14 countries in the present project were also in the Hofstede sample, and we considered it worthwhile to make cross-national comparisons between our findings regarding self-concept and sex-role ideology and Hofstede's findings regarding personal values.

As we noted in Chapter 1, Hofstede's study identified four dimensions of national culture: Power Distance, Uncertainty Avoidance, Individualism, and Masculinity. *Power distance* concerns the extent to which people within a society accept the notion that power, wealth, and prestige are unequally distributed within their organizations and society. *Uncertainty avoidance* refers to the level of tolerance for uncertainty and ambiguity. *Individualism* reflects the relationship between the individual and the collectivity in a society, the way people live together and their feelings of independence and responsibility toward each other. *Masculinity* measures the extent to which a society emphasizes more masculine values, such as assertiveness wealth, and things, in contrast to more feminine values, such as nurturance, quality of life, and people.

A preliminary review of our findings indicated that Hofstede's Uncertainty Avoidance (UAI) and Masculinity (MAS) scales showed little relationship to our findings, whereas his Power Distance (PDI) and Individualism (IDV) scales each had a number of substantial relationships. Additionally, we found that the PDI and IDV scales in our group of 12 countries were highly related in an inverse manner (r = –.79); that is, countries high in individualism tended to be low in power distance, and vice versa. This result was consistent with Hofstede's finding across all 40 of his countries (r = –.67). In order to avoid redundancy, we chose to combine the PDI and IDV scales into a single index of work-related values using the formula: IDV/PDI = IDV + (100 – PDI)/2. The numerical values used in this computation are from Hofstede (1979, p. 394).

High scores on this combined values index (C10) indicate countries in which there is an emphasis on individualism and a deemphasis on the differential distribution of power in organizations. Low scores indicate countries in which there is a deemphasis on individualism and an emphasis on power differentials. More concisely, high scores indicate countries with values that are high in individualism and low in authoritarianism, whereas low scores indicate countries with more communal and authoritarian values. In rank order, from high to low, the twelve individual country values on the combined index were: England (77.0), United States (75.5), Netherlands (71.0), Canada (70.5), Germany (66.0), Finland (65.0), Italy (63.0), Japan (46.0), India (35.5), Pakistan (29.5), Singapore (23.0), and Venezuela (15.5).

Relations Among Comparison Variables

The individual country values on each of the 10 comparison variables are shown in Table 3.3. The intercorrelations among these variables, shown in Table 3.4, reveal a number of significant correlations among the comparison variables. While we will not comment on all these relationships, we note that, with few exceptions, the correlations are less than .71, indicating that the pairs of indices have less than 50% common variance (r^2) and, therefore, are sufficiently independent to warrant consideration as separate indices. The most dramatic exception is the .90 correlation between degrees of

Table 3.4 The 10 Cultural Comparison Variables and Their Interrelations (Product-Moment Correlations with Decimal Point Omitted)

	C2	C3	C4	C5	C6	C7	C8	C9	C10
C1: *Economic-Social Development* see text (1)	36	51	66	–76	79	61	82	60	68
C2: *Catholic* % of population with Roman Catholic affiliation (2)		–08	65	–43	–09	33	40	10	02
C3: *Protestant* % of population with Protestant affiliation (2)			60	–35	66	43	25	67	58
C4: *Total Christian* % of population with Christian affiliation (2)				–61	47	43	49	61	61
C5: *Muslim* % of population with Muslim affiliation(2)					–62	–46	–68	–50	–43
C6: *Women Employed* % of women employed outside of home (3)						47	46	60	63
C7: *Women in University* % of women in university enroll-ment (1)							51	30	26
C8: *Urban* urban % of total population (1)								37	27
C9: *Latitude* latitude of capital city (4)									90
C10: *Work-Related Values* see text (5)									–

northern latitude and work-related values, indicating that, as one moves north from the equator, the expression of individualistic and antiauthoritarian values increases in a remarkably regular fashion. This finding is generally congruent with Hofstede's (1980) findings in which latitude was found to correlate .75 with individualism scores and –.65 with power distance scores across his 40 countries. Hofstede (1980, p. 123) suggested that the relation of latitude and values may be attributable to the relation of latitude to climate and to the different adjustment strategies that have evolved in societies living under different (cold versus tropical) climatic conditions.

CRITIQUE OF THE METHOD

Having described our research procedures, we will now undertake a critical evaluation of the method, considering what we believe to be its stronger and weaker points. Although such a critique by the authors themselves might be considered to be potentially self-serving, we have spent a great deal of time reflecting on the method, and we feel it may be valuable to the reader to hear our appraisal which, of course, does not have to be accepted. We will consider a number of features of the method, moving generally from the relative strengths to the relative weaknesses.

The Sample of Countries

It is desirable that the particular countries involved in a cross-cultural study be reasonably diverse, particularly, in the present instance, in terms of the sex stereotypes on the basis of which M/F is to be assessed. Fortunately, the cooperating researchers who volunteered to participate in the present project were from a group of countries that are generally representative of the larger group of countries involved in our earlier sex-stereotype project.

In the earlier project, the findings in the 25 countries were classified in terms of the degree of qualitative *differentiation* in the sex stereotypes, that is, the degree to which men and women were viewed as differing in their psychological makeup (Williams & Best, 1982, p. 251). An examination of these differentiation scores for the countries in the present project reveals a wide range. Differentiation was relatively high in the Netherlands, Malaysia, and Nigeria, suggesting that in these countries women and men are considered to differ a great deal in their psychological makeup. On the other hand, differentiation was relatively low in India and Venezuela, indicating more similarity in the views of women and men in these countries.

A second summary analysis in the sex-stereotype project was concerned with the degree to which the stereotypes in each country were typical of the findings in all 25 countries (Williams & Best, 1982, p. 253). When the typicality scores of the countries in the present study were examined, it was found that the stereotype findings in the United States, Canada, and England were relatively typical whereas those in Japan and Nigeria were relatively atypical, with the other countries being intermediate. From the foregoing, we conclude that the countries in the present project can be viewed as generally representative of the larger group of countries in the sex-stereotype project. This is a conclusion of some consequence for the present study, particularly for the masculinity/femininity analyses.

Comprehensive Self-Descriptions and Ideal Self-Descriptions

In any cross-cultural project involving self-descriptions it seems advisable to use a large pool of items in order to allow persons in different cultures to find items which they consider self-descriptive. An item that is frequently used in Culture A may not be used in Culture B, and vice versa. In the method of the present project, the subjects were asked to consider 300 adjectives, indicating those that were descriptive of self, and later, of ideal self. The use of such a large item pool, in contrast to the relatively small number of items on most M/F scales (e.g., Bem, 1974; Heilbrun, 1981; Spence & Helmreich, 1978), seems more likely to lead to useful self-descriptive data because subjects are not restricted to a small group of items, some of which may be culturally inappropriate.

It is true that the 300 item ACL (Gough & Heilbrun, 1965, 1980b) was developed for use in the United States and, hence, might be suspected of being "American biased." In response, we note that neither in our 25-country sex-stereotype study nor in the present 14-country study has there been any complaint from either our cooperating researchers or the student respondents that the item pool was not adequate for the description of persons in their cultures. Furthermore, the ACL has been used successfully as a personality measure in clinical and organizational settings in a number of countries (e.g., Italy, France).

Scoring Masculinity/Femininity Relative to Local Sex Stereotypes

Perhaps the most distinctive feature of the present method is the scoring of masculinity/femininity in a particular culture relative to the sex stereotypes in that culture. It is our view that the alternate strategy of studying masculinity/femininity by developing a scale based on the sex stereotypes in one culture, and administering the scale in another culture, is severely limited in usefulness. The psychological traits considered to be manlike and womanlike differ appreciably from culture to culture; for example, *enthusiastic* is associated with women in Italy and Germany and with men in Malaysia and Pakistan; *conservative* is associated with women in Singapore and Malaysia and with men in Germany and Norway. It seems that only by using culture-specific definitions of sex stereotypes can one make meaningful cross-cultural comparisons of masculinity/femininity; that is, stereotypes for each culture must first be determined, then, using these items, masculinity/femininity can be examined in each culture and, subsequently, can be compared between cultural groups.

Examination of Both Self and Ideal Self

Studies of masculinity/femininity typically have been concerned only with the individual's description of the perceived or "typical" self (i.e., the person you *are,* not the person you would like to be). On the other hand, psychologists have long believed that additional information about an individual is obtained by having the person describe his or her ideal self (i.e., the person you *would like to be*, not the person you are) (Block, 1984). Rogers (1951) and others have contended that the study of differences between self and ideal self are particularly revealing of important aspects of human personality, despite the fact that the ideal self may be influenced by cultural ideals and somewhat less reflective of individual differences (Wylie, 1974, 1979). Consequently, the examination of the masculinity/femininity of the perceived self and the ideal self, and the differences between them, provides a dimension not usually found in masculinity/femininity studies.

In a cross-cultural investigation, the examination of both perceived self and ideal self takes on additional significance. In the United States, there is clear distinction between these concepts; Americans always describe the ideal self at least somewhat differently from the perceived self. Is this distinction emic in nature, that is, peculiar to the United States or, perhaps, other Western countries? Or is this an etic distinction that will be found to be meaningful in all cultures studied?

Use of Scaled Items in Scoring M/F

In most contemporary measures of M/F, subjects are asked to respond self-descriptively to two classes of items—male-associated and female-associated. Thus, an individual might indicate that 12 of 20 male-associated items, and 8 of 20 female-associated items are self-descriptive. Note that in such a procedure the number of items is limited and no allowance is made for the fact that, among the items associated with a given gender, some are more highly associated than are others.

By contrast, the M% scores obtained from our sex-stereotype project provide a continuous index of the degree to which given traits are associated with one gender or the other. The assessment of M/F by reference to this continuous distribution of scores has two important consequences. The first is that it is possible to compute a mean M% for the endorsed items for use as an index of the "central tendency" of the self-description (i.e., whether the overall description is weighted toward male-associated or female-associated attributes). Hence, it is possible to obtain mean scores which vary widely along the M% dimension. Psychometrically, such mean scores seem likely to be more useful than central tendency scores obtained by combining the frequencies of endorsed male-associated and female-associated items, as is often done. We also note the apparent isomorphism between mean scores based on weighted sex-stereotyped characteristics and the popular concept of M/F in which persons appear to assess an individual's status on M/F by a "summation" of male-associated and female-associated traits, with some traits being given more weight than others. Although isomorphism between scientific concepts and popular conceptions is not essential, it is nonetheless comforting.

Use of Composite M/F Scores

We noted, in Chapter 2, that most recent M/F researchers have avoided the "bipolar assumption" under which masculinity and femininity are viewed as opposite ends of a single dimension. This has been done by designing M/F procedures so that the assessment of masculinity and femininity are operationally independent and the subject can obtain high or low scores on either or both factors.

Our M/F procedure is similarly designed in that the subjects are free to endorse as many high M% (masculine) and as many low M% (feminine) items as they choose. Actually, we could easily have employed *separate* masculinity and femininity scores as LeVerrier (1987) did (see Chapter 2). Our decision to use a combination score (the mean M%) was due to our interest in characterizing each self-description and ideal self-description as, generally, more manlike or more womanlike, which we consider to be isomorphic to the popular conception of M/F. This decision also had the practical advantage of simplifying our data analyses which, with the addition of separate M and F scores, would have been much longer and more complex.

Scoring for Intrasubject Diversity in M/F

A second major consequence of the use of scaled sex-stereotype items in the assessment of M/F is that it is possible to compute, for the items in a given self-description, the variance of the M% scores around the mean M% score. For example, it is possible for two self-descriptions to have identical mean M% scores but widely different variances attributable to differences in the degree to which the more extreme (high or low) M% scores are used in the self-descriptions. One description, having a large variance, may have both highly male-associated and highly female-associated items, whereas the other description with a smaller variance may be composed of items with less strong gender association.

Our assessment of individual differences in M/F variance is, to our knowledge, novel in the area of M/F research and relatively unusual in personality research in general. M/F measures based on categorically classified items do not permit the computation of variance scores. On the other hand, several researchers using measures with categorical items have found it useful to subdivide the persons obtaining "balanced" M/F scores (obtaining similar scores for male- and female-associated items) into two categories: *androgynous* persons, who express a relatively high degree of endorsement of both types of items; and *undifferentiated* persons who express a relatively low degree of endorsement of both.[7] It seems to us that this classification is an effort to deal with a special case of the variance concept in our method. We could, for example, identify a group of persons with mean M% scores near 50% (balanced descriptions) and subdivide these into those with relatively high (androgynous) and relatively low (undifferentiated) variances. The advantage in using the more general variance concept is that it can be applied throughout the range of mean M% scores rather than being confined to the special case of balanced self-descriptions. For these reasons, we have not employed the androgynous/undifferentiated concept in the current project.

Use of M% Scores Instead of Standard Scores

We noted, in Chapter 1, the sizable observed differences among countries in the means and variances of the M% scores for the total 300-item pool (see Table 1.1). We remarked that these differences appeared to reflect, at least in part, bona fide cultural variation because the distributions of means and variances were each related to several cultural comparison variables. On the other hand, some of the observed variation among countries, particularly in variances, might reflect differences in the subjects' approach to the task. If, for some reason, the subjects in a given country were somewhat careless in marking the items as male- or female-associated, this might lead to less extreme M% scores and, hence, to a lower variance for the item pool as a whole. Should we view the variance differences primarily as artifactual or bona fide? If the former view prevailed, it would be possible to equalize the variances (and means) by the use of standard scores instead of raw M% scores.[8]

We were aided in making this decision when we realized that the item pool contained two adjectives that could be considered "marker" items concerning variances in a sex-stereotype study; namely, the adjectives *masculine* and *feminine*. For the five countries with the largest variances (see Table 1.1), the M% scores for the adjective *masculine* ranged from 92% to 99% (mean M% = 95.0%), and in the five countries with the smallest variances they ranged from 91% to 99% (mean M% = 95.8%). Similarly, for the five countries with the large variances, the M%s for *feminine* ranged from 0% to 15% (mean M% = 6.2%), and in the five small variance countries they also ranged from 0% to 15% (mean M% = 5.6%). Because the responses of the subjects in the high and low variance countries were so similar on these marker items, we saw no reason to believe that there would be any difference in their general approach to the other items. As a result, we concluded that the different variances should be considered as bona fide cultural phenomena and that the raw M% scores should be used in scoring the self-descriptions and ideal self-descriptions for M/F.

Having decided that standard scores should not be used as statistical corrections for artifactual differences, it was still possible to use them in a supplementary manner to answer different questions concerning M/F in the various countries. As we have chosen to treat the variation in M% means and variances as reflecting bona fide phenomena, there are important differences among the item pools in the amount of "available M/F" in the different countries. In this context, the use of standard scores, by adjusting for differences in means and variances, provides an indication of the manner in which subjects employ the "available M/F" in the respective scoring systems. As an illustration, the mean M% for the item pool in Italy is 63.5% whereas the corresponding mean in Nigeria is 46.3%, indicating that there is "more masculinity" available in the Italian scoring system than in the Nigerian scoring system. Thus, a Nigerian man who obtains a mean M% score of 55% for his self-description is using a higher proportion of the "available masculinity" than an Italian man with the same mean score.

For the reasons discussed, we will employ the raw M% scores in our principal analyses of M/F in the present project. We will, however, make occasional use of standard scores as a supplementary measure of the utilization of available M/F in self-descriptions and ideal self-descriptions (see Chapter 6).

Translation of Materials

In countries where a language other than English was employed, the translated versions of the 300 adjectives used in the self-descriptions and ideal self-descriptions were those that had been made for the earlier sex-stereotype study. As described elsewhere (Williams & Best, 1982, pp. 30, 55f), the translation of these items was an enormously demanding task, particularly because of the large number of items, many with nearly synonymous meanings, which the translators had to attempt to differentiate (consider: *steady*, *stable*, *unemotional*, and *unexcitable*). While not claiming the translations were perfect—probably an unrealizeable goal—we felt that they were certainly adequate for use in defining the sex stereotypes in the various countries.

With regard to the scoring of self-descriptions and ideal self-descriptions for masculinity/femininity, the question of translation fidelity of the ACL items is not of great concern in the present study. This is because it was the items, *as translated*, which were used in the sex-stereotype study to obtain the M% scores, that were subsequently used in scoring for M/F. When an individual chooses a set of translated adjectives as self-descriptive, it is the M% values of the translated items that are used in scoring, not M% scores associated with their English equivalents. Only if a large number of items were so badly translated that the total item pool became inadequate for self-description, would translation fidelity become a problem. We are persuaded that this is not the case with the adjective translations that we have employed.

The translated versions of the Sex-Role Ideology measure were specially made for this project. Each translation was arranged by the local cooperating researcher utilizing the judgment of several persons who were familiar with English and the language into which the translation was being made. Sometimes a committee approach was used; in other cases, a back-translation approach was employed in which one or more bilingual persons translated the material from English to the other language and other bilingual persons translated the product back into English, with any discrepancies resolved by subsequent discussion (Brislin, 1980).

As usual, we have no objective basis for assessing translation fidelity and must rely on the care which our cooperating researchers took in doing the translations. Of some help, however, is the nature of the SRI items shown in Table 4.1. First, it is much easier to translate sentences than individual words and, second, most of the items have overt behavioral references which are more easily translated than abstract concepts or ideas. There is the further consideration that our analyses are based on total scores derived from the individual's responses to all 30 items. In such a circumstance, it is unlikely that one or two badly translated items would invalidate the total score.

The Sex-Role Ideology Measure

In selecting the Kalin Sex-Role Ideology measure (Kalin & Tilby, 1978) for use in the project, we were concerned about the appropriateness of the items for use in our various cultural groups. Recognizing that the items were not exhaustive of the realm of sex-role ideology, we invited each cooperating researcher to consider either adding additional culturally relevant items and/or deleting any culturally inappropriate items from the standard set. As noted earlier in this chapter, none of our local researchers chose to add items but in three countries a small number of inappropriate items was eliminated.

It would, of course, have been desirable to have revalidated the items in each country using a version of the "known-groups" strategy employed by Kalin in the original Canadian validity study, but this task was beyond our capability. As a result, our confidence in the measure must rest upon the original validity study (Kalin & Tilby, 1978), and the high degree of "face validity" of the items for the assessment of sex-role ideology along a traditional (male dominant) to modern (egalitarian) dimension.

The Affective Meaning Scoring System

The Affective Meaning Scoring System, mentioned in Chapters 1 and 2 and described in more detail in Chapter 5, was used to assess the strength, activity, and favorability of the self-descriptions and ideal self-descriptions of the subjects from the different countries. This system was developed using English language speaking persons in the United States and we need to consider the applicability of this scoring system to self-descriptions obtained in other countries, particularly when languages other than English are employed.

At a conceptual or theoretical level, there seems no problem in assessing self-descriptions in terms of these three factors. The scoring system is patterned after Osgood's three factors of affective meaning (evaluation, potency, and activity), which have been shown to have cross-cultural generality (Osgood et al., 1975); thus, there seems no reason to think of these concepts as peculiarly American. The questions arise at the level of the individual scale values used in determining the mean strength, activity, and favorability of a given self-description. The scale values represent the mean ratings of the English adjectives by American judges. Strictly speaking, when we obtain affective meaning scores for a self-description in a language other than English, the scores represent not the affective meanings of the translated adjectives but, rather, the affective meanings of the English language items from which the translation was made.

Ideally, the translated ACL items would have been rescaled for strength, activity, and favorability by persons in each country where a translated version was employed—an enormous task that was beyond our capability. Therefore, one must have some confidence that affective meanings were taken into account in the original translation of the adjectives from English to the second language, so that translated items carry affective meanings similar to the English items from which they were translated. This is not an unreasonable assumption. When translators are attempting to choose an equivalent of a given English adjective from among several possibilities, we suspect that variations in the affective meanings of the alternatives often influence their final choice.

It is not necessary that one assume that each adjective used in another language would have an identical strength rating as in the English version in order for the American scoring system to be meaningful in cross-cultural analysis. We must, however, be able to make the more general assumption that, if the translated items were judged for strength by local subjects, the resulting ratings would show a substantial positive correlation with the strength ratings from the United States. Poortinga's (1975) distinction between functional equivalence and score equivalence in cross-cultural measures is relevant here. Functional (or dimensional) equivalence indicates that the measure assesses the same attribute in different groups. Score equivalence goes a step further and indicates that given quantitative values mean the same thing in different groups. In these terms, we must assume functional equivalence, but need not assume score equivalence, in order to gain meaningful information from the use of our American-based scoring systems.

The principal emphasis in our affective meaning analysis is on *differences* between the self-descriptions and the ideal self-descriptions of women and men obtained *in the same country*. Thus, in Country X, we compare the mean strength score of the men's self-descriptions with that of the women's self-descriptions and determine which is relatively stronger. If we make a similar male-female difference analysis in Country Y, we can then compare the *relative* strength of the descriptions in the two countries. In this case, the assumption of functional equivalence seems sufficient in order for this to be a meaningful analysis. On the other hand, if we compute the mean strength scores of the men's self descriptions in Country X and in Country Y and compare them directly, we must make the additional assumption of score equivalence. For this reason, our treatment of the affective meaning data stresses the former rather than the latter type of comparison.

Use of University Students as Subjects

We turn now to a consideration of what some might consider the major weakness in our method—the use of university students as subjects in a cross-cultural study of self-concept. There are, in general, both advantages and disadvantages in using university students as subjects in psychological research. Among the advantages are: their intelligence, which enables them to comprehend abstract tasks; their intellectual orientation, which enables them to appreciate the value of research and to be willing to cooperate in it; and their accessibility.

The disadvantages of using university students as research subjects are attributable to their being a select group, which cannot be considered representative of the general adult population in any country. In addition to their obvious atypicality regarding age and intelligence, they are also likely to differ from the general population in socioeconomic status, achievement motivation, values, and exposure to cultures other than their own. There is a further complication when university students are used in cross-cultural research. Although university students in all countries are select groups, they are more atypical in some countries than in others because the proportion of young people going to university differs substantially from country to country. This makes it difficult for the researcher to know if the students from various countries are comparable. One can assume, however, that college students may be more alike across various cultures than would be representative samples of the general populations in those countries.

The appropriateness of the use of university students as subjects also depends on the nature of the research. For example, in our earlier sex-stereotype project, university students were asked to serve as "cultural reporters" of traits considered to be male-associated and female-associated. Regarding this we wrote (Williams & Best, 1982, p. 53):

> For this type of task, it is our opinion that the characteristics which distinguish university students from the general population make them superior subjects. University students are likely to have given more attention and thought to the question of the different statuses and roles occupied by women and men and to have become sensitized to the psychological traits attributed to men and women in their respective countries. Many university students have—or like to think that they have—a relatively egalitarian view of women and men, which may include the belief that men and women actually differ very little in their psychological makeup. The juxtaposition of this belief with the evidence of stereotypes in the culture probably sharpens their perception of the latter and makes them more aware of the differences in psychological characteristics ascribed to men and to women. . . . Thus, although it is true that the university students were used, in part, because of their accessibility, we believe that they constitute adequate, if not superior, subjects for this particular project.

It is quite another matter when one asks university students in different countries to report on their own *personal* characteristics with the idea of relating the findings to differences in cultural background. We have already admitted that university men and women cannot be considered representative of men and women in their cultures. How then can we rationalize their use in a project such as this?

We believe the concept of university students as "cultural carriers" is a valid one. Despite their atypicality, university students were exposed to cultural variables during their formative years with many effects persisting into young adulthood. Although their exposure to other cultures may have influenced them in significant ways, they still possess many characteristics attributable to their own cultural upbringing.

The authors' personal observations of university students in India may serve as an illustration. India has had centuries of exposure to Western culture particularly through the 200 year period of the British raj. During this time, a western educational system was installed, and English became the common language of educated Indians. Ambitious young Indians went to England, and later to the United States and Canada, for their education, often returning to teach in the Indian universities.

What is the impact of all this? Little more than to produce a thin Western veneer over the strong Indian cultural values. The great majority of Indian university students still expect their marriages to be arranged by their families. Indian university graduates go to great lengths to obtain employment in the geographical area of their ancestral homes and extended families. Professional men seek the advice of their older brothers before making important personal decisions. And so on. University students in India are very "Indian" in many basic respects, including their views of women and men and social relations between the sexes. The popular idea that relatively brief exposures to Western culture result in the obliteration of deeply rooted cultural values is a Western conceit! Thus, it is our view that university students in different countries remain products of their national cultures and therefore may be viewed as cultural carriers for research purposes.

The use of atypical groups of persons from different cultures to study cultural variation has been addressed by Hofstede (1980) in the context of his cross-cultural study of work-related values. This study of 40 countries was based on attitude survey data obtained from the employees of subsidiaries of one large, multinational business organization, coded as HERMES. The employees surveyed were primarily from the managerial, professional, and technical ranks of the company. The great majority of the subjects were male.

How can such highly selected groups be considered appropriate for the cross-cultural study of values? Hofstede (1979, p. 392) addresses this question as follows:

> Valid comparisons of samples of individuals from countries should either be very broad (representative of entire populations) or narrow but very well matched (functionally equivalent in each country). The HERMES samples belong to the second category. Respondents from country to country are

similar in many respects (education level, occupation, actual work done, company policies and superstructure); they only differ in their nationality. An analysis comparing HERMES employees in one country to those in another should therefore reveal the effect of nationality quite clearly. Because the respondents have so much in common, the differences found within HERMES should in fact be a conservative estimate of the differences to be found elsewhere.

On balance, we believe that, although university students may not be ideal subjects for a cross-cultural study of self-concept, they constitute useful samples of persons from their respective cultures. We wish, however, to be conservative about this and we suggest that the reader remember that the findings reported in the subsequent chapters relate to cross-cultural similarities and differences in the self-concepts of university students.

SUMMARY

In this chapter, we described the method employed in the current project including the subjects who participated and the questionnaire materials employed. We also described the various cultural comparison variables to which the findings of the study would be related, for example, economic-social development. This was followed by a critique of the method involving a consideration of such factors as: the sample of countries; the assessment of both self and ideal self; the use of scaled items which permits the assessment of both means and variances in self-descriptions; the translation of materials; the use of scoring system developed in the United States; and the use of university students as subjects.

NOTES

1. In the previous sex-stereotype project, there were six published papers in which the single or first author was one of our cooperating researchers: Bhana (1980); Edwards & Williams (1980); Haque (1982); Tarrier & Gomes (1981); Ward (1985); Ward & Williams (1982). The foregoing were in addition to cooperative papers written at the initiative of the present authors: Best et al. (1977); Williams et al. (1979, 1981); Williams, Best, Haque, Pandey, & Verma (1982); Williams, Giles, & Edwards (1977); Williams, Giles, Edwards, Best, & Daws (1977).

2. Saburo Iwawaki, our cooperating researcher in Japan, notes that the direct question, "What is your religion?" is considered strange or inappropriate by many Japanese persons who may participate in several different religious traditions. Standard questionnaires on religion, such as those used in the United States, are not always relevant in Japan.

3. Correlations across all 14 countries for the percentage of Catholics in the subject sample (Table 3.2) versus country values (Table 3.3) = .81. Similar correlations for percentage of

Muslims = .96, for percentage of Protestants = .53, for percentage Urban = .39, and for percentage of Women (mothers) Employed = .62.

4. (1) Sivard (1982). (2) Barrett (1982). (3) *Yearbook of labor statistics* (1976). (4) *World book encyclopedia* (1963). (5) Hofstede (1980).

5. Health and education indicators represent both input of national effort (e.g., public expenditures, teachers) and output (e.g., literacy, infant mortality). Input factors credit efforts that will determine social progress but may not yet be visible in slower-acting indicators of results. Other indicators could have been included in the index, such as housing and nutrition but many of these are reflected in related measures already included (e.g., mortality, life expectancy). Only one indicator (% women in total university enrollment) reflects the unequal distribution of resources within countries (Sivard, 1982, p. 37).

6. The economic-social development scores for our 14 countries correlates .62 with their PQLI scores.

7. Myers and Sugar (1979) discussed the problems involved in the use of such categories, including the variations from study to study in the cutoff scores used in establishing the categories. Further, they suggested that the undifferentiated category is not a meaningful classification. Other researchers (e.g., Kelly & Worell, 1977) have suggested that undifferentiated individuals so classified on scales with only positive items may be persons with negative self-concepts.

8. Standard scores are raw scores expressed in terms of their deviation from the mean of the distribution divided by the standard deviation (square root of the variance) of the distribution. Thus, a standard score of 1.0 indicates that the corresponding raw score was one standard deviation above the mean.

PART III

Discoveries

4

SEX-ROLE IDEOLOGY

Sex-role ideology refers to an individual's beliefs about proper role relationships between women and men. All human societies consist of men and women who must interact with one another, usually on a daily basis, and who have developed customs embracing prescriptive beliefs about the manner in which men and women are to relate to one another. These belief systems are sometimes explicit and specific and at other times implicit and general, but it appears that human societies generally find it necessary to provide some regulations regarding the manner in which the two sexes are to interact. As all human societies are predicated on male-female interaction, at least in the context of the sexual act, it is not surprising that sex-role prescriptions are an important facet of all human societies, and that individual persons who choose to violate the established norms are subject to social disapproval and perhaps sanctions.

Although there are a number of ways in which sex-role ideologies might be classified across cultures, we have chosen to classify them along a continuum ranging from *traditional* to *modern*. Traditional ideologies hold that men are more "important" than women and that it is proper for men to exercise control and dominance over women. Modern ideologies represent a more egalitarian viewpoint in which women and men are viewed as being of equal importance and reject the idea that one should be generally dominant over the other. The egalitarian viewpoint is sometimes labeled a *feminist* viewpoint, as this is the position often advocated by proponents of the women's liberation movement.

In this project, the individual subjects in each country were asked to indicate degree of agreement with statements relating to role-relationships between women and men, and other related matters. In later chapters, we will consider these data at the individual subject level to determine whether sex-role ideology scores are related to self-concept measures. In this chapter, we will be concerned with the typical sex-role ideology scores found for men and women in each country. Of interest here will be the question of whether women tend generally to be more liberal than men in sex-role ideology, as has been found in a number of previous investigations (e.g., Kalin et al., 1982; Spence & Helmreich, 1978). The men's and women's ideology scores also will be examined for variation across the 14 countries, and this variation will be studied in relationship to our cultural comparison variables.

We have chosen to report our principal findings regarding sex-role ideology prior to our findings regarding self-concept. In a sense, we view sex-role ideology as another cultural comparison variable, and by considering these findings first we can then treat sex-role ideology as a comparison variable in our analyses of self-concepts in Chapters 5, 6, and 7.

Summary of Method

The sex-role ideology instrument and the instructions to the subjects have been described in Chapter 3. Briefly, the subjects were asked to consider each of the 30 declarative statements shown in Table 4.1 and to indicate, along a 7-point scale, their degree of agreement or disagreement with the statements. It will be observed that some of the items are phrased in a traditional direction, indicated by the letter T in parenthesis, whereas others are phrased in a nontraditional or modern manner, as indicated by the letter M in parenthesis. In deriving a total score for the individual subjects, ratings on the traditional items were reversed so that high total scores are always indicative of a modern position and low scores are indicative of a traditional position. Scored in this manner, the possible range of mean scores was from 1.0 (most traditional) to 7.0 (most modern). It was noted in Chapter 3 that two items were excluded in Singapore and Malaysia, and three items in Pakistan, because they were considered to be culturally inappropriate. In addition, one item was unintentionally omitted from the Italian version. In these countries, the mean scores were based on the remaining items.

As we begin our consideration of the empirical findings of the project, let us comment on a matter of general organization of the remainder of the book. In this chapter and the other chapters dealing with results (Chapters 5-7), we report the findings with a minimum of interpretation. Having completed the examination of the results, we will return to the major findings in Chapter 8, where we will attempt to interpret what we have found. This approach is to us both more efficient and more meaningful than to attempt to discern the significance of each isolated finding as it is reported.

Mean Sex-Role Ideology (SRI) Scores

The mean ratings for each item by the women and men subjects in each country are found in Appendix B. In addition, a mean Sex-Role Ideology (SRI) score was obtained for each subject based on the responses to all items, with ratings for traditional items reversed so that higher scores

Table 4.1 Items of the Sex-Role Ideology Scale (T = Traditional Items; M = Modern Items)

1	The husband should be regarded as the legal representative of the family group in all matters of law. (T)
2	A wife's activities in the community should complement her husband's position. (T)
3	A woman should have exactly the same freedom of action as a man. (M)
4	The best thing a mother can teach her daughter is what it means to be a girl. (T)
5	A married woman should feel free to have men as friends. (M)
6	Woman's work and man's work should not be fundamentally different in nature. (M)
7	Swearing by a woman is no more objectionable than swearing by a man. (M)
8	A woman is not truly fulfilled until she has been a mother. (T)
9	When a man and woman live together she should do the housework and he should do the heavier chores. (T)
10	A normal man should be wary of a woman who takes the initiative in courtship even though he may be very attracted to her. (T)
11	It is an outdated custom for a woman to take her husband's name when she marries. (M)
12	Women should be paid a salary by the state for the work they perform as mothers and homemakers. (M)
13	Women should be much less concerned about make-up, clothing, and body care. (M)
14	Every child should be taught from an early age to feel a special honour and respect for Motherhood. (T)
15	A woman should be appreciative of the glances and looks she receives as she walks down the street. (T)
16	It should be perfectly alright for a mature woman to get involved with a young man. (M)
17	Marriage should not interfere with a woman's career any more than it does with a man's. (M)
18	A man's main responsibility to his children is to provide them with the necessities of life and discipline. (T)
19	A woman should be careful how she looks, for it influences what people think of her husband. (T)
20	A woman who dislikes her children is abnormal. (T)
21	Homosexual relationships should be as socially accepted as heterosexual relationships. (M)
22	More day-care centers should be available to free mothers from the constant caring for their children. (M)
23	Women should be allowed the same sexual freedom as men. (M)
24	A man's job is too important for him to get bogged down with household chores. (T)
25	A woman should be no more concerned with her physical appearance on the job than a man. (M)
26	Abortion should be permitted at the woman's request. (M)
27	The first duty of a woman with young children is to home and family. (T)
28	For the good of the family, a wife should have sexual relations with her husband whether she wants to or not. (T)
29	A woman should be more concerned with helping her husband's career than having a career herself. (T)
30	Women should not expect men to offer them seats in buses. (M)

Table 4.2 Mean SRI Scores of Men and Women in 14 Countries

	Men	*Women*
Canada	4.09	4.54
England	4.73	5.15
Finland	5.30	5.69
Germany	5.35	5.62
India	3.81	3.88
Italy	4.54	4.90
Japan	3.70	4.01
Malaysia	4.05	4.01
Netherlands	5.47	5.72
Nigeria	3.11	3.39
Pakistan	3.34	3.30
Singapore	3.61	4.39
United States	4.05	4.66
Venezuela	4.51	4.90

indicate more modern views. These scores were then averaged separately for the women and men in each country with the resulting mean scores shown in Table 4.2. These mean scores are also presented in Figure 4.1 in which the data have been arranged so that the countries with more modern scores are toward the left and the countries with more traditional scores are toward the right. Here it can be seen that the highest mean scores (i.e., most modern ideologies) were found in the Netherlands, Germany, and Finland, whereas the lowest mean scores (i.e., most traditional ideologies) were found in Pakistan and Nigeria.

The analyses of the data seen in the table and figure revealed several noteworthy findings. First, the general variation in SRI scores across countries was highly significant. The average response along the 7-point scale for subjects in the Netherlands was 5.59, whereas the average in Nigeria was 3.25. A second general finding was that the mean SRI scores tended to be generally similar for the men and women in the individual countries; across the 14 countries, the correlation between men's and women's means seen in Table 4.2 was .95. Another way to put this is that the variation between cultures appears to affect the men and women in a similar manner with the result that the cultural effects are much greater than the gender effects.

The foregoing statement does not, however, mean that there were not gender effects. As can be seen in the table and figure, there was a general tendency for the women to obtain higher (more modern) scores than the men. This effect was statistically significant in eight countries (Canada, England, Finland, Italy, Japan, Singapore, the United States, and Venezuela) and was not significant in the six other countries. In no country was there evidence that the men had more liberal scores than the women. The general

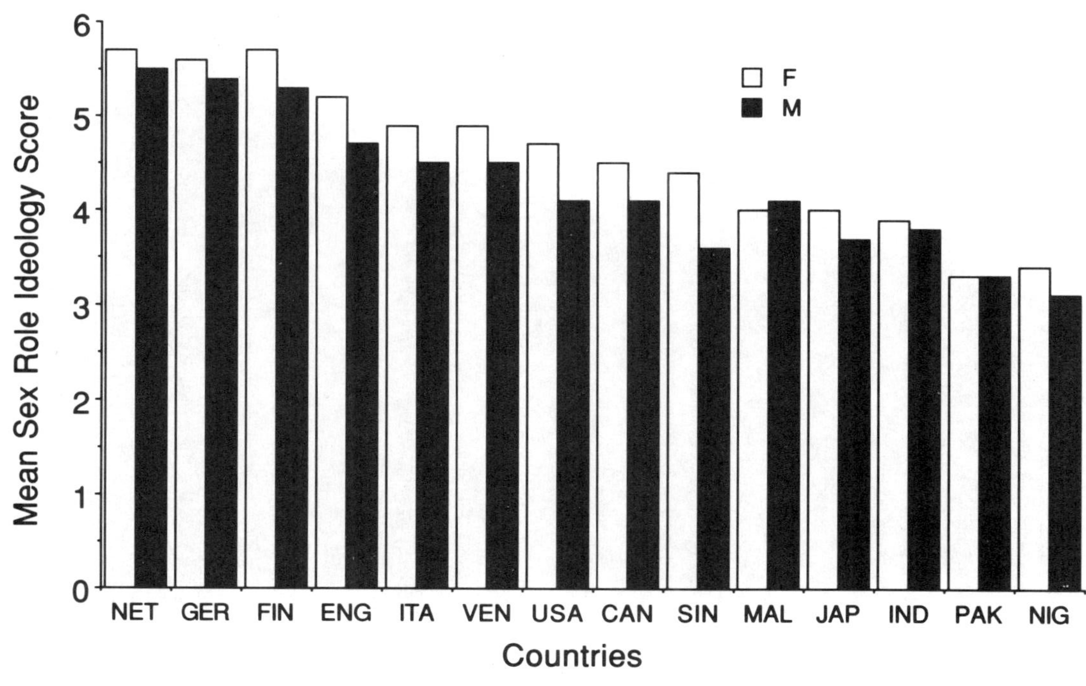

Figure 4.1. Mean Sex-Role Ideology Scores for Female (F) and Male (M) Subjects in 14 countries

Table 4.3 Sex-Role Ideology Items on which Women and Men Agreed and Disagreed

	Mean Rating	
	Women	*Men*
Items Agreed to More by Women Than Men		
5 A married woman should feel free to have men as friends.	5.5	4.9
6 Woman's work and man's work should not be fundamentally different in nature.	4.9	4.3
12 Women should be paid a salary by the state for the work they perform as mothers and homemakers.	3.9	3.3
Items Agreed to More by Men Than Women		
1 The husband should be regarded as the legal representative of the family group in all matters of law.	2.2	2.8
4 The best thing a mother can teach her daughter is what it means to be a girl.	2.6	3.2
18 A man's main responsibility to his children is to provide them with the necessities of life and discipline.	2.7	3.4
20 A woman who dislikes her children is abnormal.	2.2	3.1
24 A man's job is too important for him to get bogged down with household chores.	1.2	2.1
28 For the good of the family, a wife should have sexual relations with her husband whether she wants to or not.	1.5	2.1
Items with Greatest Agreement Between Men and Women		
11 It is an outdated custom for a woman to take her husband's name when she marries.	3.7	3.8
14 Every child should be taught from an early age to feel a special honour and respect for Motherhood.	4.1	3.9
16 It should be perfectly alright for a mature woman to get involved with a young man.	4.9	5.0
27 The first duty of a woman with young children is to home and family.	3.8	3.9
30 Women should not expect men to offer them seats in buses.	4.4	4.5

finding that women tend to be somewhat more liberal than men in sex-role ideology is consistent with the findings from a number of other studies. Kalin et al. (1982) report similar findings in England, Ireland, and Canada; Spence and Helmreich (1978) found evidence of this effect in Lebanon, Brazil, and the United States.

We examined our data further to determine whether the tendency for women to be more liberal was evident on all 30 items or tended to be restricted to certain items. This was done by computing a mean for each item across all 14 countries, separately for men and for women. The women's and men's overall means were then examined to determine how similar they were. The results of this analysis are shown in Table 4.3 in which three sets of items are listed: three items (all modern) that women agreed to more than

Table 4.4 Correlations of SRI with Cultural Comparison Variables

Economic-Social Development	.75**
Religion	
% Catholic	.46+
% Protestant	.62*
% Christian	.77**
% Muslim	–.69**
Status of Women	
% employed outside home	.50+
% women in university population	.46+
General Demographics	
urban	.67**
latitude	.70**
Values (Individualism)	.57*

+$p < .10$, *$p < .05$, **$p < .01$

men; six items (all traditional) that men agreed to more than women; and five items (two traditional, three modern) on which the agreement levels for men and women were quite similar. By examining the content of these item groups, the reader may gain some appreciation of the nature of the issues which, panculturally, men and women view differently in the general domain of sex-role ideology. Note that two of the three items agreed to more by women than men pertain to work issues, whereas most of the items agreed to more by men than women concern the higher status of men compared with women.

SRI and Cultural Comparison Variables

Having determined that there was substantial variation across countries in typical sex-role ideology along the traditional to modern continuum, we now proceed to examine the variation among countries in relation to our cultural comparison variables, previously described in Chapter 3. In view of the high degree of correspondence between mean SRI scores for the men and women in each country, we used in this analysis a total mean score for each country that was the average of the men's and women's mean SRI scores.

The cross-country correlations between mean SRI scores and the cultural comparison variables are shown in Table 4.4. Before examining the substantive findings, let us comment upon the manner in which we have chosen to indicate the statistical significance of these findings and the similar sets of correlation coefficients in the analyses reported in subsequent chapters. As can be seen, we have reported three levels of significance: .10, .05, and .01. This practice allows the reader some choice in being more conservative or more liberal in judging the reliability of the findings. For our commentary, we have generally employed the .05 level but have occasionally noted findings at the .10 level, particularly when they seemed supportive of other more significant results. The reader should also remember that in computing such large numbers of coefficients some will certainly appear significant by chance alone, tending to create Type I errors (i.e., concluding that a significant relationship exists when, in fact, it does not).

Turning now to the substantive findings in Table 4.4, it can be seen that there was a substantial relationship between sex-role ideology and economic-social development. As one moves from less developed to more developed countries, sex-role ideology shifts from a more traditional to a more modern orientation. Sex-role ideology was also related to religion; ideology tends to be more liberal in highly Christian countries and more traditional in highly Muslim countries. Liberality in sex-role ideology tended to be positively associated with both the percentage of women employed outside of the home and the percentage of women in the university. Heavily urbanized countries tended to be more liberal in ideology as did countries more distant from the equator. The Values correlation indicated that sex-role ideology is more liberal in countries where a high value is placed on individualism and a low value on authoritarian power structures. Stating the inverse of this, the relations between men and women are more traditional in countries in which a high value is placed on communal relationships and in which power differentials in organizational settings are viewed as legitimate.

From the foregoing it is clear that national differences in sex-role ideology do not exist in a vacuum but are importantly related to a variety of cultural differences. We will reexamine these findings later in the book after we have examined the relationships of our other measures to cultural comparison variables.

This completes our examination of cross-national differences in sex-role ideology. We will, however, return to sex-role ideology scores in subsequent chapters as we examine the relationship between sex-role ideology and our various measures of self-concept.

SUMMARY

In this chapter, we examined the cross-national findings regarding sex-role ideology assessed along a traditional/modern dimension. Significant variation was found among the countries in typical sex-role ideology. The SRI scores of women and men subjects were found to correlate highly across countries. There were, however, indications of gender effects: In 8 of the 14 countries women's views were more liberal than the men's views; in the remaining 6 countries there were no differences in the mean scores for men and women. Groups of items were identified to which the responses of men and women subjects differed. The variations in SRI scores across countries were found to correlate with a large number of cultural comparison variables; for example, the ideology scores were more modern (egalitarian) in countries higher in economic-social development.

5

AFFECTIVE MEANINGS OF SELF-CONCEPTS

The Adjective Check List (ACL), which we have used for the assessment of perceived self and ideal self, is a method widely used in the United States and other countries, particularly Italy and France. It is frequently employed in clinical settings to obtain a personality assessment that may be of use in working with individual clients. It has also been used in a great variety of research settings; a bibliography for the ACL lists 701 citations (Gough & Heilbrun, 1980a). The single-word item format of the ACL makes it easy to use in the assessment of concepts other than perceived self; thus, by simply changing the instructions to refer to the person an individual would like to be, one can obtain a description of the ideal self.

An individual's ACL description of perceived self or ideal self may be scored in terms of three comprehensive, alternative systems. The standard and most widely used scoring system generates a personality description in terms of 15 psychological needs (Gough & Heilbrun, 1980b). A second system summarizes the personality in terms of the five functional ego states of Transactional Analysis (William & Williams, 1980). The third scoring system, patterned after Osgood's three factors of affective meaning, describes the personality in terms of its relative favorability, strength, and activity (Best et al., 1980; Williams & Best, 1977). We employed all three of these alternative systems in our earlier cross-cultural study of sex stereotypes (Williams & Best, 1982). For the present project, we have chosen to use the affective meaning scoring system primarily because of the pancultural generality of the three affective meaning dimensions, as demonstrated in the work of Osgood and his associates (Osgood et al., 1975).

The findings from our study of sex stereotypes enabled us to propose a pancultural model of the psychological characteristics differentially associated with men and women when evaluated in terms of affective meaning. The findings on which the model is based are illustrated in Figure 5.1.

In each of our 25 countries, we identified the focused male and female stereotypes, which were the sets of adjectives that were associated with one gender at least twice as often as with the other gender. In each country, the male-stereotype items and the female-stereotype items were then scored to obtain mean strength, activity, and favorability scores. For strength, high scores represented greater strength; for activity, high scores represented greater activity; and for favorability, high scores represented greater favorability. The bars shown in Figure 5.1 represent the range of scores

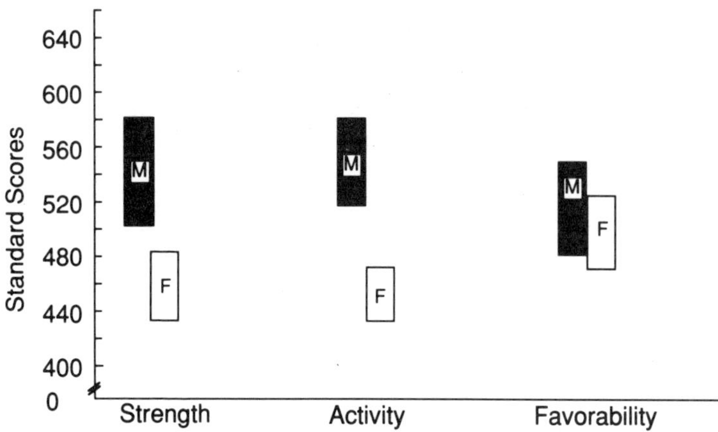

Figure 5.1. Ranges of Mean Scores for Strength, Activity, and Favorability for Male (M) and Female (F) stereotypes in 25 countries

obtained (highest to lowest) in the 25 countries for the three affective meaning factors.

It can be seen that in all countries the characteristics associated with men were both stronger and more active than the characteristics associated with women. No pancultural effect was found regarding the relative favorability of the sex stereotypes; rather, it was found that in certain countries the male-stereotype characteristics were more favorable than the female, whereas in other countries the reverse effect was found. There was, however, an interesting relationship between the relative favorability of the stereotypes and the strength and activity differences. In countries where the strength and activity differences were most pronounced, the male stereotype was viewed more favorably than the female stereotype, whereas in countries where the strength and activity differences were relatively small, the female stereotype was viewed as more favorable than the male stereotype. Stating this another way: In countries where women are seen more favorably than men, there is less perceived difference in the strength and activity of the sexes; in countries where women are seen less favorably than men, they are also seen as much weaker and more passive than men.

In this chapter, we will examine the self-descriptions and ideal self-descriptions of the men and women in our 14 countries with regard to their relative strength, activity, and favorability. With regard to strength and activity, we will note whether or not the differences in self-descriptions of men and women echo the findings from the sex-stereotype study, that is, do men describe themselves as stronger and more active than women? The favorability scores derived from the self-descriptions may be viewed as a rough index of self-esteem (LeVerrier, 1987). A comparison of the relative favorability of the self-descriptions of men and women in different countries may, therefore, provide us with information concerning the relative self-esteem of the two sexes. After examining the relative strength, activity, and favorability of the self-descriptions of men and women in the different countries, we will then relate these differences to our cultural comparison variables in order to gain insight into possible determinants of the observed differences in self-perceptions of women and men.

Scoring System

We discussed, in Chapter 3, the problems associated with the use of affective meaning ratings provided by American students in the scoring of self-descriptions of persons from other cultures, particularly when a translated version of the ACL is being employed. Our conclusion from this was that the scoring system may provide useful information when we are making *relative* comparisons between the self and ideal-self data for men and women in a particular country but that we must be much more cautious in making direct comparisons of mean scores between countries; for example, in comparing the mean favorability of men's self-concepts in one country with those of men in another country.

Detailed accounts of the studies in which the 300 ACL items were scaled for favorability, strength, and activity are available elsewhere (Best et al., 1980; Williams & Best, 1977). Here we will provide only a brief summary taken from our earlier book on sex stereotypes (Williams & Best, 1982, p. 85):

> Three independent studies were conducted with 100 American university students (50 men and 50 women) serving as subjects in each. In the first study, the students were presented with the 300 ACL items and were asked to rate the favorability of each item along a five-point scale: 1, very unfavorable; 2, moderately unfavorable; 3, neutral; 4, moderately favorable; and 5, very favorable. In the second and third studies, the subjects made similar five-point ratings along weak/strong and passive/active dimensions.
>
> The data from each of the three rating studies were handled in a similar manner; the favorability-rating data provide an illustration. The first step in analysis was to determine the mean of the favorability ratings assigned to each of the 300 items. The 300 mean item scores were then placed in a distribution and the mean and standard deviation were computed. Finally, the item means were converted to standard scores by setting the overall mean equal to 500 and the standard deviation equal to 100 and computing the standard score corresponding to each individual item. Thus, an item that received a standard

score of 600 (one standard deviation above the mean) was a favorable item, while an item with a score of 400 (one standard deviation below the mean) was an unfavorable item. Items with scores near 500 were neutral with regard to relative favorability.

In a similar manner, standard scores were also established for the data from the strength study and the activity study. For the strength ratings, scores above 500 were indicative of relative strength, while scores below 500 were indicative of relative weakness; for the activity ratings, scores above 500 were indicative of relative activity, while scores below 500 were indicative of relative passivity. In this way, three affective meaning scores were developed for each of the ACL items.

The favorability, strength, and activity scores associated with each of the 300 ACL items are presented in Appendix A. There it can be seen, for example, that the adjective aggressive has a favorability score of 504 (neutral), a strength score of 713 (very strong), and an activity score of 712 (very active), whereas the adjective gentle has a favorability score of 635 (very good), a strength score of 492 (neutral), and an activity score of 362 (very passive).

In the present study, mean favorability, strength, and activity scores were computed for the items endorsed by each subject in providing the self-descriptions and ideal self-descriptions. Group means of affective meaning scores were then computed for the men subjects and for the women subjects in each country. These scores, and various difference scores computed among them, constitute the data which we will examine in the balance of this chapter.

Strength Analysis

The mean strength scores for the self-descriptions and ideal self-descriptions of the men and women in the 14 countries are presented in Table 5.1. Also shown in the table are the differences in strength scores between the men's and women's self-descriptions and ideal self-descriptions. Differences in "total" or generic[1] self-descriptions (i.e., the mean of actual self and ideal self) are included along with difference scores between ideal self and actual self for men, for women, and for both sexes (the average of the two gender groups). These difference scores reflect the *relative* strength of the concepts in each country which, as noted earlier, may be more meaningful than the direct comparison of scores across countries.

The mean strength scores for the self-descriptions of men in the 14 countries are shown at the extreme left in Table 5.1. Here it can be seen that these scores ranged from a high of 553.9 in Nigeria to a low of 500.0 in

Table 5.1 Strength Analysis

	Means				*Difference Scores*					
	Men		*Women*		*Men – Women*			*Ideal Self – Self*		
	Self	*Ideal Self*	*Self*	*Ideal Self*	*Self*	*Ideal Self*	*Total Self*	*Men*	*Women*	*Both Sexes*
Canada	544.9	571.1	542.8	576.1	2.1	–5.0	–1.5	26.2	33.3	29.7
England	531.3	575.7	540.6	578.0	–9.3	–2.3	–5.8	44.4	37.4	40.9
Finland	517.5	571.0	530.4	574.4	–12.9	–3.4	–8.1	53.5	44.0	48.8
Germany	527.1	572.1	527.6	568.6	–.5	3.5	1.5	45.0	41.0	43.0
India	547.6	572.7	531.5	566.0	16.1	6.7	11.4	25.1	34.5	29.8
Italy	529.8	567.8	521.6	567.4	8.2	.4	4.3	38.0	45.8	41.9
Japan	500.0	578.1	491.3	573.5	8.7	4.6	6.7	78.1	82.2	80.1
Malaysia	548.0	569.5	522.2	569.2	25.8	.3	13.1	21.5	47.0	34.3
Netherlands	537.9	574.0	529.3	571.0	8.6	3.0	5.8	36.1	41.7	38.9
Nigeria	553.9	572.7	543.6	564.1	10.3	8.6	9.4	18.8	20.5	19.6
Pakistan	544.3	565.2	544.3	560.5	0	4.7	2.4	20.9	16.2	18.6
Singapore	546.4	577.2	535.0	575.6	11.4	1.6	6.5	30.8	40.6	35.7
United States	552.3	578.2	549.1	576.4	3.2	2.1	2.6	26.2	27.3	26.8
Venezuela	534.3	565.5	525.9	561.7	8.4	3.8	6.1	31.2	35.8	33.5

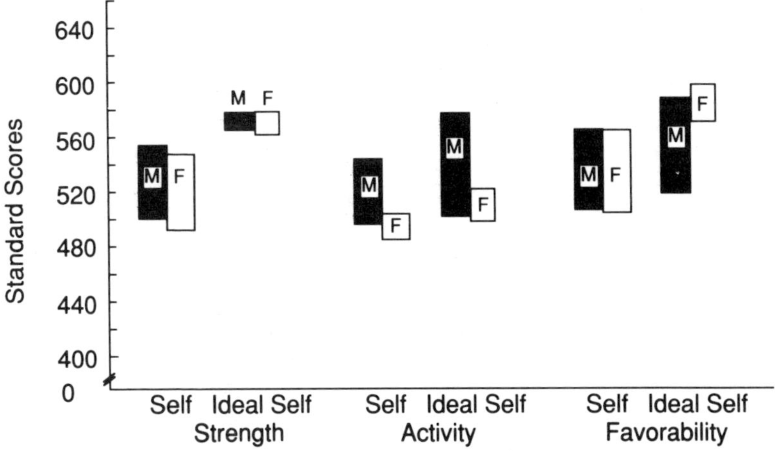

Figure 5.2. Ranges of Mean Scores for Strength, Activity, and Favorability for Male (M) and Female (F) Descriptions in 14 Countries

Japan, a range of 53.9 points. All scores, except for the Japanese, are above 500, suggesting that men's self-descriptions are relatively strong. In the next column are shown the mean strength scores for the ideal self-descriptions of the men. The highest mean (578.2) was obtained in the United States and the lowest mean in Pakistan (565.2), a range of only 13.0 points. Thus, it can be seen that the cross-country variation in men's strength scores was less for the ideal self-descriptions than for the actual self-descriptions. Also note that the ideal self-descriptions in all countries have higher strength scores than the self-descriptions, suggesting that panculturally men desire stronger characteristics.

The mean strength scores for the women's self-descriptions ranged from a high of 549.1 in the United States to a low of 491.3 in Japan, a range of 57.8 points. As in the men's data, all scores, with the exception of Japan, are above 500, suggesting relative strength in self-descriptions. For the women's ideal self-concepts, the mean scores varied from 578.0 in England to 560.5 in Pakistan, a range of 17.5 points. Again, there was less variability in mean strength scores for the ideal self-descriptions than for the self-descriptions, and ideal self-descriptions had higher strength scores than self-descriptions.

The ranges of strength scores for women's and men's self-descriptions and ideal self-descriptions are shown at the left in Figure 5.2. Here it can be seen that, for both men and women there is much more cross-national variation in the strength scores associated with self-descriptions than in the strength scores associated with ideal self-descriptions (i.e., how people see

Table 5.2 Strength Analysis: Rank Orders of Difference Scores

Men – Women						*Ideal Self – Self*					
Self		*Ideal Self*		*Total Self*		*Men*		*Women*		*Both Sexes*	
MAL	25.8	NIG	8.6	MAL	13.1	JAP	78.1	JAP	82.2	JAP	80.1
IND	16.1	IND	6.7	IND	11.4	FIN	53.5	MAL	47.0	FIN	48.8
SIN	11.4	PAK	4.7	NIG	9.4	GER	45.0	ITA	45.8	GER	43.0
NIG	10.3	JAP	4.6	JAP	6.7	ENG	44.4	FIN	44.0	ITA	41.9
JAP	8.7	VEN	3.8	SIN	6.5	ITA	38.0	NET	41.7	ENG	40.9
NET	8.6	GER	3.5	VEN	6.1	NET	36.1	GER	41.0	NET	38.9
VEN	8.4	NET	3.0	NET	5.8	VEN	31.2	SIN	40.6	SIN	35.7
ITA	8.2	USA	2.1	ITA	4.3	SIN	30.8	ENG	37.4	MAL	34.3
USA	3.2	SIN	1.6	USA	2.6	CAN	26.2	VEN	35.8	VEN	33.5
CAN	2.1	ITA	.4	PAK	2.4	USA	26.2	IND	34.5	IND	29.8
PAK	0	MAL	.3	GER	1.5	IND	25.1	CAN	33.3	CAN	29.7
GER	–.5	ENG	–2.3	CAN	–1.5	MAL	21.5	USA	27.3	USA	26.8
ENG	–9.3	FIN	–3.4	ENG	–5.8	PAK	20.9	NIG	20.5	NIG	19.6
FIN	–12.9	CAN	–5.0	FIN	–8.1	NIG	18.8	PAK	16.2	PAK	18.6

themselves is more variable from country to country than how people would like to be). Furthermore, both men and women see stronger traits as more desirable. It is interesting to note that although the strength scores for the Japanese men's and women's self-descriptions were noticeably lower than the other groups, their ideal strength scores were quite similar.

Men minus women difference scores. The six difference scores from Table 5.1 are repeated in Table 5.2, where they are arranged in rank order of magnitude. The difference scores between the men and women in each country are shown in the left half of the table, where the differences were obtained by subtracting the women's mean from the men's mean. Thus, a positive sign indicates that the men had higher strength scores than the women, whereas a minus sign indicates that the women had higher strength scores than the men.

The strength differences between the men's and women's self-descriptions are shown in the left-hand column of the table. Here, it can be seen that in most countries the men's self-descriptions were stronger than the women's self-descriptions, with this effect being most pronounced in Malaysia and India. On the other hand, there were two countries, England and Finland, in which the women's self-descriptions were noticeably stronger than the men's.

An examination of the strength differences between the ideal self-descriptions of men and women reveals, again, that in most countries the men had stronger descriptions than the women, with this effect being most pronounced in Nigeria and India. In Finland and Canada there was evidence of at least a slight tendency for the ideal self-descriptions of women to be stronger than the ideal self-descriptions of men.

If we average the strength scores for the self-concepts and ideal self-concepts for men and for women, and obtain the difference in these two averages, we obtain the total or generic self-difference scores seen in the table. These scores can be viewed as a composite of what people are and what they wish to be. These scores indicate that the generic self-descriptions for men were stronger than those for women in a majority of countries, with this effect being most pronounced in Malaysia and India. On the other hand, in England and Finland, there was a tendency for the generic self-descriptions of women to be stronger than the generic self-descriptions of men.

In our earlier sex-stereotype study (Williams & Best, 1982, p. 93), it was found that the male stereotype was stronger than the female stereotype in all 14 of the countries in the current study. Relative to this, we note that the direction of the stereotype differences is repeated in the self-descriptions and ideal self-descriptions in most countries but not in all. Considering the findings in England and Finland, it appears that the fact that male-associated characteristics are said to be stronger than female-associated characteristics in a given country does not necessarily mean that men will perceive themselves as being stronger than women. Apparently, other factors can, at times, counteract the models provided by general sex stereotypes.

Ideal-self minus self differences. The difference scores between ideal self and self are shown at the right-hand side of Table 5.2, where the difference scores are always computed by subtracting the self-strength score from the ideal-self-strength score. A general observation is that all of the ideal-self/self difference scores are positive indicating that, without exception, the subjects in all countries wished to be stronger than they perceived themselves to be. A second general observation is that the magnitude of the difference scores between ideal self and self are of a much greater magnitude than the differences previously reviewed between men and women. In other words, the difference between what people *are* and what people *want to be* is greater than the difference in gender.

The ideal-self/self difference scores may be conceptualized as indexing the degree to which persons in different countries desire to be stronger than they are. For the men, this effect appeared greatest for the Japanese and the Finns and smallest for the Malaysians, Pakistanis, and Nigerians. For the women, the effects were greatest in Japan and Malaysia and smallest in Pakistan and Nigeria. If one averages the difference scores for men and women one obtains the difference score for both sexes seen in the right-hand column of the table. This distribution of scores indicates that, for persons generally, the desire to be stronger than one is appears most pronounced in Japan and Finland and least pronounced in Nigeria and Pakistan.

From these analyses, we conclude that persons of both genders in all countries would like to be stronger than they are, but that the magnitude of this effect shows considerable variation across countries.

Table 5.3 Strength Analysis: Correlation of Difference Scores with Comparison Variables

	Men – Women			*Ideal Self – Self*		
	Self	*Ideal Self*	*Total Self*	*Men*	*Women*	*Both Sexes*
Economic-Social Development	–.40	–.66**	–.54*	.55*	.46+	.53*
Religion						
% Catholic	.00	–.10	–.04	–.08	–.06	–.07
% Protestant	–.64*	–.41	–.65*	.26	–.05	.13
% Christian	–.58*	–.45	–.62*	.10	–.16	–.02
% Muslim	.22	.36	.30	–.51+	–.47+	–.52+
Status of Women						
% women employed outside home	–.52+	–.58*	–.61*	.67**	.49+	.61*
% women in university population	–.40	–.77**	–.57*	.02	–.04	–.01
General Demographics						
urban	–.33	–.40	–.40	.47+	.37	.45
latitude	–.71	–.46	–.73**	.49	.16	.35
Values	–.51+	–.56+	–.57*	.20	.05	.14
Sex-Role Ideology	–.71**	–.46+	–.73**	.40	.20	.33

+$p < .10$, *$p < .05$, **$p < .01$

Strength difference scores and comparison variables. We have noted, in Chapter 3 and elsewhere, that affective meaning *difference* scores are more meaningful for cross-cultural comparisons than are the affective meaning scores themselves. For this reason, difference scores were used in all analyses involving cultural comparison variables. The cross-country distributions of strength difference scores were correlated with the 10 cultural comparison variables described in Chapter 3, and with the sex-role ideology scores from Chapter 4. The results of this analysis are shown in Table 5.3. It can be seen that the patterns of correlations were quite similar for the self and ideal-self difference scores and for the men's and women's difference scores. To avoid redundancy, we will confine our commentary to the strength difference scores between men and women for the total or generic self and to the ideal-self/self difference scores for both sexes.

The strength difference scores between generic self for men and generic self for women were found to be related to a number of comparison variables. As can be seen, strength differences between men and women were negatively correlated with economic-social development; as one moves from less developed to more developed countries, the strength differential in the self-perceptions of men and women diminishes and, perhaps, tends to reverse. This means that in less developed countries women describe themselves as much weaker than men, but in more developed countries they see themselves as more similar to how men see themselves in terms of strength. The strength differential between men and women was also related to the percentage of the population indicating a Protestant Christian affiliation; strength differences are less pronounced in highly Protestant countries. Hence, men and women saw themselves more similarly in these countries.

The strength difference scores were also related to both status of women variables; strength differences are smaller in countries in which there are high percentages of women employed outside the home and high percentages of women in the universities; where women spend more time outside the home in school or work, their self-perceptions are more similar to men's self-perceptions with regard to strength. The strength differential in men's and women's self-concepts were also related to latitude; these differences are greatest in countries close to the equator and diminish as one moves away from the equator. A negative correlation was found between the values measure and the strength differential between the sexes; there is less difference in the self-perceptions of men and women in countries that are more individualistic and less authoritarian. Finally, strength differences were also significantly related to sex-role ideology; the tendency for men to view themselves as stronger than women perceive themselves is greater in more traditionally oriented countries than in countries where the sex-role ideology is more egalitarian.

Correlations between the ideal-self/self difference scores for both sexes are shown in the right-hand columns of Table 5.3. Only two correlations reached statistical significance. The strength differential between how people see themselves and how they would like to be tends to be greater in more developed than less developed countries, and in countries where a higher percentage of women are employed outside the home. Perhaps greater development and more exposure of women to influences outside the home lead to less self-satisfaction and a greater desire to be stronger and perhaps more effective. There was also the suggestion that the strength differential between self and ideal self was less pronounced in highly Muslim countries. Inspection of the mean scores suggests that this effect may be attributable to women in Muslim countries seeing strong characteristics as somewhat less desirable than do women in other non-Muslim countries.

Activity Analysis

The mean activity scores for the self-concepts and ideal self-concepts of men and women in the 14 countries are shown at the left in Table 5.4.

The activity associated with the men's self-concepts ranged from a high of 544.0 in Venezuela to a low of 493.1 in Japan, a range of 50.9 points.

Table 5.4 Activity Analysis

	Means				*Difference Scores*					
	Men		*Women*		*Men – Women*			*Ideal Self – Self*		
	Self	*Ideal Self*	*Self*	*Ideal Self*	*Self*	*Ideal Self*	*Total Self*	*Men*	*Women*	*Both Sexes*
Canada	506.9	513.3	502.1	512.4	4.8	.9	2.9	6.4	10.3	8.4
England	502.6	514.5	505.7	504.0	–3.1	.5	–1.3	11.9	8.3	10.1
Finland	504.3	523.7	507.2	520.5	–2.9	3.2	.2	19.4	13.3	16.4
Germany	497.9	518.5	507.9	515.8	–10.0	2.7	–3.7	20.6	7.9	14.3
India	508.5	515.7	502.2	511.6	6.3	4.1	5.2	7.2	9.4	8.3
Italy	498.8	509.8	499.8	508.4	–1.0	1.4	.2	11.0	8.6	9.8
Japan	493.1	517.0	487.2	507.5	5.9	9.5	7.7	23.9	20.3	22.1
Malaysia	506.5	516.9	493.6	510.5	12.9	6.4	9.7	10.4	16.9	13.7
Netherlands	506.4	513.9	502.1	515.2	4.3	–1.3	1.5	7.5	13.1	10.3
Nigeria	503.7	508.8	490.1	498.4	13.6	10.4	12.0	5.1	8.3	6.7
Pakistan	495.7	506.4	495.5	508.1	.2	–1.7	–.8	10.7	12.6	11.7
Singapore	504.9	511.5	494.7	508.3	10.2	3.2	6.7	6.6	13.6	10.1
United States	509.8	515.4	504.4	510.4	5.4	5.0	5.2	5.6	6.0	5.8
Venezuela	544.0	577.1	507.5	514.5	36.5	62.6	49.6	33.1	7.0	20.1

Most of the scores indicated relatively active self-descriptions. The activity associated with men's ideal self-concepts ranged from a high of 577.1 in Venezuela to a low of 506.4 in Pakistan, a range of 70.7 points. Thus, there was a relatively high degree of variability in activity scores across countries for both the men's self-concepts and their ideal self-concepts. Both the self-concepts and ideal self-concepts reflect relatively active descriptions, with the ideal scores generally being somewhat more active.

The mean activity scores associated with women's self-concepts ranged from a high of 507.9 in Germany to a low of 487.2 in Japan, a range of 20.7 points. Thus, these scores clustered around 500, indicating relatively neutral activity scores for women's self-descriptions. The activity associated with the women's ideal self-concept ranged from a high of 520.5 in Finland to a low of 498.4 in Nigeria, a range of 22.1 points. Women's ideal descriptions were also mostly neutral in terms of activity scores.

The ranges of activity scores of the men's and women's self-concepts and ideal self-concepts are shown in the center section of Figure 5.2, which illustrated the findings that the men's self and ideal self were both higher and more variable than the women's. On the face of it, it would appear that the activity of men's self-concepts varies more across cultures than does the activity of women's self-concepts. Could this be attributable to a greater heterogeneity in men's roles than in women's roles across cultures?

Men minus women difference scores. The activity difference scores between men and women, and between ideal self and self, are presented in rank order in Table 5.5. The activity differences for the self-descriptions of men and women, seen at the extreme left in Table 5.5, indicate that in a majority of countries the men view themselves as more active than the women. This effect was particularly pronounced in Venezuela. On the other hand, there were countries in which the women viewed themselves as more active than the men viewed themselves, with this effect being strongest in Germany.

The activity difference scores for the ideal self of men and women indicated that in a majority of countries the men's ideal self was somewhat more active than the women's ideal self. Once again, this effect was more pronounced in Venezuela with a slight suggestion of a reversal of this effect in the Netherlands and Pakistan.

Considering the activity difference scores for the generic or total self, it can be seen that in a majority of countries men's total self was more active than women's total self. This effect was particularly pronounced in Venezuela, with a suggestion of a reversal in England and Germany.

The findings of the earlier sex-stereotype study (Williams & Best, 1982, p. 92) had indicated that men were viewed as more active than women in all countries. The findings just reviewed indicate that this does not necessarily result in men having more active self-concepts than women.

Table 5.5 Activity Analysis: Rank Orders of Difference Scores

Men – Women						*Ideal Self – Self*					
Self		*Ideal Self*		*Total Self*		*Men*		*Women*		*Both Sexes*	
VEN	36.5	VEN	62.6	VEN	49.6	VEN	33.1	JAP	20.3	JAP	22.1
NIG	13.6	NIG	10.4	NIG	12.0	JAP	23.9	MAL	16.9	VEN	20.1
MAL	12.9	JAP	9.5	MAL	9.7	GER	20.6	SIN	13.6	FIN	16.4
SIN	10.2	MAL	6.4	JAP	7.7	FIN	19.4	FIN	13.3	GER	14.3
IND	6.3	USA	5.0	SIN	6.7	ENG	11.9	NET	13.1	MAL	13.7
JAP	5.9	IND	4.1	USA	5.2	ITA	11.0	PAK	12.6	PAK	11.7
USA	5.4	SIN	3.2	IND	5.2	PAK	10.7	CAN	10.3	NET	10.3
CAN	4.8	FIN	3.2	CAN	2.9	MAL	10.4	IND	9.4	ENG	10.1
NET	4.3	GER	2.7	NET	1.5	NET	7.5	ITA	8.6	SIN	10.1
PAK	.2	ITA	1.4	ITA	.2	IND	7.2	ENG	8.3	ITA	9.8
ITA	−1.0	CAN	.9	FIN	.2	SIN	6.6	NIG	8.3	CAN	8.4
FIN	−2.9	ENG	.5	PAK	−.8	CAN	6.4	GER	7.9	IND	8.3
ENG	−3.1	NET	−1.3	ENG	−1.3	USA	5.6	VEN	7.0	NIG	6.7
GER	−10.0	PAK	−1.7	GER	−3.7	NIG	5.1	USA	6.0	USA	5.8

Ideal-self versus self differences. The ideal-self minus self difference scores for men, women, and both sexes in each country are shown at the right in Table 5.5. We note that all of the differences have a positive sign indicating that in all cases persons wish to be somewhat more active than they in fact see themselves to be. On the other hand, we note that the general magnitude of these differences are substantially less than the comparable differences between ideal self and self for strength noted earlier in Table 5.2. Apparently, persons wish to be both more active and stronger than they are, but the magnitude of this effect is greater for strength than for activity.

Among the men's groups, the shift in activity from self to ideal self was greatest in Venezuela and Japan and least in the United States and Nigeria. Among the women's groups, the activity shift was greatest in Japan and Malaysia and least in Venezuela and the United States. Note the interesting contrast between the ideal-self/self differences of men and those of women in Venezuela; the men's is the largest of the countries studied and the women's one of the smallest. Furthermore, Venezuelan men had the highest self and ideal-self mean activity scores, suggesting a strong emphasis upon activity for this group. Considering the combined data for both sexes, the self to ideal-self activity increase was greatest in Japan and Venezuela and least in Nigeria and the United States.

Activity difference scores and comparison variables. The correlations of the activity difference scores with the cultural comparison variables are presented in Table 5.6. Once again we will confine our commentary on the men minus women difference scores to those for the total or generic self. The activity difference scores for generic self were found to correlate with

Table 5.6 Activity Analysis: Correlation of Difference Scores with Comparison Variables

	Men – Women			*Ideal Self – Self*		
	Self	*Ideal Self*	*Total Self*	*Men*	*Women*	*Both Sexes*
Economic-Social Development	–.40	–.16	–.36	.35	–.01	.24
Religion						
% Catholic	–.37	–.24	–.37	–.09	–.53*	–.32
% Protestant	–.41	–.16	–.36	.29	–.11	.15
% Christian	–.57*	–.31	–.54*	.04	–.62*	–.27
% Muslim	.31	–.04	.21	–.23	.21	–.05
Status of Women						
% women employed outside home	–.32	.19	–.16	.55*	.11	.45
% women in university population	–.35	–.38	–.40	–.01	–.26	–.13
General Demographics						
urban	–.40	–.29	–.41	.24	–.06	.14
latitude	–.67**	–.44	–.66**	.39	–.15	.20
Values	–.31	–.21	–.34	.06	–.20	–.05
Sex-Role Ideology	–.69**	–.46+	–.69**	.33	–.25	.11

+ $p < .10$, * $p < .05$, ** $p < .01$

three comparison variables. The activity difference between men and women tends to be smaller in highly Christian countries, in countries farther removed from the equator, and in countries where there is a relatively liberal sex-role ideology. Stating this inversely, greater activity differences in the self-descriptions of men and women tend to be found in countries with relatively traditional sex-role ideologies, in countries closer to the equator, and in countries where there is a relatively small percentage of Christian religious affiliation.

The correlations involving the ideal-self minus self difference scores are shown at the right of Table 5.6. For women, the ideal-self minus self activity differential was smaller in highly Christian—particularly Catholic—countries. For men, this differential was greater in countries with a higher percentage of women employed outside the home—where more women work outside the home, men wish to be more active than they are!

Favorability Analysis

The mean favorability scores associated with the self-concepts and ideal self-concepts of the men and women in the various countries are shown at the left in Table 5.7. As we review these findings, the reader may wish to keep in mind that the mean favorability of self-descriptions may be considered as an index of self-esteem (LeVerrier, 1987).

The favorability associated with the self-concepts of the men ranged from a high of 567.3 in Nigeria to a low of 507.2 in Venezuela, a range of 60.1 points, with all scores on the favorable side of the midpoint of 500. The favorability associated with men's ideal self also showed substantial variability ranging from a high of 593.4 in Japan and the United States to a low of 518.7 in Venezuela, a range of 74.7 points. Again, all scores were favorable, with the ideal-self scores being generally more favorable than the self scores.

Considering the favorability of the women's self-descriptions, the results revealed that all self scores were on the favorable side, with women in Nigeria having the most favorable self-concepts (566.6) and the women in Japan having the least favorable (505.6), a range of 61.0 points. The favorability means for the ideal self-descriptions of women showed much less variability ranging from a high of 597.7 in England to a low of 571.6 in Venezuela, a range of 26.1 points. As with the men's scores, all ideal scores were very favorable and generally more favorable than the self scores.

The ranges of favorability scores for women's and men's self-concepts and ideal self-concepts are shown at the right in Figure 5.2. Note particularly the greater consistency among the women's ideal-self scores than among the men's. Women in all 14 countries show a more uniform desire to have more favorable ideal self-descriptions. Apparently, in some countries, men incorporate somewhat less favorable characteristics into their ideal self-descriptions, resulting in greater variation in favorability of ideal self-concepts across countries.

Men minus women difference scores. The men minus women favorability difference scores for self, ideal self, and total self are shown in rank order at the left in Table 5.8. For all three self-measures, it can be observed that there are some countries in which the men's self-descriptions are noticeably more favorable than the women's self-descriptions, and other countries in which the reverse effect occurs. This variability is similar to that obtained in our earlier study of sex stereotypes (Williams & Best, 1982, p. 90) in which no general pancultural favorability effect was found but, rather, in some countries the male stereotype was more favorable than the female stereotype, whereas in other countries the reverse was true.

Table 5.7 Favorability Analysis

	Means				*Difference Scores*					
	Men		*Women*		*Men – Women*			*Ideal Self – Self*		
	Self	*Ideal Self*	*Self*	*Ideal Self*	*Self*	*Ideal Self*	*Total Self*	*Men*	*Women*	*Both Sexes*
Canada	556.4	582.9	561.8	594.8	–5.4	–11.9	–8.7	26.5	33.0	29.8
England	543.3	592.4	555.5	597.7	–12.2	–5.3	–6.9	49.1	42.2	45.7
Finland	521.3	578.1	537.9	587.3	–16.6	–9.2	–12.9	56.8	49.4	53.1
Germany	540.4	581.9	537.3	583.5	3.1	1.4	2.3	44.5	46.2	45.4
India	557.1	585.1	543.5	578.7	12.6	6.4	10.0	28.0	35.2	31.6
Italy	538.1	577.9	530.4	581.2	7.7	–3.3	2.2	39.8	50.8	45.3
Japan	512.9	593.4	505.6	597.0	7.3	–3.6	1.9	80.5	91.4	86.0
Malaysia	559.7	577.9	540.1	584.8	19.6	–6.9	6.4	18.2	44.7	31.5
Netherlands	544.8	588.1	545.3	588.3	–.6	–.5	.6	43.4	43.3	43.4
Nigeria	567.3	587.1	566.6	586.1	.4	1.0	.7	19.8	19.2	19.5
Pakistan	561.4	580.7	564.1	577.5	–2.7	3.2	.3	19.3	13.4	16.4
Singapore	558.2	590.7	554.8	595.0	3.4	–4.3	–.5	32.5	40.2	36.4
United States	562.1	593.4	565.3	596.9	–3.2	–3.5	–3.4	31.3	31.6	31.5
Venezuela	507.2	518.7	536.6	571.6	–29.4	–52.9	–41.2	11.5	35.0	12.3

Table 5.8 Favorability Analysis: Rank Orders of Difference Scores

Men – Women						*Ideal Self – Self*					
Self		*Ideal Self*		*Total Self*		*Men*		*Women*		*Both Sexes*	
MAL	19.6	IND	6.4	IND	10.0	JAP	80.5	JAP	91.4	JAP	86.0
IND	12.6	PAK	3.2	MAL	6.4	FIN	56.8	ITA	50.8	FIN	53.1
ITA	7.7	GER	1.4	GER	2.3	ENG	49.1	FIN	49.4	ENG	45.7
JAP	7.3	NIG	1.0	ITA	2.2	GER	44.5	GER	46.2	GER	45.4
SIN	3.4	NET	–.5	JAP	1.9	NET	43.4	MAL	44.7	ITA	45.3
GER	3.1	ITA	–3.3	NIG	.7	ITA	39.8	NET	43.3	NET	43.4
NIG	.4	USA	–3.5	NET	.6	SIN	32.5	ENG	42.2	SIN	36.4
NET	–.6	JAP	–3.6	PAK	.3	USA	31.3	SIN	40.2	IND	31.6
PAK	–2.7	SIN	–4.3	SIN	–.5	IND	28.0	IND	35.2	MAL	31.5
USA	–3.2	ENG	–5.3	USA	–3.4	CAN	26.5	VEN	35.0	USA	31.5
CAN	–5.4	MAL	–6.9	ENG	–6.9	NIG	19.8	CAN	33.0	CAN	29.8
ENG	–12.2	FIN	–9.2	CAN	–8.7	PAK	19.3	USA	31.6	NIG	19.5
FIN	–16.6	CAN	–11.9	FIN	–12.9	MAL	18.2	NIG	19.2	PAK	16.4
VEN	–29.4	VEN	–52.9	VEN	–41.2	VEN	11.5	PAK	13.4	VEN	12.3

An examination of the men's minus women's favorability scores for self-descriptions indicates that men viewed themselves more favorably than women viewed themselves in such countries as Malaysia and India, whereas women had relatively more favorable self-descriptions in Finland and Venezuela. Regarding differences in favorability of ideal self, men had more favorable ideal self-concepts in India, whereas women had more favorable ideal self-concepts in such countries as Canada and Venezuela. One notes that in 10 of the 14 countries the women's ideal self was more favorable than the men's; in most of the countries, women aspire to be "better people" than do men.

Ideal-self minus self differences. An examination of the relative favorability of ideal self and self shown in the right-hand portion of Table 5.8 reveals, as one might expect, that persons in all countries wish to be more favorable than they perceive themselves to be. There were, however, some noteworthy differences in the magnitude of this effect. For the men, the favorability shift from self to ideal self was greatest in Japan and smallest in Venezuela. For the women's groups, the favorability shift from self to ideal self was largest, again, in Japan and smallest in Pakistan. Merging the difference scores for men and women, the average shift from self to ideal self was greatest in Japan and least in Venezuela. It would appear from these analyses that there are some major differences among countries in the degree to which people aspire to have characteristics that are more favorable than the ones they perceive themselves to have.

Favorability difference scores and comparison variables. Table 5.9 presents the correlations between the various favorability difference scores just

Table 5.9 Favorability Analysis: Correlation of Difference Scores with Comparison Variables

	Men – Women			*Ideal Self – Self*		
	Self	*Ideal Self*	*Total Self*	*Men*	*Women*	*Both Sexes*
Economic-Social Development	–.37	–.70**	–.51+	.58*	.52+	.57*
Religion						
% Catholic	.11	.13	.13	–.06	–.05	–.05
% Protestant	–.67**	–.52+	–.67**	.30	.03	.17
% Christian	–.54*	–.36	–.52+	.16	–.08	.04
% Muslim	.16	.43	.27	–.58*	–.53*	–.58*
Status of Women						
% women employed outside home	–.48+	–.47+	–.61*	.67**	.57*	.64*
% women in university Population	–.37	–.53*	–.46+	.04	.00	.02
General Demographics						
urban	–.28	–.50+	–.39	.51+	.41	.47+
latitude	–.61**	–.53*	–.63*	.54*	.27	.41
Values	–.54+	–.58*	–.60*	.26	.14	.20
Sex-Role Ideology	–.37	–.32	–.38	.45	.27	.37

$+p < .10$, $*p < .05$, $**p < .01$

noted and the cultural comparison variables. For the men minus women difference scores, the pattern of correlations with the comparison variables was similar for self, ideal self, and total self. To avoid redundancy, we will confine our comments to the relationships for total or generic self. The findings suggested that the women's total self was relatively more favorable than the men's in countries which are: high in percentage of Protestant affiliation; high in the percentage of women employed outside the home; farther from the equator; and high in individualistic values. In addition, correlations approaching statistical significance suggested that the women's total self was more favorable than men's in more developed countries and in countries with a high percentage of women attending the university. It can also be noted that the favorability difference scores for total self did not correlate significantly with sex-role ideology, contrary to the significant correlations found for the difference scores on both strength and activity. These correlations suggest that women develop more positive feelings about themselves in cultures where more opportunities are available to them and where there is greater economic development.

The magnitude of the favorability shift from self to ideal self appeared to be correlated with four variables. The shift was relatively small in highly

Muslim countries where self-descriptions were highly favorable. On the other hand, the shift was relatively large in countries with high socioeconomic development, in countries in which a high percentage of women are employed outside the home, and in relatively urbanized countries. In these countries, the ideal self-descriptions were the most favorable, suggesting greater aspirations toward being better people.

A Comparison of Ranges for the Three Affective Meaning Factors

Having examined all three sections of Figure 5.2, it is interesting to note the different types of results observed when the ranges of the three affective meaning factors are compared. The ranges of strength scores revealed a "main effect" of concept (i.e., ideal self was higher and less variable than self for both sexes). The ranges of activity scores suggested a "main effect" of gender (i.e., the men's scores were higher and more variable than the women's for both concepts). Finally, the ranges of favorability scores revealed an "interaction effect," with the women's ideal selves being higher and less variable than the men's, whereas the two actual-self ranges were quite similar. One final effect can be noted in the figure: The ranges for women's ideal self are always small whereas, in two out of three instances, the ranges for men's ideal self are relatively large. From this it would appear that, cross-culturally, there is more agreement among women than among men as to the characteristics of the ideal self.

Affective Meaning Composite Scores

The discerning reader may have noticed considerable similarity in the correlational patterns between the cultural comparison variables and the strength, activity, and favorability difference scores noted in Tables 5.3, 5.6 and 5.9. The reason for this is that there are significant correlations among the difference scores for the three affective meaning factors, as well as among some of the comparison variables (see Chapter 3). For the men minus women total-self scores, strength differences and activity differences correlate .68, strength differences and favorability differences correlate .90, and activity differences and favorability differences correlate .38. For the ideal-self minus self difference scores for both sexes, strength differences correlate with activity differences .84, the strength differences correlate with the favorability differences .99, and the activity differences correlate with the favorability differences .79. These relationships suggested the existence of *general* differences in affective meaning and we decided that it would be worthwhile to form composite affective meaning difference scores which would take into account all three of the affective meaning factors simultaneously.

A composite score for the men minus women affective differences was obtained in the following manner. First, constants were added to the difference scores shown in Tables 5.2, 5.5, and 5.8 to remove negative numbers. The three resulting scores were then averaged. Computed in this manner, high scores would be obtained in countries where the total self-descriptions of men were relatively stronger, more active, and more favorable than those of women. Low scores on the composite would be found in countries where there was little difference, or a slight difference favoring women, in strength and activity and in which the favorability of the women's self-concepts was greater than that of the men's. The composite affective meaning score for the ideal-self minus self differences was both easier to compute and simpler to interpret. The composite score was computed by averaging the "both sexes" difference scores in Tables 5.2, 5.5 and 5.8. High scores on this composite occurred in countries where the affective meaning shift from self to ideal self was relatively large; low scores occurred in countries where this shift was relatively small.

The correlations between these two composite affective meaning difference scores and the comparison variables are shown in Table 5.10. For purposes of exposition, let us define two types of countries in terms of their status on the men minus women affective meaning composite scores. Type A countries are those in which the composite score is relatively high; in these countries the total self-concepts of men relative to women tend to be more favorable, much stronger, and much more active. Type B countries are those in which the composite score is relatively low; here, the women's self-concepts are more favorable and there is relatively little difference in the strength and activity in the men's and women's self-concepts, or a slight tendency for the women's concepts to be stronger and more active than the men's. Employing this conceptualization, we can make a number of observations based on the correlations between the men minus women difference scores and the comparison variables seen in the left-hand column of Table 5.10.

Type A countries, where the men's self-concepts are more favorable, much stronger, and more active, tend to be: relatively low in economic social development; relatively low in the percentage of Christian (especially Protestant) religious affiliation; relatively low in the percentages of women in the universities and employed outside the home; and relatively close to the equator. In the Type A countries the emphasis on individualism is relatively low and the general social orientation tends to be more authoritar-

Table 5.10 Correlations of Affective Meaning Composite Difference Scores with Comparison Variables

	Men – Women Total Self	*Ideal Self – Self Both Sexes*
Economic-Social Development	–.54*	.52+
Religion		
% Catholic	–.07	–.09
% Protestant	–.66**	.14
% Christian	–.63*	–.03
% Muslim	.30	–.50
Status of Women		
% women employed outside home	–.55*	.61*
% women in university population	–.54*	–.01
General Demographics		
urban	–.45	.43
latitude	–.76**	.37
Values	–.61*	–.14
Sex-Role Ideology	–.58*	.32

+$p < .10$, *$p < .05$, **$p < .01$

ian. Also, Type A countries tend to have a relatively traditional sex-role ideology orientation.

Stating these relationships in the reverse manner, Type B countries, where the women's self-concepts are more favorable and where the usual strength and activity differentials are low or perhaps slightly reversed, tend to be: relatively more developed socioeconomically; relatively high in the percentage of Christian (especially Protestant) religious affiliation; relatively high in the percentages of women in the universities and employed outside the home; and relatively far removed from the equator. In these countries, the emphasis on individualistic values tends to be relatively high and the general sex-role ideology orientation tends to be rather modern. Thus, we see that there is a sizable constellation of cultural variables which are related to the affective meaning composite difference scores.

The composite ideal-self minus self affective-meaning difference scores showed less relationship to cultural variables. They were significantly related only to the percentage of women employed outside the home; in countries where this percentage is large, there tends to be a greater shift in overall affective meaning from self to ideal self, or a greater difference between how people see themselves and what they aspire to be. The correlation with socioeconomic development, which approached statistical significance, suggested a tendency for the overall shift in affective meaning from self to ideal self to be greater in more developed countries. Perhaps the psychological climate in more developed countries encourages people to aspire to greater personal change than in less developed countries; in more developed countries, it may be easier to say, "I wish to be different from what I am."

SUMMARY

In this chapter, we examined the self-concepts and ideal self-concepts of the men and women subjects in the different countries in terms of affective meaning: strength, activity, and favorability. We also examined the descriptions in terms of a composite score based on all three affective meaning factors. A number of interesting findings were observed: for example, a tendency for the men's self-descriptions and ideal self-descriptions to be stronger and more active than the women's, with no general difference for favorability; a tendency for ideal self to be stronger, more active, and more favorable than self for both men and women in all countries. Differences in the affective meanings associated with the self-concepts and ideal self-concepts of men and women were found to have important relationships to several cultural comparison variables; for example, in countries low in economic-social development, the self-concepts of women and men were more differentiated in terms of overall affective meaning than in more highly developed countries.

NOTE

1. See Chapter 2 for a discussion of generic self-concepts as the sum of actual and ideal self-concepts. We are using the terms *total* and *generic* interchangeably.

6

MASCULINITY/FEMININITY OF SELF-CONCEPTS

Manlike or womanlike—this is the essential meaning of the twin concepts of masculinity/femininity (M/F). If a person behaves in a manlike manner, the person is said to be masculine; if a person behaves in a womanlike manner, the person is said to be feminine. The question of cross-cultural variation in M/F is an intriguing one and conventional wisdom suggests that such differences may exist. Consider the phenomenon of machismo in Latin American countries; aren't males in Venezuela more masculine than males in, say, Finland? What about the relation of masculinity to sex-role ideology? Aren't men more masculine in traditional countries with a male-dominant ideology than in more modern countries with a relatively egalitarian ideology?

A number of investigators have attempted to address the question of variations in M/F across cultures. Usually, the approach has been to take an M/F scale developed in one country (often the United States) and administer it to men and women from one or more other countries, using translated items if necessary. These data are then examined to see if men and women from the other cultures display more or less M/F than those in the original culture.

A study reported by Spence and Helmreich (1978) illustrates this approach. These researchers had developed their Personal Attributes Questionnaire (PAQ) from M/F studies which they conducted in the United States (see Chapter 2). As noted earlier, they found that the self-descriptions of American male university students revealed similar means on the masculinity (M = 21.69) and femininity scales (M = 22.43), whereas the self-descriptions of American female university students revealed lower masculinity scores (M = 19.54) and higher femininity scores (M = 24.37) (Spence & Helmreich, 1978, p. 50). They then translated their scale into Portuguese and administered it to university students in Brazil. The pattern of findings for the female students in Brazil was generally similar to that in the United States: The typical woman had a mean femininity score of 23.27 and a mean masculinity score of 18.53. The Brazilian men, however, were found to differ from the American men in that they obtained higher femininity scores (M = 21.61) than masculinity scores (M = 18.98). Findings similar to these also were reported by Basow (1984) who administered an English-language version of the PAQ to university students in Fiji and found that the women obtained mean femininity and masculinity scores of 23.0 and 20.4, respectively, whereas the men obtained a femininity mean of 24.2 and a masculinity mean of 21.6. Can we compare the findings for men in the three countries and conclude that Brazilian men and Fijian men are "more feminine" than American men? Hardly, because all groups were responding to items that had been selected as female- and male-associated *in the United States*. Only by comparing the self-descriptions of Brazilian and Fijian men with traits that are associated with women and men in their respective countries would it be possible to obtain findings that might permit such a conclusion.

A study by Gough (1966) serves as another example of this approach. Gough had developed a 38-item femininity scale in conjunction with the development of the California Psychological Inventory (CPI). This scale consisted of items which men and women subjects in the United States used with differential frequency in self-description; items that women endorsed more frequently than men were scored positively and items that men endorsed more frequently than women were scored negatively. As a result, high scores on the scale were taken as an index of femininity and low scores on the scale were taken as an index of masculinity. For purposes of this particular study, the femininity scale was translated into French, Italian, Spanish, and Turkish and was administered to subjects in France, Italy, Venezuela, and Turkey.

Viewed at a general level, the results of this study were as expected in that the male subjects in each country obtained significantly lower (more masculine) scores than did the female subjects in the same country. On the other hand, the difference between the mean scores for men and women differed appreciably from country to country. In the United States the women's mean was 23.36 and the men's mean was 16.26 for a difference of 7.10 points. In Turkey the men's mean was 22.25 and the women's mean was 18.17 for a difference of 4.08 points. Can we conclude from these findings that women and men in the United States are more highly differentiated in terms of masculinity/femininity than are men and women in Turkey? The answer is negative. Gough's analysis indicates that, although most of the CPI items "worked" in the appropriate direction in Turkey, some did not. Thus, the item "I want to be an important person in the community," which is agreed to more frequently by men than women in the United States, reverses in Turkey where it is agreed to more frequently by women than by men. The item "I like adventure stories better than romantic stories," which is agreed to more frequently by men in the United States, is agreed to more frequently by women in Turkey. In other words, these two items that are "masculine" in the United States are "feminine" in Turkey. Similar findings were obtained in Romania by Pitariu (1981) who translated the CPI femininity scale into Romanian and found that, of the 38 items, 31 differentiated significantly in the proper direction and 3 showed significant reversals.[1]

Even more dramatic evidence of failure of translated items to work in another culture is reported by Kaschak and Sharratt (1983) who were interested in developing a Spanish-language Latin American Sex-Role Inventory based on the responses of university students in Costa Rica. Included in the preliminary pool of 200 items were Spanish translations of the items from the Spence and Helmreich (1978) PAQ and the Bem (1974) SRI. It is reported that only two of the PAQ items were found to discriminate between men and women. The Bem items fared better with approximately half of the items found to be discriminating. From these findings it is clear that many items which represented masculinity and femininity in the United States did not do so in Costa Rica. Similar conclusions were reached by Ward and Sethi (1986) from BSRI studies conducted in South India and Malaysia and by Lara-Cantu and Navarro-Arias (1987) from a BSRI study conducted in Mexico.

The findings from the studies just discussed illustrate the general problems involved in the use of translated scales in cross-cultural studies of masculinity/femininity. Whereas some items appear to work very well across cultures, others do not. Some items may be inappropriate because of their content, whereas others may not work because of translation problems. In either case, because there are items which do not work cross-culturally, the total masculinity and femininity scores obtained from persons in different cultures cannot be directly compared to judge the relative masculinity/femininity of persons from different cultures. What is needed is a method for assessing M/F in a given culture in terms of the attributes that are male-associated and female-associated *in that culture* (i.e., locally defined sex stereotypes).

We noted in Chapter 2 our view that a proper operational definition of masculinity/femininity requires a consideration of three factors: a method for determining in a particular culture what is considered manlike and womanlike; a means for assessing the behavior of individual persons in the culture; and a way to evaluate or "score" the behavior of individual persons in terms of the cultural definition of what is manlike and womanlike. In the present project, what is manlike and womanlike is defined in terms of the findings from our previous sex-stereotype project (Williams & Best, 1982) in which we determined the characteristics more frequently associated with men and the characteristics more frequently associated with women in each country. The behavior of interest in this project consists of the self-descriptions and ideal self-descriptions of men and women in different countries. The third requirement is met in the current project by scoring the self-descriptions and ideal self-descriptions from a given country in terms of the locally defined sex stereotypes to determine the degree to which the self-perceptions of the women and men reflect the local stereotype characteristics.

For each of the 14 countries in the present project, the earlier sex-stereotype project yielded a set of M% scores that indicated the degree to which each of the 300 items from the Adjective Check List are differentially associated with men and women in that country. M% scores near 50% indicate items that are equally associated with men and women. As one moves upward from 50%, the items become progressively more strongly associated with men than with women, with scores in the 90s indicating adjectives that are much more highly associated with men than with women. As one moves to M% scores below 50%, the items become progressively more strongly associated with women so that items with M% scores around 10% are much more highly associated with women than with men. The M% value for each of the 300 items in the 14 countries in the current study are presented in Appendix A.

For purposes of our masculinity/femininity analyses, the self-descriptions and ideal self-descriptions of the men and women in each country were scored using the M% values for that particular country. This means that the self-descriptions and ideal self-descriptions are being scored, not in terms of some general scoring system, but in terms of the local stereotype definitions of what is manlike and womanlike in each culture. This definition of masculinity/femininity in culture-specific terms is one of the more novel features of the current project.

The scoring of each self-description and ideal self-description was accomplished by computing, for the set of endorsed items, the mean of the M% scores and the variance of the M% scores. Our examination of mean M% scores represents a conventional approach to the study of masculinity/femininity in which the analysis is directed toward summarizing a self-description in terms of whether it is, on the average, more masculine, more feminine, or balanced between the two. The examination of individual variance scores is a more novel approach concerned with summarizing the variability of the item values used by an individual in a self-description. The variance score for an individual description indicates the relative *diversity* in the M% scores of the items endorsed by the individual; individuals with high variance scores are persons who endorsed items with considerable numbers of extreme (high or low) M% scores; persons with relatively small variances tended to select items with M% scores closer to 50%. We will examine in this chapter our findings related to the mean M/F scores. Our findings concerning the variance M/F scores will be presented in Chapter 7.

Group Means of Individual Mean M% Scores

One mean M% score was computed for each subject's self-description and another for the subject's ideal self-description using the appropriate country values from Appendix A. In each sample of subjects, these individual subject mean scores were combined to obtain group mean scores for the self-descriptions and ideal self-descriptions of the women and men subjects in each country. These group means are shown in Table 6.1 together with marginals representing total or generic self (see Chapter 2), and self versus ideal self for all persons.

In each country separately, the data were analyzed to assess variations in the mean M/F scores associated with the self-descriptions and ideal self-descriptions of the women and men subjects.[2] In all countries, the analyses revealed a significant overall effect of gender indicating that, with self-descriptions and ideal self-descriptions combined into a total or generic self measure, the men's descriptions tended to have higher or more masculine M% scores than did the women's descriptions. In all countries, there was also a significant overall difference between the self-concepts and the ideal self-concepts: With the two gender groups combined, there was a general tendency for the M% means for ideal self to be higher than the M% means for self. Thus, in all countries, the generic self-concepts of men tended to be more masculine than the generic self-concepts of women, and the ideal self tended to be more masculine than the self.

In three countries—the Netherlands, Malaysia, and Canada—there was an interaction between the concept and the gender variables. This was attributable to the fact that, in these countries, the increase in M% scores from self to ideal self was greater for women than for men, suggesting that women in these countries saw a greater discrepancy between themselves and their ideals than did the men. In the other 11 countries the increase from self to ideal self was comparable in both gender groups.

The findings just reviewed reveal a high degree of pancultural generality. In all countries, men's self-concepts were significantly more masculine than women's self-concepts. In all countries, persons of both sexes wish to be somewhat more masculine (or less feminine) than they perceive themselves to be. These two effects are summarized in Figure 6.1 in which are plotted the ranges of the means for 14 countries for the actual and ideal self-concepts of the women and men subjects.

Correlations Among Self and Ideal-Self Means Within Countries

Do persons who have relatively masculine self-concepts also have relatively masculine ideal self-concepts? This question was addressed, sepa-

Table 6.1 Group Means of Mean M% Scores for Self (S) and Ideal Self (IS)

	Canada				England		
	S	*IS*	*S + IS*		*S*	*IS*	*S + IS*
Men	48.34	51.40	49.87	Men	51.91	54.85	53.38
Women	43.81	48.87	46.34	Women	49.45	53.19	51.32
All Persons	46.07	50.14		All Persons	50.68	54.02	
	Finland				**Germany**		
	S	*IS*	*S + IS*		*S*	*IS*	*S + IS*
Men	51.79	53.57	52.68	Men	51.56	55.17	53.37
Women	48.27	50.92	49.60	Women	48.65	53.64	51.15
All Persons	50.03	52.25		All Persons	50.12	54.36	
	India				**Italy**		
	S	*IS*	*S + IS*		*S*	*IS*	*S + IS*
Men	55.72	57.84	56.78	Men	61.03	63.71	62.37
Women	53.63	57.00	55.32	Women	57.61	61.22	59.46
All Persons	54.68	57.42		All Persons	59.32	62.47	
	Japan				**Malaysia**		
	S	*IS*	*S + IS*		*S*	*IS*	*S + IS*
Men	50.39	64.86	57.63	Men	53.33	57.33	55.33
Women	47.90	61.26	54.58	Women	46.17	55.23	50.70
All Persons	49.15	63.06		All Persons	49.75	56.28	
	Netherlands				**Nigeria**		
	S	*IS*	*S + IS*		*S*	*IS*	*S + IS*
Men	54.88	58.36	56.62	Men	51.33	56.73	54.03
Women	45.98	54.06	50.02	Women	46.63	52.39	49.51
All Persons	50.43	56.21		All Persons	48.98	54.56	
	Pakistan				**Singapore**		
	S	*IS*	*S + IS*		*S*	*IS*	*S + IS*
Men	52.65	55.00	53.83	Men	52.13	57.49	54.18
Women	50.22	53.10	51.66	Women	48.92	56.03	52.48
All Persons	51.44	54.05		All Persons	50.53	56.76	
	United States				**Venezuela**		
	S	*IS*	*S + IS*		*S*	*IS*	*S + IS*
Men	52.69	53.92	53.30	Men	53.51	54.30	53.91
Women	48.02	50.55	49.28	Women	51.48	53.30	52.39
All Persons	50.35	52.23		All Persons	52.49	53.8	

rately in each country, by obtaining the correlation between the mean M% scores for ideal self and for self, separately for the men and women subjects. The results of this analysis are shown in Table 6.2. An examination of the correlation coefficients for men indicated a range from .55 in India to –.20 in Nigeria. The women's coefficients ranged from .56 in the United States to

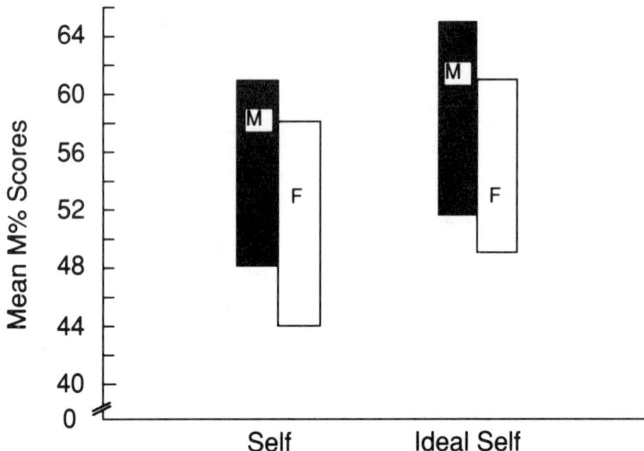

Figure 6.1. Ranges of Mean M% Scores for the Self-Descriptions and Ideal Self-Descriptions of Men and Women in 14 Countries

–.06 in Italy. Considering these arrays, two general observations can be made. First, we note that 11 of the 14 men's coefficients were positive in sign as were 13 of the 14 women's coefficients. These findings indicate a tendency in most countries for persons with relatively masculine self-concepts to have relatively masculine ideal self-concepts. On the other hand, we observe that the magnitude of the correlations are rather small in most countries suggesting that the effect just described is a rather weak one; indeed, in some countries there appears to be no relationship at all. This reinforces the notion that ideal self-descriptions incorporate desired M/F traits that the individuals do not perceive in their self-descriptions.

Correlations of Means with Sex-Role Ideology Scores Within Country

Within each country studied, there were variations among individual persons in their sex-role ideology scores and in the M/F of their self-concepts. Are these variables related? Do relatively masculine men and relatively feminine women tend to be more traditional in their sex-role orientations? In each country, this question was examined by correlating the sex-role ideology scores of individual subjects with the mean M% of their self-descriptions and ideal self-descriptions. These correlations were computed separately for the women and men subjects in each country. The results of these analyses are shown in Table 6.3. Viewed as a whole, the

Table 6.2 Correlations of Mean Self and Mean Ideal Self Within Country

Country	*Men*	*Country*	*Women*
India	.55*	United States	.56*
Netherlands	.48*	Nigeria	.43*
Canada	.42*	England	.34*
Finland	.28*	Singapore	.31*
England	.27*	Netherlands	.29*
United States	.26	Finland	.27*
Italy	.15	Germany	.18
Germany	.12	Pakistan	.16
Pakistan	.09	Venezuela	.16
Japan	.02	Canada	.15
Malaysia	.01	India	.15
Singapore	–.06	Japan	.06
Venezuela	–.11	Malaysia	.04
Nigeria	–.20	Italy	–.06

*$p < .05$

coefficients reported in the table indicate that there is generally little relationship between masculinity/femininity and sex-role ideology. With regard to the correlations between the masculinity/femininity of self-description and sex-role ideology, we note that for the men's groups the sign of the correlation coefficient was negative in 10 out of 14 instances, whereas for the women subjects the correlations were positive in 13 out of the 14 instances. Bearing in mind that low sex-role ideology scores are relatively traditional scores, this suggests a weak cross-cultural trend for more masculine men to be more traditional in sex-role ideology and for more feminine women to be more conservative in sex-role ideology—which was perhaps the common sense expectation with regard to these findings. A comparable examination of the ideal-self correlations indicates that the signs of the correlations were negative in 9 of the 14 instances for the men and were positive in 11 of the 14 instances for women. This provides weak evidence of a tendency for men who wish to be more masculine and women who wish to be more feminine to be somewhat more traditional in sex-role ideology.

There were only two instances where both the men's and the women's data showed significant support for the hypothesis: the self-descriptions of both sexes in Pakistan, and the ideal self-descriptions of both sexes in England. Although these particular findings may be worthy of further study, we must conclude that panculturally there is little evidence of a link between individual differences in sex-role ideology and individual differences in M/F of self-concepts.

Table 6.3 Correlations of Mean Self M/F and Mean Ideal-Self M/F with SRI

	Mean Self		*Mean Ideal Self*	
	Men	*Women*	*Men*	*Women*
Canada	–.17	.05	–.13	.14
England	–.08	.21	–.32*	.30*
Finland	–.26	.06	–.28*	.20
Germany	.09	.02	–.13	.25
India	.00	.16	.08	–.32*
Italy	–.23*	–.08	.18	.16
Japan	–.09	.13	.03	.16*
Malaysia	.30*	.34*	–.02	.27*
Netherlands	–.06	.00	–.11	.15
Nigeria	.14	.20	–.11	.26
Pakistan	–.37*	.43*	.18	.15
Singapore	–.19	.35*	–.03	–.02
United States	–.03	.16	–.18	.20
Venezuela	–.14	.27*	.05	–.10

*$p < .05$

Rank Orders of Group Means

The individual country mean scores previously shown in Table 6.1 are displayed again in Table 6.4 where, for each of the four types of scores, the country means are arranged in descending order from highest to lowest. An examination of the distributions for the men's and women's self-descriptions, in columns 1 and 2, indicates that the mean M% scores were highest in Italy and lowest in Canada. The scores in columns 4 and 5 indicate that the ideal self for both men and women was highest in Japan and lowest in Canada. Taken at face value, the four distributions indicate considerable cross-country variation in the relative masculinity/femininity of the self-concepts and ideal self-concepts.

The men minus women difference scores in each country are presented in columns 3 and 6. All difference scores are positive in sign, reflecting, for both self and ideal self, our earlier observation of greater masculinity for the men than for the women. It is also interesting to note that there appears to be less average difference between men and women for ideal self (column 6, mean = 2.41) than for self (column 3, mean = 3.89), that is, the ideal selves of women and men appear somewhat more similar in terms of M/F than do their selves.

A comparison of the rank orders of countries seen in columns 1, 2, 4, and 5 indicates considerable similarity in the four arrays. This was confirmed by computing correlations between pairs of arrays: The correlation across countries between the men's and women's self-concepts (columns 1 and 2)

Table 6.4 Mean M% Scores: Group Means for Men (M) and Women (W) Arranged in Rank Order from Highest to Lowest

Self						*Ideal Self*						*Ideal Self – Self*			
M (1)		*W* (2)		*M – W* (3)		*M* (4)		*W* (5)		*M – W* (6)		*M* (7)		*W* (8)	
ITA	61.0	ITA	57.6	NET	8.9	JAP	64.9	JAP	61.3	NIG	4.3	JAP	14.5	JAP	13.4
IND	55.7	IND	53.6	MAL	7.1	ITA	63.7	ITA	61.2	NET	4.3	SIN	5.4	MAL	9.1
NET	54.9	VEN	51.5	NIG	4.7	NET	58.4	IND	57.0	JAP	3.6	NIG	5.4	NET	8.1
VEN	53.5	PAK	50.2	USA	4.7	IND	57.8	SIN	56.0	USA	3.4	MAL	4.0	SIN	7.1
MAL	53.3	ENG	49.5	CAN	4.5	SIN	57.5	MAL	55.2	FIN	2.7	GER	3.6	NIG	5.8
PAK	52.7	SIN	48.9	FIN	3.5	MAL	57.3	NET	54.1	CAN	2.5	NET	3.5	CAN	5.1
USA	52.7	GER	48.7	ITA	3.4	NIG	56.7	GER	53.6	ITA	2.5	CAN	3.1	GER	4.9
SIN	52.1	FIN	48.3	SIN	3.2	GER	55.2	VEN	53.3	MAL	2.1	ENG	2.9	ENG	3.7
ENG	51.9	USA	48.0	GER	2.9	PAK	55.0	ENG	53.2	PAK	1.9	ITA	2.7	ITA	3.6
FIN	51.8	JAP	47.9	JAP	2.5	ENG	54.9	PAK	53.1	ENG	1.7	PAK	2.4	IND	3.4
GER	51.6	NIG	46.6	PAK	2.5	VEN	54.3	NIG	52.4	GER	1.5	IND	2.1	PAK	2.9
NIG	51.3	MAL	46.2	ENG	2.4	USA	53.9	FIN	50.9	SIN	1.5	FIN	1.8	FIN	2.6
JAP	50.4	NET	46.0	IND	2.1	FIN	53.6	USA	50.6	VEN	1.0	USA	1.2	USA	2.5
CAN	48.3	CAN	43.8	VEN	2.0	CAN	51.4	CAN	48.9	IND	.8	VEN	.8	VEN	1.8

was .81; the correlation between the men's and women's ideal self-concepts (columns 4 and 5) was .95; the correlation between men's self-concepts and men's ideal self-concepts (columns 1 and 4) was .51; the correlation between women's self-concepts and women's ideal self-concepts (columns 2 and 5) was .59. These findings indicate that in countries where the men's self-concepts were relatively masculine the women's were also, with a comparable finding for ideal self. In countries where the women's self-descriptions were relatively masculine their ideal self-descriptions also tended to be masculine, with a similar finding for men.

Let us pause to consider a methodological issue related to the correlations just observed. We noted in Chapter 1 that the findings from the sex-stereotype project in which the M% scores were derived indicated that there was substantial variation across countries in the mean M% score for the total set of 300 adjectives (see Table 1.1). For example, the mean M% for the total item pool in Italy was 63.5%, whereas that in Nigeria was 46.3%. To what degree are the between-country differences in the arrays we have been examining related to the between-country differences in the item-pool means? When the item-pool means from Table 1.1 were correlated with the self-description variables from Table 6.4, the following correlations were obtained: men's self, .80; women's self, .86; men's ideal self, .47; women's ideal self, .58. Thus, all of the between-country differences that we have been examining in Table 6.3 are related to some degree to the between-country differences in overall item-pool mean M% scores. This means that in countries where the item pool is seen to be more masculine, men and women describe themselves in more masculine terms. In countries where the item pool is considered more feminine, self-descriptions and ideal self-descriptions are more feminine. Given these across-country differences, should we attempt some sort of statistical "correction" for the differences in item-pool means? We will return to this question later in the chapter.

Correlations of Group Means with Comparison Variables

The eight score arrays from Table 6.4 were each correlated with our cultural comparison variables. The results of this analysis are seen in Table 6.5, where it will be observed that only two correlations reached statistical significance. A negative correlation was obtained between the percentage Protestant variable and the mean M% scores for the ideal self of women; in highly Protestant countries, women tend to have more feminine ideal selves. The second significant correlation was between the values variable and the difference in mean M% for the ideal selves of men and women; in countries that are more individualistic and less authoritarian in values, there is a greater difference in the relative masculinity of the male and female ideal self-descriptions. Correlations of borderline significance suggested that differences in M/F between the self and the ideal self tended to be less in highly Christian countries for both men and women subjects.

Although the observed correlations are interesting, the most general observation to be made regarding Table 6.5 is the relative lack of relationships of the between-country differences in masculinity/femininity with the cultural comparison variables. From this, we conclude that we have little evidence of true cross-cultural variation in the self-concepts of women and men when they are scored in terms of average masculinity/femininity defined separately for each cultural group. Note the contrast between this conclusion and the findings from Chapter 4 where the variations in self-concepts of men and women scored in terms of affective meaning were found to be related to a large number of cultural comparison variables. We will discuss this further in Chapters 8 and 9.

Masculinity/Femininity Adjusted for Item-Pool Means and Variances

We discussed, in Chapters 1 and 3, the question of whether the differences between countries in the means and variances of the item pool should be considered artifactual, and corrected for statistically, or should be consid-

Table 6.5 Correlations of Group Means with Comparison Variables

	Mean M%							
	Self			Ideal Self			IS – S	
	M (1)	W (2)	M – W (3)	M (4)	W (5)	M – W (6)	M (7)	W (8)
Economic-Social Development	–.13	–.23	.20	–.02	–.09	.23	.08	.13
Religion								
% Catholic	.40	.34	.00	.00	.03	–.10	–.36	–.34
% Protestant	–.26	–.36	.24	–.44	–.55*	.30	–.27	–.24
% Christian	.03	–.04	.12	–.41	–.46+	.15	–.48+	–.48+
% Muslim	–.06	–.07	.04	–.09	–.09	–.04	–.04	–.01
Status of Women								
% employed outside home	–.38	–.32	–.01	–.11	–.19	.23	.21	.13
% women in university population	–.02	.04	–.09	–.44	–.36	–.30	–.47+	–.45
General Demographics								
urban	–.13	–.12	.01	.01	.01	.01	.12	.13
latitude	–.00	–.02	.04	–.10	–.17	.23	–.11	–.17
Values	–.06	–.32	.49+	–.13	–.29	.56*	–.09	.00
Sex-Role Ideology	.16	.03	.19	–.13	–.13	–.00	–.29	–.19

$+p < .10$, $*p < .05$, $**p < .01$

ered to reflect bona fide cultural variation. We decided in favor of true cultural variation because our sex-stereotype project indicated that the differences between countries in item-pool means and variances were related to certain cultural variables. Statistical equation of the mean M% scores in different countries might very well exclude important cultural variation.

In this section, however, we would like to examine the mean M% scores when they are corrected for the differences in item-pool means and variances. One might conceptualize this correction in terms of "available masculinity/femininity" in a given country. For example, in a country such as Italy, where the mean M% for all 300 items is substantially above 50%, it is relatively "easy" for a person to select items that yield a mean self-description score above 50. According to our definition, such a score would be classified as masculine. By contrast, in Nigeria where the item-pool mean was below 50, it would be more "difficult" to obtain a self-description mean above 50 and to be classified as masculine.

Consider the self-descriptions of two hypothetical male subjects, one from Italy, where the item-pool mean is 63.5, and the other from Nigeria where the item-pool mean is 46.3. Assume that these two men check exactly the same items on the Adjective Check List as being self-descriptive. Because of the M% differences reflected in the item-pool means, the Italian man would probably obtain a higher mean M% for his self-description than would the Nigerian man. By our general definition, we would be forced to conclude that the Italian man was "more masculine" than the Nigerian man. On the other hand, we could examine the two self-descriptions relative to the item-pool means for the respective countries. We could see whether the two self-descriptions were above or below the item-pool means. With the item-pool correction, we might find that the Italian and Nigerian men's self-descriptions were, in fact, quite comparable in terms of relative masculinity or we may even find that the Nigerian man was relatively more masculine than the Italian man.

The corrected (item-pool adjusted) scores employed in this supplemental analysis were obtained in the following manner. In a given country, the mean M% for men's self-descriptions was expressed as a standard score by obtaining the difference between the men's mean and the item-pool mean and dividing this difference by the standard deviation (square root of the variance) of the item-pool M% scores in that country. (The item-pool mean and variance for each country are shown in Table 1.1.) For each country:

$$\frac{\text{Male M\% Mean for Self-Description in Country X} - \text{Item-Pool M\% Mean for Country X}}{\text{Item-Pool Standard Deviation for M\% Scores in Country X}}$$

Similar corrections were made for the mean M% for the men's ideal self in each country as well as for the self-descriptions and ideal self-descriptions of the women. Computed in this way, the standard score corresponding to a given group mean indicates whether the group mean was above (+) or below (–) the item-pool mean with the difference expressed in terms of the item-pool standard deviation (standard deviation is the unit of measurement).

The group means from columns 1, 2, 4, and 5 of Table 6.4 were converted in the foregoing manner to produce the standard scores presented, in rank order, in Table 6.6. Looking at column 1, the standard scores for the men's self-descriptions were highest in Nigeria, Malaysia, and Singapore and lowest in Italy and India. Thus, in terms of our concept of "relative masculinity," one can say that the self-descriptions of the men in the former group are more masculine than in the latter. In the fourth column, standard scores corresponding to the men's ideal self-concepts are shown. These scores indicate that relative masculinity was highest in Japan and Nigeria and lowest in Italy and India. Thus, we observe that men in the former group of countries wish to be relatively more masculine than do men in the latter group.

Table 6.6 Rank Orders of Group Means of M% Scores Expressed Relative to Item-Pool Means and Variances

Self						*Ideal Self*					
M (1)		*W* (2)		*M – W* (3)		*M* (4)		*W* (5)		*M – W* (6)	
NIG	.19	NIG	.01	NET	.29	JAP	.51	JAP	.36	NIG	.17
MAL	.16	SIN	–.01	MAL	.27	NIG	.40	SIN	.31	JAP	.15
SIN	.15	VEN	–.07	USA	.19	SIN	.37	MAL	.23	NET	.14
NET	.09	FIN	–.08	NIG	.18	MAL	.30	NIG	.23	USA	.13
VEN	.07	PAK	–.08	CAN	.17	NET	.21	NET	.07	ITA	.11
FIN	.04	MAL	–.11	SIN	.16	PAK	.12	VEN	.05	CAN	.10
PAK	.02	ENG	–.16	ITA	.15	VEN	.12	PAK	.04	FIN	.09
USA	.02	USA	–.17	VEN	.14	FIN	.10	FIN	.01	PAK	.08
CAN	–.03	GER	–.19	FIN	.12	CAN	.09	CAN	–.01	ENG	.07
ENG	–.06	JAP	–.19	GER	.11	ENG	.06	ENG	–.01	MAL	.07
GER	–.08	NET	–.20	ENG	.10	USA	.06	GER	–.01	VEN	.07
JAP	–.09	CAN	–.20	JAP	.10	GER	.05	USA	–.07	GER	.06
ITA	–.10	ITA	–.25	IND	.10	ITA	.01	ITA	–.10	SIN	.06
IND	–.18	IND	–.28	PAK	.10	IND	–.08	IND	–.12	IND	.04

The standard score equivalents for the women's self-concepts and ideal self-concepts in the different countries are shown in columns 2 and 5. Here, scores toward the bottom of each column are relatively more feminine. Thus, the self-descriptions of women are relatively more feminine in Italy and India and relatively less feminine in Nigeria and Singapore. Considering the ideal self, once again the women in India and Italy appear most feminine, whereas the women in Japan and Singapore appear relatively masculine.

The relationships among the relative masculinity/femininity scores were examined with the results shown in Table 6.7 where several intriguing relationships are observed. We note first that, across the 14 countries, there was no relationship between the relative masculinity of the men's self-concepts and the women's self-concepts. In addition, there was no relationship between the relative masculinity of the men's self-concepts and the men's ideal self-concepts. On the other hand, there was a significant relationship between the masculinity of the men's self-concepts and the women's ideal self-concepts—in countries where the men's self-descriptions were relatively masculine the women wished to be relatively more masculine.

A parallel finding was obtained for the women's self-concepts. The relative masculinity of the women's self-concepts was not related to the relative masculinity of the men's self-concepts nor was the relative masculinity of the women's self-concepts related to the relative masculinity of the women's ideal self-concepts. However, the relative masculinity of the

Table 6.7 Correlations Among Relative M/F Measures

	Self			*Ideal Self*		
	M	*W*	*M – W*	*M*	*W*	*M – W*
Self						
M	–	.12	.92**	–.15	.73**	.12
W		–	–.26	.65*	.25	.14
M – W			–	–.36	.60*	.09
Ideal Self						
M				–	.44	.48
W					–	.29
M – W						–

*$p < .05$, **$p < .01$.

women's self-concepts was significantly correlated with the relative masculinity of the men's ideal self-concepts—in countries where the women described themselves as relatively masculine, the men wished to be relatively more masculine.

Two other interesting relationships are seen in the table, both of which involve the masculinity difference score for the self measure. In countries where the relative difference between men's and women's self-perceptions is greatest, men tend to have relatively masculine self-perceptions and women tend to have relatively masculine ideal self-perceptions. In other words, in countries where men perceived themselves to be much more masculine than women perceived themselves to be, the men "are" more masculine and the women "wish to be" more masculine. Overall, the relationships seen in Table 6.7 suggest some important and complex cross-sex dynamics in self-perceptions and ideal self-perceptions.

Each of the six distributions of relative masculinity/femininity scores were correlated in turn with each of our cultural comparison variables. The results of this analysis are shown in Table 6.8. Significant relationships were found involving two of the comparison variables. The correlations involving latitude indicate that the relative masculinity of the women's self-perceptions tends to be less in the higher latitudes; women in countries further from the equator tend to have relatively more feminine self-descriptions. The second finding regarding latitude was that the men's ideal self-descriptions tended to be relatively less masculine in the high latitudes. In other words, in countries close to the equator women described themselves in a more masculine/less feminine manner and men wished to be more masculine/less feminine. These findings should be viewed with caution, however, since similar results were not found in the main M/F analyses discussed earlier.

The other comparison variable of interest was sex-role ideology. In countries with a relatively traditional ideology men wished to be more

Table 6.8 Correlations of Relative Masculinity/Feminity Scores With Comparison Variables

	Self			Ideal Self		
	M *(1)*	*W* *(2)*	*M – W* *(3)*	*M* *(4)*	*W* *(5)*	*M – W* *(6)*
Economic-Social Development	–.08	.29	–.19	.15	–.04	–.09
Religion						
% Catholic	.04	–.26	.15	–.39	–.25	.01
% Protestant	.19	–.04	.18	.32	–.11	.00
% Christian	.11	–.21	.17	–.51+	–.34	.06
% Muslim	.09	.45	–.08	.27	.11	.01
Status of Women						
% employed outside home	–.19	–.11	–.15	.10	–.08	.19
% women in university population	–.19	–.04	–.16	–.27	–.44	–.33
General Demographics						
urban	.15	–.15	.16	–.11.	.18	–.10
latitude	–.10	–.62*	.09	–.57*	–.31	.01
Values	–.10	.49	–.31	.38	.17	–.31
Sex-Role Ideology	.22	–.42	.33	–.62*	–.09	–.32

+$p < .10$, *$p < .05$, **$p < .01$

masculine. Somewhat surprisingly, there was also a tendency for the self-descriptions of women to be more masculine in traditional countries although the relationship did not reach statistical significance.

Viewed more generally, the paucity of relationships between the relative M/F measures and the cultural comparison variables mirrors the findings for the uncorrected M/F measures. By either definition, there was little evidence that the observed differences between countries in masculinity/femininity were related to the cultural variables. Thus, within the limitations of the study, we feel that there is little evidence of appreciable *cross-cultural* variation in average masculinity/femininity. This conclusion is in stark contrast to the findings reported in Chapter 4 where self-perceptions and ideal self-perceptions scored for affective meaning were seen to be related to many of the cultural comparison variables.

SUMMARY

In this chapter, the self-concepts and ideal self-concepts of men and women in each country were scored for masculinity/femininity defined by reference to the sex stereotypes in that country as determined in the earlier study by Williams and Best (1982). Among the results were the findings that: men's self and ideal self were more masculine than women's self and ideal self in all countries; the ideal self was more masculine than the self for both men and women in all countries; in countries where the men's self-concept was relatively masculine, the women's ideal self was relatively masculine; and in countries where the women's self-concept was relatively masculine, the men's self was relatively masculine. A relatively small number of relationships were found between men's and women's self and ideal self scored for masculinity/femininity and the cultural comparison variables.

NOTES

1. Other cross-cultural studies of the CPI femininity scale have been conducted by Gough, Chun, and Chung (1968) in Korea; Levin and Karni (1971) in Israel; and Nishiyama (1975) in Japan.

2. In each country, a split-plot analysis of variance was done, with the two concepts (self and ideal self) as the within-subjects variable and the two sexes as the between-subjects variable. The .05 level was used for statistical significance.

7

DIVERSITY IN MASCULINITY/FEMININITY OF SELF-CONCEPTS

The terms *masculinity* and *femininity*, as ordinarily employed, refer to whether a person's behavior is typically, or on the average, more manlike or womanlike. In most studies of psychological masculinity/femininity, persons are asked to respond to a series of items that have been previously determined to be manlike or womanlike and a summation or average of the person's responses across all items is taken as reflecting the individual's masculinity/femininity. It is this typical, or average, masculinity/femininity that we examined in Chapter 6 via our analysis of the mean M% scores derived from the self-descriptions and ideal self-descriptions of individual subjects. We will now turn our attention to intrasubject diversity in masculinity/femininity.

Personality psychologists have paid little attention to the general question of intrasubject diversity in the behaviors they study.[1] A principal reason for this is the categorical classification of items employed in many personality assessment procedures, for example, the standard scoring of the ACL (Gough & Heilbrun, 1980b). In the area of masculinity/femininity, all of the better-known assessment methods (e.g., Bem, 1974; Berzins et al., 1978; Heilbrun, 1981; Spence & Helmreich, 1978) involve the recording of the subjects' responses to two item sets—one manlike and one womanlike—with no allowance made for the fact that, within each set, some items are more highly related to the criterion than are others (e.g., some of the manlike items are more highly associated with men than are others). When this approach is used, there is no opportunity to study intrasubject variability.

In the present study, we employ items that have been scaled as to the *relative degree* to which they are manlike or womanlike, as reflected in the M% scores. As described in the previous chapter, M% scores near 50% indicate items that are equally associated with men and women. As one moves upward from 50%, the items are progressively more male-associated, and as one moves down from 50% the items are progressively more female-associated. Using the M% values, it is possible to compute an index of the *diversity* of the items the individual used for a self-description.

Let us consider the hypothetical self-descriptions of two American men. Tom describes himself with adjectives such as: ambitious (M% = 89%), artistic (22%), assertive (85%), civilized (29%), deliberate (71%), and considerate (26%); Brock describes himself with adjectives such as: adaptable

(41%), alert (59%), calm (57%), clever (56%), dependable (55%), and distractible (53%). If we note the M% values in the parentheses, it is clear that the adjectives Tom has used to describe himself are more *diverse*, in terms of M% values, than the adjectives used by Brock. Tom has used some adjectives that are highly associated with men and some which are highly associated with women; Brock has used adjectives that are not highly associated with either gender. The computed variance for Tom's items is 981.57, whereas that for Brock's items is 41.47. This sort of difference in persons' self-descriptions, computed across the 100 or so items typically chosen, is what we mean by *diversity* of masculinity/femininity. In passing, let us note that the average (mean) M% for Tom's adjectives is 53.7% whereas Brock's average is 53.5%. Thus, the *average* masculinity/femininity of the two descriptions is quite similar, both being a bit on the masculine side. If we were attending only to average scores, we would conclude that Tom and Brock are quite similar in masculinity/femininity whereas, in fact, their descriptions are quite different in terms of the types of items endorsed. We have noted, in Chapter 2, that our concept of diversity in masculinity/femininity has some similarity to the concepts of *androgynous* versus *undifferentiated* self-descriptions, as these terms have been employed by other researchers, such as Bem (1974) and Spence and Helmreich (1978).

The data to be examined in this chapter consist of the variance of the M% scores for the self-descriptions and ideal self-descriptions. For a given description, this measure is obtained by considering the M% values of the items endorsed and computing a standard variance measure (the square of the standard deviation), as described in any statistical reference book. Computed in this way, the variance score becomes an index of the intrasubject diversity in the M% values of the endorsed items.

Independence of Means and Variances

The reason for studying the variance scores is that they may constitute a different facet of M/F from that provided by the average or mean scores. Obviously, this idea is valid only to the degree that the means and variances obtained for individual subjects are generally independent of one another. This important question was explored in the following manner. Within each of the 14 countries separately, we computed correlation coefficients across subjects between the mean M% and the variance M% for self-description and between the mean M% and the variance M% for ideal self-description. Because these correlations were computed separately for men and women subjects in each country, this resulted in a total of 56 correlation coefficients dealing with the question of the independence of means and variances in individual descriptions. The range of the distribution of 56 correlation coefficients was from .67 to –.78 with a median of –.19 suggesting, perhaps, a slight tendency for higher means to be associated with lower variances. On the other hand, the low magnitude of this median correlation was taken to indicate that, generally, the means and variances are essentially independent and, thus, the variances do provide an additional index related to psychological masculinity/femininity.

A different question concerning the relationship of means and variances involves the degree to which the total country means and total country variances correlate with one another across the 14 countries. We will return to examine this question later in the chapter.

Grand Means of Variance M% Scores

The mean variance scores for the self-concepts and ideal self-concepts of the men and women in each of the 14 countries are shown in Table 7.1. In addition to the four cell means, the table also shows two marginal effects; at the right are shown the total-self variance scores for men and women (self and ideal self pooled); at the bottom are shown the total-self and ideal-self variances (men and women subjects pooled). Total-self scores can be considered to be indicators of overall self-perceptions, including both currently perceived and desired traits; self and ideal-self scores that are pooled across sex provide indicators of the nature of these concepts irrespective of gender. The data in each country were subjected to an analysis to determine which of the observed effects were statistically significant.[2]

Let us deal first with the differences in total self between men and women in the various countries. In 10 of the 14 countries the observed effects (right-hand marginals) indicated that the women had more variable total self-concepts than the men; this effect was statistically significant in Malaysia, Venezuela, Japan, and Italy and nonsignificant in Finland, Germany, India, Netherlands, Nigeria, and Pakistan. In 4 of the countries, the observed effect was for the men's total self to be more variable than the women's; this effect was statistically significant in Canada and nonsignificant in England, Singapore, and the United States. Viewed overall, it appears that, in most countries, women tended to describe themselves with a set of adjectives that were more diverse, relative to M/F, than were those used by the men. This is true for both self-concepts and ideal self-concepts when examined together.

Let us now consider the observed differences in overall variances for self-concepts and ideal self-concepts, with the data for men and women combined (lower marginals). In 11 of the 14 countries, the ideal self-concepts were observed to be more variable in terms of M/F than the self-concepts; this effect was statistically significant in the Netherlands, the United

Table 7.1 Group Means of Individual Variance Scores for Self (S) and Ideal Self (IS)

	Canada				**England**		
	S	*IS*	*S + IS*		*S*	*IS*	*S + IS*
Men	652.48	690.12	671.30	Men	554.01	586.52	570.27
Women	605.97	669.99	637.98	Women	560.12	576.26	568.19
All Persons	629.23	680.06		All Persons	557.07	581.39	
	Finland				**Germany**		
	S	*IS*	*S + IS*		*S*	*IS*	*S + IS*
Men	724.94	762.16	743.55	Men	681.31	721.68	701.50
Women	747.43	768.85	758.14	Women	694.88	751.20	723.04
All Persons	736.19	765.51		All Persons	688.10	736.44	
	India				**Italy**		
	S	*IS*	*S + IS*		*S*	*IS*	*S + IS*
Men	432.57	453.73	443.20	Men	513.36	553.52	533.44
Women	460.62	447.09	453.86	Women	552.08	581.60	566.84
All Persons	446.60	450.41		All Persons	532.72	567.56	
	Japan				**Malaysia**		
	S	*IS*	*S + IS*		*S*	*IS*	*S + IS*
Men	519.87	562.06	540.97	Men	706.68	715.27	710.98
Women	514.60	607.28	560.94	Women	722.85	743.52	733.19
All Persons	517.24	584.67		All Persons	714.77	729.40	
	Netherlands				**Nigeria**		
	S	*IS*	*S + IS*		*S*	*IS*	*S + IS*
Men	812.76	866.38	839.57	Men	769.95	749.40	759.68
Women	837.92	903.05	870.49	Women	771.03	784.43	777.73
All Persons	825.34	884.72		All Persons	770.49	766.92	
	Pakistan				**Singapore**		
	S	*IS*	*S + IS*		*S*	*IS*	*S + IS*
Men	532.27	547.81	540.04	Men	565.00	540.60	552.80
Women	530.92	558.30	544.61	Women	545.76	534.45	540.11
All Persons	531.60	553.10		All Persons	555.38	537.53	
	United States				**Venezuela**		
	S	*IS*	*S + IS*		*S*	*IS*	*S + IS*
Men	651.04	689.48	670.26	Men	208.73	201.15	204.94
Women	639.36	676.06	657.71	Women	229.84	212.78	221.31
All Persons	645.20	682.77		All Persons	219.29	206.97	

States, Finland, England, Canada, Pakistan, Japan, Germany, and Italy and nonsignificant in India and Malaysia. In three of the countries, the observed effect was for the ideal self-concept to be less variable than the self-concept; this effect was significant in Venezuela and Singapore and nonsignificant in

Nigeria. Viewed overall, these findings suggest that, as a rule, the ideal self (what people want to be) is more diverse in terms of M/F than is the actual self (what they perceive themselves to be).

There were two countries in which there was a significant interaction of the gender and concept variables. In India, the men's ideal self-concepts were more diverse than the self-concepts, whereas the women's ideal self-concepts was less diverse than the self-concepts. In Japan, the ideal self was more diverse than the self for both men and women, but this effect was much more pronounced for women than for men.

The findings were that, in most of our countries, the women's self-concepts were more diverse in terms of M/F than the men's, and that the ideal self-descriptions were more diverse than the self-descriptions. Thus, women tend to see themselves with both strongly male-associated and strongly female-associated traits, whereas men choose less strongly differentiated M/F items to describe themselves. Both men and women chose a greater variety of masculine and feminine words to describe their ideal selves than their selves. These findings suggest that the use of our novel measure of intraperson variance may provide useful new information concerning the self-perceptions and ideal self-perceptions of men and women.

Correlation of Self and Ideal-Self Variances Within Each Country

Do persons who give more variable self-descriptions also give more variable ideal self-descriptions? In other words, do persons who include both masculine and feminine items in their self-descriptions do the same for their ideal self-descriptions? Within each country, the variance of self-description was correlated with the variance of ideal self-description separately for the men and women subjects. The resulting correlations are shown in Table 7.2.

An examination of the tabled values leads to two general observations. First, there is considerable variation among countries in the degree to which self and ideal-self variability are correlated. Second, we note that, with one exception, all correlations are positive in sign. Overall, we can conclude that there appears to be a general tendency for persons with more variable self-concepts to have more variable ideal self-concepts with this effect being quite strong in some countries but being weak or nonexistent in others. Generally speaking, persons who have more diverse views of what they are in terms of M/F tend to have more diverse views of what they wish to be.

Table 7.2 Correlation of Self and Ideal-Self Variances Within Each Country

Country	*Men*	*Country*	*Women*
United States	.70*	Canada	.49*
India	.46*	Germany	.45*
Venezuela	.42*	England	.43*
Finland	.38*	United States	.43*
Singapore	.37*	Finland	.34*
Pakistan	.35*	Nigeria	.32
Netherlands	.32*	Pakistan	.27*
Germany	.28*	Venezuela	.24
Italy	.28	Italy	.17
Canada	.25	Singapore	.11
Nigeria	.23	India	.10
Malaysia	.10	Netherlands	.10
Japan	.00	Japan	.08
England	–.05	Malaysia	.05

*$p < .05$

Correlations of Variances with Sex-Role Ideology Within Countries

Do persons who are relatively modern in personal sex-role ideology tend to have more or less variable self-concepts? If we view diversity of M/F in self-concept as related to androgyny, the question then is whether androgynous individuals are more modern in their sex-role ideology or are more traditional. This question was explored, within each country, by correlating the self and ideal-self variance scores with sex-role ideology scores, separately for men and women. The results of this analysis are shown in Table 7.3.

The paucity of significant correlations in the table leads to the general conclusion that, in most countries, there is little if any relationship between personal sex-role ideology and diversity in M/F of self-description and ideal self-description. Significant correlations were found in only four countries. In Canada, more modern women tended to have more variable self-concepts and ideal self-concepts. In Italy, there was no relationship to variability of self-concept but for ideal self-concept more ideologically modern men and women tended to have less variable descriptions. In Japan, the only significant finding was the tendency for more ideologically modern women to have less diverse ideal self-concepts, a finding that was also repeated in Singapore.

Overall, it appears that there is little systematic relationship between an individual's personal beliefs concerning proper role relations between men and women, along a traditional/modern dimension, and the diversity of their

Table 7.3 Correlations of Self and Ideal-Self Variances with Sex-Role Ideology Scores within each Country

	Self		*Ideal Self*	
	Men	*Women*	*Men*	*Women*
Canada	−.10	.30*	−.02	.41*
England	.00	.09	−.05	.08
Finland	.18	−.03	.17	.08
Germany	−.18	−.02	−.24	−.23
India	.04	.02	−.14	.26
Italy	−.09	−.11	−.24*	−.32*
Japan	−.14	.01	.01	−.17*
Malaysia	−.03	.19	.09	−.20
Netherlands	.14	.23	.06	.08
Nigeria	−.04	.02	−.03	.10
Pakistan	−.07	.24	.04	.20
Singapore	.07	.20	−.06	−.27*
United States	−.03	.13	−.03	.04
Venezuela	.14	−.12	.15	−.05

*$p < .05$

self-concepts and ideal self-concepts along the masculinity/femininity dimension. If, as suggested in Chapter 2, our measure of diversity may be related to the concept of psychological androgyny, then there would appear to be no support for the idea that androgynous persons tend to be more modern or egalitarian in sex-role ideology.

Rank Orders of Mean Variance Scores

The country means of the self and ideal-self variance scores of men and women presented in Table 7.1 are shown again in Table 7.4 where the scores have been arranged in rank order from highest to lowest. In examining the table, one is struck at once by the high degree of correspondence in the rank orders for the men's and women's self-concept and ideal self-concept variances; for example, in each array the scores from the Netherlands had the largest mean variance and the scores from Venezuela had the smallest mean variance. The similarities in rank order are most easily explained with reference to the item-pool variances from the earlier sex-stereotype study (Williams & Best, 1982), which are reproduced in column 9 of the table, where they also are presented in rank order from highest to lowest (see Chapters 1 and 6 for a more complete discussion of the item-pool differences across countries). A comparison of the item-pool variances with the variances for the men's and women's self-descriptions and ideal self-descriptions indicates, not surprisingly, that in countries where the item pool was highly diverse in terms of M% values, the self-descriptions and ideal self-descriptions had larger variances, whereas in countries where there was less dispersion in the M% scores of the item pool, the self-descriptions reveal less diversity. Thus, when the personality traits in the item pool are seen as differing widely in terms of M/F, men and women describe themselves with both more masculine and more feminine items than in countries where the item pool is seen as more constricted in masculinity and femininity.

The substantial differences in item-pool variances from country to country pose an interesting methodological problem. The question is whether the differences in item-pool variances are to be considered legitimate findings or are to be treated as artifactual in nature. After considering this question in some detail in Chapter 3, we decided that the former view was the proper one. A principal consideration was the fact that, in the sex-stereotype study, differences in item-pool variances (i.e., in the general dispersion of M% scores through the score range) were found to be correlated with a number of cultural variables; for example, item-pool variances tend to be larger in Protestant countries, smaller in Catholic countries, and smaller in relatively authoritarian countries (Williams & Best, 1982). Such findings suggest that attempting to compensate for the differences in variances by some statistical means could obscure important cultural differences.

Let us consider for a moment the psychological meaning associated with the item-pool variances. A high variance indicates a large dispersion of M% scores, which in turn indicates a highly differentiated view of the psychological characteristics associated with the sexes. A low variance, on the other hand, indicates less dispersion in the M% values, which in turn indicates less differentiation in the psychological characteristics associated with men and women. From this point of view, the similarities in rank orders for the variances for men's and women's self-descriptions and ideal self-descriptions take on more meaning. In countries where the stereotypic perceptions of men and women are more highly differentiated, the self-perceptions of men and women are more highly differentiated; in countries where the psychological characteristics typically associated with men and women are less differentiated, the self-perceptions in these countries are less differentiated. Thus, the degree of diversity in masculinity/femininity in the self-concepts and ideal self-concepts of persons in a particular country tends to mimic the degree of differentiation in the psychological characteristics stereotypically associated with women and men in that country.

Correlation of Mean Variances with Comparison Variables

Correlations were computed across the 14 countries between the mean variance scores for the men's and women's self-concepts and ideal self-con-

Table 7.4 Rank Order of Self and Ideal-Self Variance Means

Self			*Ideal Self*			*Ideal Self – Self*		*Item-Pool*
M (1)	*W* (2)	*M – W* (3)	*M* (4)	*W* (5)	*M – W* (6)	*M* (7)	*W* (8)	*Variances* (9)
NET 812.76	NET 837.92	CAN 46.51	NET 866.38	NET 903.05	CAN 20.13	NET 53.62	JAP 92.68	NET 934
NIG 769.95	NIG 771.03	SIN 19.24	FIN 762.16	NIG 784.43	USA 13.42	JAP 42.19	NET 65.13	FIN 831
FIN 724.94	FIN 747.43	USA 11.68	NIG 749.40	FIN 768.85	ENG 10.26	GER 40.38	CAN 64.02	GER 756
MAL 706.68	MAL 722.85	JAP 5.57	GER 721.68	GER 751.20	IND 6.64	ITA 40.38	GER 56.32	MAL 756
GER 681.31	GER 694.88	PAK 1.35	MAL 715.27	MAL 743.52	SIN 6.15	USA 38.44	USA 36.70	NIG 692
CAN 652.48	USA 639.36	NIG –1.08	CAN 690.12	USA 676.06	FIN –6.69	CAN 37.64	ITA 29.52	USA 670
USA 651.04	CAN 605.97	ENG –6.11	USA 689.48	CAN 669.99	PAK –10.49	FIN 37.22	PAK 27.38	CAN 631
SIN 565.00	ENG 560.12	GER –13.57	ENG 586.52	JAP 607.28	VEN –11.63	ENG 32.51	FIN 21.42	JAP 592
ENG 554.01	ITA 552.08	MAL –16.17	JAP 562.06	ITA 581.60	ITA –28.08	IND 21.16	MAL 20.67	ENG 589
PAK 532.27	SIN 545.76	VEN –21.11	ITA 553.52	ENG 576.26	MAL –28.25	PAK 15.54	ENG 16.14	SIN 582
JAP 519.87	PAK 530.92	FIN –22.49	PAK 547.81	PAK 558.30	GER –29.52	MAL 8.59	NIG 13.40	ITA 571
ITA 513.36	JAP 514.30	NET –25.16	SIN 540.60	SIN 534.45	NIG –35.03	VEN –7.58	SIN –11.31	PAK 555
IND 432.57	IND 460.62	IND –28.05	IND 453.73	IND 447.09	NET –36.67	NIG –20.55	IND –13.53	IND 430
VEN 208.73	VEN 229.84	ITA –38.82	VEN 201.15	VEN 212.78	JAP –45.22	SIN 24.40	VEN –17.06	VEN 221

Table 7.5 Correlations of Group Variances with Comparison Variables

	Self			*Ideal Self*			*IS – S*	
	M (1)	*W* (2)	*M – W* (3)	*M* (4)	*W* (5)	*M – W* (6)	*M* (7)	*W* (8)
Economic-Social Development	.28	.21	.12	.30	.18	.12	–.56*	–.43
Religion								
% Catholic	–.38	–.35	–.20	–.34	–.50	.18	.27	.40
% Protestant	.56*	.57*	–.02	.60*	.58*	–.02	.34	–.01
% Christian	.12	.13	–.05	.17	.04	.25	.42	.23
% Muslim	.09	.08	.10	.02	.10	–.21	–.44	–.24
Status of Women								
% women employed outside home	.29	.28	.12	.36	.34	.03	.41	.17
% women in university population	–.10	–.13	.26	–.06	–.19	.69*	.24	.07
General Demographics								
urban	–.02	–.06	.21	.02	–.01	.12	.28	.23
latitude	.31	.33	–.12	.43	.29	.15	.84*	.44
Values	.73*	.73*	.06	.77*	.58*	.12	.78*	.45
Sex-Role Ideology	.15	.20	–.33	.23	.14	.04	.56*	.24

*$p < .05$

cepts and our cultural comparison variables. Correlations were also computed between a number of difference scores computed between pairs of the scores shown in Table 7.4. The obtained correlation coefficients are shown in Table 7.5.

Significant correlations were found between the percentage Protestant variable and the self and ideal-self variance scores, for both men and women. In predominantly Protestant countries, men's and women's self-concepts and ideal self-concepts tend to be more diverse in terms of masculinity/femininity. It can also be seen that the reverse pattern tended to occur in the highly Catholic countries, although the coefficients did not reach statistical significance. It was noted above that the item-pool variance findings from the sex-stereotype study revealed that the general stereotypic views of men and women are more differentiated in Protestant than in Catholic countries. We have speculated elsewhere (Williams & Best, 1982, pp. 260-263) about the different roles of men and women in the two religious traditions, which may be responsible for the stereotype differences and, in a similar manner, for the self-concept differences noted here.

The work-related values index also correlated positively with the variance scores of the self-concepts and ideal self-concepts of men and women; in more individualistic and less authoritarian countries, men and women show greater diversity in self-concept. Although the correlations between economic-social development and diversity of self-concept and ideal self-concept were all positive in sign, none reached statistical significance. More substantial relationships were seen when economic-social development was related to the *difference* between the self variance and the ideal-self variance; in more developed countries, there is a greater increase in diversity in moving from self to ideal self than in less developed countries. This means that in more developed countries, ideal self-concepts were more androgynous than self-concepts. A similar finding is seen in the relationship between the ideal-self minus self difference scores and latitude; the increase in diversity from self to ideal self, or the greater androgyny of ideal self, is larger in countries farther from the equator.

When sex-role ideology scores were compared with the variance scores, a pattern of weak, positive, but nonsignificant correlations was observed. On the other hand, the relationship was more substantial with regard to the ideal-self minus self difference scores where the correlation for men was significant. This suggests that, at least for men, in countries where the prevailing sex-role ideology is relatively modern, the shift in diversity from self to ideal self, or the greater androgyny of ideal self, is larger than in countries where the sex-role ideology is more traditional.

We conclude this section with the general observation that our relatively novel measure of intrasubject diversity in masculinity/femininity was related to several cultural comparison variables. This suggests that the new measure provides some interesting additional information concerning masculinity/femininity.

Correlation of Group Means and Variances Across Countries

At the beginning of this chapter, we examined the question of the relationship between means and variances among individual subjects *within* each of our 14 countries. Although appreciable variation was found with regard to these correlations, we concluded that the individual subject means and variances were sufficiently independent to make them worthy of separate analysis.

We will consider here the different question of whether there is any relationship between the variations in means and variances found across the 14 countries. In Chapter 6, we noted the mean M% scores for men's and women's self-descriptions and ideal self-descriptions in each of the 14 countries (Table 6.4). We have examined in this chapter the variance scores for men's and women's self-descriptions and ideal self-descriptions (Table 7.4). Is there any systematic relationship, on a cross-country basis, between the level of masculinity/femininity of self-concept measured by mean scores, and the diversity of masculinity/femininity measured by variance scores?

Across the 14 countries, the following correlations were obtained: self mean and self variance for women—$r = -.53$; ideal-self mean and ideal-self variance for women—$r = -.43$; self mean and self variance for men—$r = -.24$; ideal-self mean and ideal-self variance for men—$r = -.09$. For women, it appears that in countries where the self-concept is relatively masculine, it tends to be less diverse, with a similar finding for ideal self. The signs of the two correlations for men suggest a similar but weaker relationship between level of masculinity/femininity and diversity of masculinity/femininity. Viewed overall, these between-country findings are consistent with the within-country findings in suggesting a modest tendency for persons with more masculine self-concepts to have somewhat more constricted self-concepts, whereas persons with more feminine self-concepts tend to have somewhat more diverse self-concepts. Because women tend to have more feminine self-concepts than men, the findings just noted may be related to the earlier observation that in most countries women tend to have more diverse self-concepts than do men.

SUMMARY

In this chapter, we examined the self-concepts and ideal self-concepts of men and women scored for intrapersonal diversity in masculinity/femininity, a relatively novel measure. The diversity scores were found to vary widely from country to country in a manner that mimicked the diversity of the sex stereotypes in the countries as determined in our earlier study (Williams & Best, 1982). Among the results were the findings that, in most countries, the women's self-descriptions and ideal self-descriptions tended to be more diverse (more androgynous) than the men's and, in most countries, the ideal self-descriptions of men and women tended to be more diverse than their self-descriptions. The results also indicated a modest tendency for persons with more masculine self-concepts to have somewhat more constricted self-concepts, whereas persons with more feminine self-concepts tended to have more diverse self-concepts. The diversity measures were found to be related to a few of the cultural comparison variables; for example, in countries with relatively individualistic value systems, the self-concepts and ideal self-concepts of men and women tended to be more diverse.

NOTES

1. We will consider, in Chapter 9, whether intrasubject diversity as we have defined it may be related to cognitive complexity as described by Triandis (1977) and others.

2. In each country, a split-plot analysis of variance was done with the two concepts (self and ideal self) as the within-subject variable and the two sexes as the between-subject variable. The .05 level was used for statistical significance.

PART IV

Outcomes

8

SUMMARY OF FINDINGS: CROSS-CULTURAL SIMILARITIES AND DIFFERENCES

The preceding chapters have provided a detailed examination of the findings of the study relative to the self-perceptions and ideal self-perceptions of men and women and their sex-role ideologies. In this chapter, we will review the major findings that emerged from the preceding analyses and attempt to provide some conceptual integration. We will examine, first, the findings related to pancultural similarities, offering generalizations concerning the self-concepts and sex-role ideologies of men and women across our sample of countries. Following this, we will examine the findings related to cross-cultural variation by considering each of our cultural comparison variables in turn and noting any self-concept or sex-role ideology effects that appear to be associated with these variables. In the final section of the chapter, we will attempt an integration of our findings regarding cross-cultural differences.

Before beginning our summary, it is useful to note an important distinction between findings of similarities and findings of differences in cross-cultural research. Evidence of cross-cultural similarities usually can be accepted *as is*, whereas evidence of cross-cultural differences must be viewed much more cautiously, as we attempted to explain in our earlier book on sex stereotypes (Williams & Best, 1982, pp. 63-64):

> The explanation resides in the differential effect of methodological flaws on the demonstration of cross-cultural similarities and differences. Most methodological inadequacies tend to produce spurious evidence of differences which may obscure true similarities. Thus, when one finds evidence of similarity, it is occurring despite methodological problems. The situation reverses regarding cultural differences. Observed differences among cultural groups may be due solely to methodological flaws and provide no sound basis for conclusions about true cultural differences. Relevant here is Campbell's (1964) "plausible rival hypothesis" approach, in which he proposes that the cross-cultural investigator should not conclude that observed differences reflect true cultural differences unless all other likely explanations can be ruled out. For these reasons, evidence of cross-cultural similarities—particularly if they are complex and patterned—can be taken at face value, while evidence of cross-cultural differences must be interpreted with great caution.

In keeping with the foregoing rationale, we have tended to accept observed cross-cultural similarities in a relatively uncritical manner but have been much more conservative with observed cross-cultural differences. Regarding the latter, our principal strategy has been to treat observed differences between countries as important only if they were found to be associated with one or more of our cultural comparison variables.

CROSS-CULTURAL SIMILARITIES

Affective Meaning

The affective meaning analyses, described in Chapter 5, examined the perceived self-concepts and ideal self-concepts of men and women in terms of their relative strength, activity, and favorability. It was observed that, in most countries, the perceived self of men was both stronger and more active than the perceived self of women. Similar findings were obtained for the ideal self; in most countries, men described the person they would like to be as stronger and more active than did women. These findings echo, in a general way, the findings of the earlier study of sex stereotypes (Williams & Best, 1982), where it was found in all countries studied that the psychological characteristics said to be associated with men tended to be stronger and more active than the psychological characteristics said to be associated with women. If one wishes to give explanatory prominence to the sex stereotypes, one can observe that in most of the countries studied, the men's and women's self-concepts incorporated some degree of the strength and activity characteristic of the male and female sex stereotypes. On the other hand, there were certain countries where this effect did not occur; thus, there appear to be other factors that, in a given country, can lead to men's and women's self-concepts not reflecting the strength and activity differences present in that country's stereotypes.

The findings concerning the relative favorability of the perceived self of men and women did not show any consistency across countries; in some of the countries the men's perceived self was noticeably more favorable than the women's, whereas in others the reverse effect was found. We noted earlier in Chapter 5 that the mean favorability score obtained from an individual's self-description may be viewed as an index of self-esteem (LeVerrier, 1987). Hence, our findings suggest that there may be differences in the relative self-esteem of men and women from different cultures. This interpretation is inconsistent with the conclusion of Spence and Helmreich (1978, p. 149) that "the preponderance of evidence from diverse samples suggests there are no reliable sex-differences in self-esteem" and the conclusion of Wylie (1979, p. 273) that "the evidence from studies involving well-known instruments fails to support a relationship between sex and overall self-regard." It should be noted, however, that the evidence referred to is, in both instances, primarily from research conducted in the United States and, indeed, there was no evidence of an appreciable difference in self-esteem between the American women and men in the present study (see Tables 5.7 and 5.8). The substantial differences in the mean favorability (hence, self-esteem) scores of men and women in some other countries, seen earlier in Tables 5.7 and 5.8, indicate that the Spence and Helmreich statement should be taken as a culture-specific observation and not as a pancultural, etic conclusion.

Whereas there were approximately the same number of countries in which the men and the women had the higher self-esteem scores, the differences in the mean favorability of the ideal-self scores were asymmetrically distributed. In most countries, the desired self for women was more favorable than the desired self for men, that is, women usually want to be "better people" than men do.

The affective meaning analysis also revealed some noteworthy relative findings when the self-concepts and ideal self-concepts were compared with one another. First, it was found that the ideal self was uniformly more favorable than the perceived self for both men and women subjects in all countries. This was not unexpected; it would certainly be strange to find that what people want to be is not more favorable than what they perceive themselves to be. On the other hand, the strength and activity differences provide more food for thought. The ideal self-descriptions were stronger and more active than the perceived self-descriptions for both men and women in all countries. From this we might infer that people generally feel somewhat weaker and more passive than they would like to be and that, if they could become stronger and more active, they would be more effective in meeting the demands of everyday living. It is intriguing to observe that in terms of strength and activity, both men's and women's ideal selves are more similar to the male sex stereotype than the female.

Before leaving the affective meaning analyses, there is another effect to be pointed out. Across the 14 countries, the men's ideal-self scores were more variable than the women's with regard to both activity and favorability. These findings suggest that, across cultures, the influences determining the men's ideal self-perceptions are somewhat more varied than the influences upon the women's ideal self-perceptions. Cross-culturally, there is more variability in what men wish to be than in what women wish to be.

A final effect to be noted was that there was more variability across countries in the strength of perceived self than in the strength of ideal self, for both men and women subjects. Regarding strength, it appears that there is more cultural variation in what people perceive themselves to be than in what they wish to be. However people in a given country may perceive themselves, they all wish to be quite strong!

Masculinity/Femininity

The average or typical masculinity/femininity of the self-descriptions and ideal self-descriptions of the men and women subjects were examined in detail in Chapter 6. In each country, the self-descriptions and ideal self-descriptions were scored with reference to the M% scores obtained in that country in the earlier sex-stereotype study (Williams & Best, 1982). This provided the opportunity to study, in each country, the masculinity/femininity of the self-descriptions and ideal self-descriptions relative to the characteristics generally associated with men and women in that particular country. Scored in this manner, it was found that in all countries the perceived self of the men was more masculine than the perceived self of the women. This was, of course, our expectation, but there was nothing about the present method that forced such a result to emerge, and in psychological research it is always comforting to be able to prove the obvious.

The finding that, in all countries, the ideal self-descriptions of men were more masculine or less feminine than those of women is somewhat more interesting. In describing the persons they would like to be, there is still a relative difference in masculinity/femininity, as Block (1984) has reported in her study of persons in six Western countries. Thus, in each country, the sex stereotypes were echoed, to some degree, in both aspects of the self-concepts of women and men.

One of the more substantial findings observed in the masculinity/femininity analysis concerned the relative masculinity/femininity of the self-concepts and ideal self-concepts. In all countries, for both men and women, the ideal self was relatively more masculine than the self; when the subjects were asked to describe their selves and then their ideal selves, the description shifted in a relatively masculine direction. Why do all groups want to be more masculine than they perceive themselves to be? This may be related to the affective meaning differences discussed earlier, where it was noted that persons of both genders wished to be stronger and more active than they thought they were. As greater activity and strength ratings are found for adjectives stereotypically associated with men than with women, the shift toward "greater masculinity" in moving from self to ideal self may be a reflection of the shift toward a stronger and more active description of the ideal self.

A final finding from the principal masculinity/femininity analysis was that, across the 14 countries, there appeared to be less difference in the masculinity/femininity of the men's and women's ideal self-concepts than there was in the masculinity/femininity of their self-concepts; panculturally, what men and women *wish to be* is more similar, in terms of M/F, than what they *are*. It is interesting to juxtapose this finding to Wylie's (1974) observation, based on research conducted primarily in the United States, that the ideal self is somewhat less variable from person to person than is the perceived self, presumably because of shared values concerning attributes considered desirable in people.[1] The present findings, thus, suggest that there may be some pancultural agreement in the conception of what constitutes the ideal person.

Interesting findings also emerged from a secondary analysis of the average masculinity/femininity scores. It had been found in the earlier sex-stereotype project that there were substantial differences in both means and variances of the M% scores associated with the 300 adjectives in the item pools used in scoring the data from the different countries. The secondary analysis corrected the group mean scores of the women and men for these differences in item-pool means and variances with the resulting scores viewed as adjusted, or relative, indices of masculinity/femininity. The results of this analysis were, in general, similar to those of the primary analysis. In all countries, the men's self-description was relatively more masculine than the women's self-description, with a similar effect observed for the ideal self. Another parallel finding was that the adjusted masculinity/femininity scores appeared to vary more across countries for the self-concept than for the ideal self-concept for both men and women. Once again, what people wish to be, relative to masculinity/femininity, is more similar than what they see themselves to be.

The analysis of the adjusted masculinity/femininity scores yielded two other findings which deserve comment. First, let us note that there was no significant correlation across countries between the relative masculinity of the men's and women's self-perceptions, or the men's and women's ideal self-perceptions. However, there were some interesting relationships between the self-perceptions of one gender and the ideal self-perceptions of the other gender. The relative M/F of the men's self-perception was positively correlated with the M/F of the women's ideal self-concept; and the M/F of the women's self-concept was positively correlated with the M/F of the men's ideal self-concept. In countries where men described themselves as being relatively masculine, the women wished to be relatively more masculine; in countries where women described themselves as being relatively masculine, men wished to be relatively more masculine.

These findings suggest the operation of some important between-gender dynamics. Apparently, there is no pressure for persons of one gender to "match" the M/F of their self-perceptions to the M/F of the self-perceptions of persons of the other gender; similarly for the two ideal self-perceptions. On the other hand, there appears to be some "matching" between how one gender perceives itself and how the other gender wishes to perceive itself. Thus, in a given country, if the men perceive themselves in a highly masculine manner, this does not influence the women's self-perceptions but it leads the women to aspire to greater masculinity in their ideal selves.

Diversity of Masculinity/Femininity

A relatively novel feature of the present project was the scoring of men's and women's self-concepts and ideal self-concepts in terms of the diversity of masculinity/femininity. The measure of diversity was the variance of the M% scores comprising a particular description. For example, one description might consist of items that were highly associated with men and with women, whereas a second description might consist of items that were only moderately associated with men or with women. The variance, or diversity, of masculinity/femininity would be greater in the former case than in the latter, despite the fact that the average (mean) masculinity/femininity might be identical in the two descriptions.

The most interesting finding to emerge from these analyses was that in most countries both the self-concepts and the ideal self-concepts of women were more diverse than those of men. Put the other way, the self-descriptions and ideal self-descriptions of men tend to be somewhat more constricted along the masculinity/femininity dimension than were the descriptions of women. We suggested, in Chapter 2, that our diversity measure is related to the concept of androgyny (having attributes of both genders) as this term has been used by Bem (1974) and Spence and Helmreich (1978). Employing this concept, we observe a general tendency for the self-descriptions and ideal self-descriptions of women to be "more androgynous" than the self-descriptions and ideal self-descriptions of men. This is contrary to our earlier research on self-descriptions of men and women students (Williams & Best, 1982), which indicated that the men saw themselves as more androgynous than the women did.

Another noteworthy finding was the tendency, in most countries, for the ideal self-concepts of men and women to be more diverse than their self-concepts. This suggests a general tendency for persons to wish to be more variable (more androgynous) along the masculinity/femininity dimension than they in fact see themselves to be. This finding is consistent with the view that androgyny is related to psychological health and adjustment (Bem, 1974; Kaplan & Bean, 1976).

A final finding regarding diversity has to do with the relationsip of diversity and average masculinity/femininity across countries. For women, and to a lesser degree for men, in countries where the perceived self and ideal self were more masculine, the concepts tended to be less variable. Once again, we note that greater masculinity seems associated with less diversity in self-description and ideal self-description. This, in turn, is congruent with the finding noted above that, in most countries, the self-concepts of women were more diverse than the self-concepts of men. If it is generally true that boys are socialized in a more restrictive manner than are girls, as seems to be true in the United States (e.g., Fling & Manosevitz, 1972; Goodenough, 1957; Hartup & Moore, 1965; Lansky, 1967; Ruby, 1968), the effects just noted may be related to differential socialization effects for the two gender groups.

Sex-Role Ideology

Sex-role ideology is concerned with the person's views as to proper role relationships between men and women scaled along a traditional/male dominant to modern/egalitarian dimension. The analyses of the ideology scores of men and women in the 14 different countries led to several general findings. Substantial variation was found in typical sex-role ideology in the different countries, with persons in some countries being relatively modern and others relatively traditional. An important finding was that the correlation across the 14 countries for the men's and women's means was quite high; if the women in a particular country tended to have relatively modern views, the men did also. Another way to put this is that the differences between the sexes were considerably smaller than the differences between the countries, indicating that general cultural influences seem to have more impact on sex-role ideology than does gender.

Another noteworthy finding related to gender was the fact that, in most countries, the women subjects tended to be somewhat more liberal than the men subjects. Similar findings have been reported in studies conducted in the United States and other countries by other researchers (e.g., Kalin et al., 1982; Spence & Helmreich, 1978). These results suggest that women are usually somewhat more egalitarian in their views about sex-role relationships than are men, who tend to be somewhat more traditional. Feminist theorists might argue that this is not a surprising finding in light of the fact that the traditional ideology, which assigns greater importance and/or power to men, would naturally be viewed as being more agreeable to men than to women. On the other hand, we reiterate that the observed ideology differences between women and men were not great; men's and women's views were much more similar than different.

A persistent notion among researchers in the areas of masculinity/femininity and sex-role ideology is that these two variables should be systematically related. For example, one might expect relatively masculine men and relatively feminine women to be more traditional with regard to sex-role ideology, whereas less masculine men and less feminine women might be expected to be more egalitarian. Despite the intuitive appeal of this hypothesis, previous studies have found little support for it (e.g., Spence & Helmreich, 1978, 1980). In this project, findings were obtained that were consistent with the hypothesis but they were very weak; there was, at most, a very slight tendency for more masculine men and more feminine women to be more conservative in sex-role ideology. Thus, one must conclude that there is, as yet, no strong support for the hypothesis.

The findings that we have reviewed in this section on cross-cultural similarities point to a number of general effects relating to the self-concepts and sex-role ideologies of men and women. None of these observations should be taken as final conclusions but should be considered as propositions for further investigation.

CROSS-CULTURAL DIFFERENCES

In addition to an interest in cross-cultural similarities discussed in the previous section, the project was also concerned with differences in men's and women's self-concepts and sex-role ideologies that appeared to be culturally related. The general strategy here was to determine whether observed differences between countries in men's and women's self-concepts or sex-role ideologies were systematically related to a variety of cultural comparison variables. For example, one could inquire as to whether the differences in the strength of men's and women's self-perceptions were systematically related to economic-social development. In this section we will summarize the findings obtained when the self-concept and sex-role ideology differences observed in Chapters 4-7 were correlated with our cultural comparison variables.

We will deal first with the relationship between sex-role ideology scores and the other cultural comparison variables. Having done this, we will then treat sex-role ideology as an additional cultural comparison variable as we examine relationships with the various self-concept measures.

Sex-Role Ideology

The variations among countries in sex-role ideology along the traditional to modern dimension were found to be related to virtually all of the cultural comparison variables. With reference to economic-social development, ideology tended to be more modern in more highly developed countries. With regard to work-related values, ideology was more liberal in countries where values were individualistic and nonauthoritarian. Regarding the status of women, ideology tended to be more liberal in countries where a relatively large number of women were employed outside the home, and where a relatively high percentage of the women attended universities. When religion was considered, sex-role ideology tended to be relatively modern in more Christian countries and relatively traditional in more Muslim countries. When general demographics were considered, sex-role ideology was found to be more modern in relatively urbanized countries and in countries in the high latitudes (i.e., countries that are relatively far from the equator). Thus, sex-role ideology appears to be related to a wide variety of cultural variables.

Recalling that there are a number of substantial correlations among the various cultural comparison variables we have employed (see Table 3.4), one might think that the large number of significant correlations between sex-role ideology scores and the cultural comparison variables is attributable to the lack of independence among the latter measures. It will be seen, as we proceed, that this idea does not appear valid. We will observe a number of instances where, for example, economic-social development is related to a self-concept variable but religion and status of women are not. Instead, we view the large number of relationships between sex-role ideology and other cultural variables as indicating the pervasive nature of the variables that collectively influence the typical sex-role ideology in particular countries.

We will now treat sex-ideology itself as a cultural comparison variable and examine the relationship of the ideology scores to the various measures of self-concept examined in Chapters 5, 6, and 7. The differences among countries in typical sex-role ideology scores were found to be related to the affective meaning difference scores. In more traditional countries, men's and women's self-concepts and ideal self-concepts tended to be more highly differentiated in terms of affective meaning, whereas in more modern countries men's and women's self-concepts were less differentiated. These overall findings were attributable primarily to differences in strength and activity; the general tendency for men's self-concepts and ideal self-concepts to be stronger and more active than those of women was greater in more traditional countries than in more egalitarian countries.

The observed differences among countries in typical sex-role ideology were essentially unrelated to the various measures of average masculinity/femininity of self-concept reported in Chapter 6; the only significant relationship observed suggested a tendency for the men's ideal self to be more masculine in relatively traditional countries. This paucity of relationships between sex-role ideology and average masculinity/femininity *across* countries mirrors the lack of relationship *within* countries, noted above. Viewed either way, there seems little relationship between ideology and average masculinity/femininity.

The differences in sex-role ideologies across countries showed little relationship to the diversity of masculinity/femininity as examined in Chapter 6. The only significant relationship observed was a tendency for the increase in diversity from self to ideal self for men to be greater in more egalitarian countries.

In sum, we observe that the between-country differences in sex-role ideology are related to cross-national differences in self-concept when this is evaluated in terms of affective meaning, but shows little relationship to self-concept when it is scored in terms of average masculinity/femininity. Somewhat surprisingly, sex-role ideology seems to be more strongly influenced by cultural variables related to development than to self-perceptions of masculinity/femininity.

Work-Related Values

We reviewed, in Chapter 1, Hofstede's (1980) study of work-related values in 40 countries. Two of his scores, Individualism and Power Distance, were chosen for inclusion as cultural comparison variables in the present project. Because of the high negative correlation between these two variables in our sample of countries, we chose to combine these two scores into a single values index. High scores on the composite measure indicated countries where values are high on individualism and low on authoritarianism, whereas low scores indicated more communal and authoritarian societies. For purposes of explication we will refer to countries with high scores as *high individualism/low authoritarianism* (HI/LA), and countries with low composite scores will be referred to as *low individualism/high authoritarianism* (LI/HA).

The values measure was found to be related to the affective meaning difference scores in men's and women's self-concepts. The degree to which the selves and ideal selves of men and women differed in terms of affective meaning was less in the HI/LA countries that in LI/HA countries. This overall effect was attributable primarily to differences in strength and favorability. The strength difference between men's and women's self-concepts and ideal self-concepts was less in the HI/LA countries than in the LI/HA countries. In addition, in the HI/LA countries women perceived their self and ideal self as being more favorable than did the men, whereas in the LI/HA countries this effect was reversed, with the men having the more favorable self-concepts and ideal self-concepts. In countries where individualism is stressed, women seem to view themselves as more effective and more positive.

The values measure was found not to be related to the cross-country variation in average M/F scores for either men or women, for either self or ideal self. There were, however, some findings relating the values measure to the *relative* M/F of men's and women's self-concepts. For both self and ideal self, the masculinity of the men's concepts relative to the women's was greater in the HI/LA countries; the general tendency for the men's concepts to be more masculine and the women's more feminine was more pronounced in countries with more individualistic value systems. When this finding is juxtaposed to that noted in the preceding paragraph, an apparent paradox emerges: In HI/LA countries, men's and women's concepts are *more* differentiated on M/F and *less* differentiated on affective meaning. This seems inconsistent, as a major component of M/F scores is related to affective meaning, especially strength and activity. One can only speculate that there must be differences in the neutral affective-meaning components of M/F that are responsible for the relationship of the M/F differences to the values measure. Apparently, it is possible for the self-concepts of men and women to be *more* differentiated in terms of M/F and, at the same time, be *less* differentiated in terms of affective meaning.

The most striking relationship between the values measure and masculinity/femininity was found in its relationship to the M/F diversity measure. In the HI/LA countries the self-descriptions and ideal self-descriptions of both men and women tended to be more diverse (more androgynous) than in the LI/HA countries. Another finding related to diversity was that the increase in diversity from self to ideal self for men was greater in the HI/LA countries; the direction of the result for women was the same but was not significant. Thus, men and, to a less extent, women identify with a more androgynous ideal in countries where individualism is valued.

In sum, it appears that there are relationships between work-related values as defined by Hofstede and differences in the self-concepts of men and women. In countries where the value structure places a high emphasis upon individualism and a low emphasis on authoritarianism, the men's and women's self-concepts tend to be less differentiated in terms of affective meaning and more diverse, or more androgynous, in terms of relative masculinity/femininity.

Economic-Social Development

Our composite index of economic-social development was described in detail in Chapter 3. It is based on a variety of factors such as GNP per capita, several indicators of educational development and literacy, and several indicators of health. Countries that are high on the index tend to be wealthy countries with well-developed educational and health-care systems, whereas countries low on the index tend to be economically poor countries with relatively less developed educational and health systems.

Economic-social development was found to be significantly related to the affective meaning difference scores for the self and ideal self of women and men; in more highly developed countries, the men's and women's self-concepts showed less differentiation. This overall finding was attributable primarily to differences on strength and favorability. The general tendency for men's self-descriptions and ideal self-descriptions to be stronger than women's was more evident in less developed countries than in more developed countries. In the more developed countries there was a tendency for women's self-concepts to be more favorable than men's, whereas in less developed countries there was a tendency for this effect to reverse and for men to have the more favorable self-concepts. This pattern of relationships is similar to that found between the affective meaning difference scores and the values measure, suggesting that individualism is stressed in more economically developed countries and these aspects of development are related to women having stronger, more favorable self-concepts.

The economic-social development index was also related to the affective meaning differences between self and ideal self. For both sexes, there was a greater difference between what people *are* and what they *want to be* in more highly developed countries than in less highly developed countries. This effect was attributable primarily to shifts on strength and favorability. Although persons in all countries wish to be stronger and more favorable than they are, this effect was more pronounced in the more developed countries than in the less developed countries. From this, we might infer that aspirations for personal change are greater in more developed countries, perhaps attributable to the greater flexibility and potential for growth afforded by various aspects of development.

When the men's and women's self-descriptions and ideal self-descriptions were analyzed in terms of masculinity/femininity and diversity of masculinity/femininity, the observed differences between countries showed little appreciable relationship to economic-social development. The paucity of relationships is similar to that found in our earlier project when we examined the relationships between indices of economic-social development and sex stereotypes (Williams & Best, 1982). In this study, the only significant finding was for the shift in diversity from self to ideal self for men to be less in the more developed countries.

In sum, the self-concepts of men and women were found to vary systematically with economic-social development when the concepts are scored in terms of affective meaning but not when they are scored in terms of masculinity/femininity.[2]

Status of Women

There were two cultural comparison variables reflecting the relative status of women across the 14 countries: the percentage of women employed outside the home and the percentage of women in the total university population. Each of these measures may be viewed as an index of the degree to which the women in a country are "liberated" from the traditional role of homemaker.

In countries where these percentages are low, women tend to be more concerned with domestic affairs; in countries where the percentages are high, women are participating, to a greater degree, in activities outside the home. We observed in Chapter 3 that these two variables are positively associated (i.e., in countries where the percentage of women working outside the home is high, there is also a tendency for there to be a higher percentage of women in the university population). On the other hand, the magnitude of the correlation (.47) indicates that the measures are sufficiently independent to warrant their separate examination. The general question being addressed, then, is whether the self-concepts of men and women vary with the degree of extradomestic activity by women.

There were both similarities and differences in the manner in which the two status of women variables related to the self-concept data. For both variables, it was found that in countries where the women are relatively "liberated," the affective meaning differences in the self-perceptions and ideal self-perceptions of men and women were less (i.e., women and men perceived themselves in a more similar fashion). This overall difference was attributable primarily to differences in strength and favorability. In countries where women participate more in extradomestic roles, the general tendency for the women's self-concept to be weaker than the men's is diminished. Regarding favorability, in countries where women are active outside the home, women tend to have more favorable self-concepts than men, but in countries where women are confined primarily to domestic activities, they tend to have the less favorable self-concepts.

Differences were found in the manner in which the two status of women variables related to the affective meaning discrepancy scores between self and ideal self. In countries where more women work outside the home, there was a greater overall affective meaning difference between self and ideal self *for both women and men* (i.e., there is a greater gap between how people saw themselves and what they would like to be). Once again, the overall affective meaning differences were attributable primarily to the stength and favorability variables. The usual tendency for people to wish to be stronger and more favorable than they are was greater in countries where many women work outside the home. On the other hand, the second status of women variable, the percentage of women in the university population, was not related to self/ideal-self differences.

The status of women variables showed little relationship to the masculinity/femininity variables. The only significant relationship observed was the somewhat puzzling finding that, in countries where there was a relatively high percentage of women in the university population, the ideal self-descriptions of the women tended to be more diverse (more androgynous) than the men. Perhaps in countries where women have greater opportunity to advance educationally, their ideals become more androgynous, incorporating more masculine traits.

Religion

Religion is usually considered to be a powerful cultural variable that influences the person's perception of the world and the people who live in it. The prescriptive aspects of religion address what people are like and what they should be like and often speak to relations between men and women. We have already noted that the religious comparison variables were related to sex-role ideology. Here we will examine the degree to which religion may be related to the self-concepts of men and women. Let us note that, because of uneven distribution of various religions across countries, our examination is a limited one, dealing only with possible relationships to the Christian and Muslim faiths.

The influence of religion as a cultural variable was explored through the use of four indices: the percentage of the population in a country that was Catholic Christian, Protestant Christian, total Christian, and Muslim. The relationships among these indices were examined in Chapter 3 (see Table 3.3). There it was noted that there was no significant correlation between the percentage Protestant and percentage Catholic indices that justified their treatment as separate measures. Both the Protestant and the Catholic indices correlated with the total Christian percentage; thus, findings involving the latter index are not entirely independent of findings involving the two former indices. All three of the Christian indices correlated negatively with the Muslim index.

The percentage Muslim measure was found to be related to the self/ideal-self difference scores in the affective meaning analysis; in highly Muslim countries, there was more similarity between what people *are* and what they *wish to be*. Another way to put this is that there appeared to be less aspiration for personal change in highly Muslim countries. The percentage Muslim scores were not related to the affective meaning differences between men's and women's self-concepts, nor were they related to any of the masculinity/femininity indices.

The percentage Christian scores were related to several of the affective meaning difference scores. Overall, the men's and women's total self-concepts were less differentiated in more Christian countries. This effect, which was more pronounced for the perceived self than for the ideal self, was evident on all three affective meaning dimensions—strength, activity, and favorability. In more non-Christian countries, the tendency for men to see themselves as stronger, more active, and more favorable than women was greater than in more Christian countries. The comparison of the percentage Christian indices with the masculinity/femininity indices revealed only a few relationships of borderline significance. For both men and women, the difference in average masculinity/femininity scores between self and ideal self was less in highly Christian countries. In addition, there was a tendency for the ideal selves of men and women to be less masculine in more highly Christian countries. Finally, for women, the overall similarity of self and ideal self appeared to be greater in highly Christian countries.

The findings relating the percentage Protestant scores to the affective meaning difference scores were generally similar to those described above for the percentage Christian scores. In more Protestant countries, the self-descriptions and ideal self-descriptions of men and women were less differentiated in terms of affective meaning. The usual tendency for men's self-concepts and ideal self-concepts to be stronger than the women's concepts was diminished in more Protestant countries. Regarding favorability, in highly Protestant countries women tended to have more favorable self-concepts and ideal self-concepts than did men, but in countries with a low Protestant percentage men tended to have more favorable self-concepts and ideal self-concepts than women.

The percentage Protestant scores were also found to be strongly related to the diversity of masculinity/femininity measure; in highly Protestant countries, both men and women tended to give more diverse, more androgynous, self-descriptions and ideal self-descriptions. There was the suggestion that this effect may be attributable to the Protestant orientation rather than the general Christian orientation, as comparable effects were not found for the percentage Christian measure discussed above.

The percentage Catholic measure showed little relationship to the self-concept measures. There was a suggestion that in more Catholic countries women's self-perceptions and ideal self-perceptions differed less in activity than in countries with a low Catholic percentage. There was also the suggestion of less diversity in women's ideal self in more Catholic countries. It can be noted that this effect is opposite to that described above for the Protestant index. Combining these two results, we can note that in more Protestant countries the ideal self-concept of women tends to be more diverse, more androgynous, whereas in more Catholic countries it tends to be less diverse.

Urbanization

We have already noted that sex-role ideology tends to vary with degree of urbanization, with more liberal views being held in more highly urbanized countries. When the urbanization measure was compared with the self-concept measures, only a few relationships were observed. There was a relatively weak tendency for the men's and women's self-concepts in the more urbanized countries to be less differentiated in terms of affective meaning. This means that the tendency for men's self-concepts to be higher on strength and activity was less pronounced in more urban countries. There was also the suggestion that the affective meaning discrepancy between self and ideal self was somewhat greater in the more urbanized countries. No relationships were observed between the masculinity/femininity measures and urbanization.

Latitude

The latitude measure indexes each country's distance north of the equator. We noted earlier that this rather arbitrary sounding index was employed in our study because of the findings of other investigators (e.g., Hofstede, 1980) indicating substantial relationships between latitude and various psychological measures. High scores on the latitude measure indicate countries that are relatively far removed from the equator (e.g, Finland), whereas low scores indicate countries that are relatively close to the equator (e.g., Singapore).

We have already observed that sex-role ideology varies with latitude; more modern ideologies are found in countries further removed from the equator. The latitude measure was also related to the affective meaning difference scores. In higher latitude countries, there is less overall difference in men's and women's self-descriptions and ideal self-descriptions than in countries in the lower latitudes; the general tendency for men's self-descriptions to be stronger and more active than women's self-descriptions diminishes as one moves away from the equator. In addition, in countries closer to the equator, the men's self-concepts and ideal self-concepts are likely to be more favorable than the women's, whereas in the higher latitude countries the women's self-descriptions and ideal self-descriptions tend to be more favorable. The findings also suggested that as one moves away from the equator the self-descriptions of women become more feminine and the ideal self-descriptions of men also become more feminine. The only other finding regarding latitude and masculinity/femininity involved the diversity measure. It was found that as one moves away from the equator, there is a tendency for the diversity difference between the men's self-concepts and their ideal self-concepts to increase.

Why should self-concept and sex-role ideology vary with latitude? We propose in the following section that this effect may best be understood in terms of the relation of latitude to socioeconomic development. The interested reader may also wish to review Hofstede's (1980) speculations concerning the relationship of latitude to work-related values.

An Integration of Findings Regarding Cross-Cultural Differences

The foregoing review has indicated that our self-concept and sex-role ideology measures were related to a number of cultural comparison variables. These cannot be viewed as independent findings because of the considerable number of interrelationships existing among the cultural comparison variables themselves (see Table 3.4). Although we believe it has been useful to examine each cultural comparison variable separately, we now feel a need to attempt to integrate the findings regarding cross-cultural differences.

How are we to summarize the findings regarding cross-cultural differences with relation to cultural variation? The initial thought when looking at such an enormous amount of data would be to conduct multivariate analyses, such as multiple regression or factor analyses, to see which cultural variables predict self-concept or sex-role ideology scores. Examining our data more closely, we see that our cultural variables represent intercountry variation rather than intracountry variation; each subject in Japan has the same economic-social ranking, each subject in Nigeria has the same score for percentage of women employed outside the home, and so forth. Therefore, rather than looking at individual subject scores, analyses of cross-cultural variation would have to treat each country as a "subject" or "case," which would result in a sample size of only 14. With such a small sample, it is almost impossible to meet the assumptions of most multivariate analyses (e.g., most texts recommend four to five times as many cases as independent variables). Because of these limitations, we have chosen a straightforward and commonsensical way to examine cultural variation by identifying a key comparison variable that seems to account for much of the observed variation in self-concept and sex-role ideology. We will refer to other cultural comparison variables only when the findings cannot be adequately explained with reference to our key variable.

The key cultural comparison variable that we identified was our measure of economic-social development. The principal reason for determining this measure to be our key variable is the fact that it was related to more of the other cultural comparison variables than was any other single variable. An examination of the interrelationships among the cultural comparison variable measures, seen in Table 3.4, reveals that economic-social development showed an appreciable relationship to eight of the other nine variables; in addition, it was also significantly related to the sex-role ideology measure. Thus, it appears that the economic-social development measure has more in common with our other cultural comparison variables than does any other single variable. An additional reason for focusing upon the economic-social development measure is the fact that it is generally considered to be an important cultural variable by social scientists in a variety of fields, and is often assigned an explanatory role in the interpretation of cross-cultural findings. Furthermore, as a composite measure encompassing education, health, and economic factors, it is a good overall descriptor of the cultures being studied.[3]

The economic-social development measure (see Chapter 3) is based on such factors as the relative wealth of a country and the degree of development of its educational and health-care systems. More developed countries tend to be from the higher latitudes (i.e., further from the equator) and to be relatively urbanized. In more developed countries, there tends to be a higher percentage of women employed outside the home and a higher percentage of women in the university enrollment. Regarding religious tradition, more developed countries tend to be more Christian (particularly Protestant Christian) and tend to have relatively low percentages of Muslim affiliation. In relatively developed countries, work-related values tend to be more individualistic and less authoritarian than in less developed countries. In addition, in more developed countries sex-role ideology tends to be more modern or egalitarian than in less developed countries. There is, thus, a considerable constellation of cultural differences which tend to cluster around the economic-social development variable.

When we reexamine the self-concept findings in relation to economic-social development, the following conclusions can be noted. In relatively less developed countries, the self-perceptions of men and women tend to be more highly differentiated in terms of affective meaning than in the more highly developed countries; a similar conclusion applies to the men's and women's ideal self-concepts. These findings are consistent with the idea that, as economic-social development proceeds, the self-concepts of men and women become more similar.

Another major conclusion relates to the similarity of perceived self and ideal self (i.e., between how people see themselves and how they would like to be). In relatively less developed countries the self-descriptions and ideal self-descriptions are somewhat more similar, whereas in more developed countries there is a greater difference between self and ideal self. This might be viewed as indicating a higher "psychological aspiration level" in the more developed countries. In all countries, persons wish to be stronger and more favorable than they perceive themselves to be. The fact that this effect is more dramatic in more developed countries may be related to the greater societal fluidity in more developed countries. In the more traditionally oriented, relatively less developed countries, the prospect for change is generally less, and this is reflected in lower aspirations for personal change. In sum, it appears to the authors that the economic-social development concept provides an reasonable way of summarizing the findings related to self-concept differences as assessed via affective meaning.

The observed linkage between economic-social development and self-concept is too remote to be satisfying. What are the factors that mediate this relationship? What are the differences in experiences that lead persons in more developed countries to perceive themselves differently from persons in less developed countries? Although we cannot offer conclusive answers to these questions, the concept of *individual modernity*, as developed by Inkeles and Smith (1974), may provide a useful point of departure.

These authors and their associates worked in six developing countries where they conducted studies of the personal changes occurring in men as a result of contact with various "modernizing" influences such as education, mass-media exposure, and occupation, particularly "experience with large-scale modern productive enterprises such as the factory" (p. 19). After comparing men with varying degrees of exposure to such influences, the authors conclude that experiences of this sort tend to move people in the direction of increasing "individual modernity." How is the modern man characterized? Inkeles and Smith (1974, pp. 19-25) note 12 defining characteristics, among which are such traits as: openness to new experience, readiness for social change; awareness of diversity of attitude and opinion in others; orientation to present and future, not past; belief that environment can be controlled; belief that people and insitutions can be relied on to meet their obligations; and so forth.

Regarding the relationship of modernization to women's rights, Inkeles and Smith (1974, p. 26) state:

> We predicted that the liberating influence of the forces making for modernization would act on men's attitudes, and incline them to accord to women status and rights more nearly equal to those enjoyed by men. We tested the men's

orientation through questions on a woman's right to work and to equal pay, to hold public office, and to freely choose her marriage partner.

The finding in the current project that men in more developed countries have more egalitarian views of sex roles seems quite congruent with Inkeles's and Smith's expectations. The fact that women also show a similar effect is a point that they do not address.

In his review of psychological factors related to social and cultural change, Berry (1980c) has noted the importance of distinguishing between the *processes* of change and the *states* that exist at some point during the process. Whereas Inkeles and Smith's study of more and less modernized subgroups within each of their developing countries is clearly aimed at understanding the process of change, our findings can be considered, at most, to relate to different states of modernity, as these may be reflected in the relative standing of our countries in terms of economic-social development.

Let us assume, for the moment, that our between-country differences in economic-social development can be viewed as reflecting, among other things, differences in states of modernity, with our more developed countries being more modern and our less developed countries being less modern. Following Inkeles and Smith's logic, persons exposed to "more modern" cultures should be "more modernized" in terms of attitudinal and personality variables. How do the results of the present project appear when viewed in this manner? Our findings suggest that, as modernity increases, there is a decrease in the differences in the self-perceptions of men and women, there is an increase in the discrepancy between how persons view themselves and how they view their ideal selves, and there is movement toward more egalitarian sex roles. We might add our findings based on Hofstede's measures and note that, with increasing modernity, work-related values become increasingly individualistic and decreasingly authoritarian. All these findings seem congruent with the changes expected and found by Inkeles and Smith (1974) to result from exposure to modernizing influences within developing countries. While recognizing that individual modernity is a complex, and at times, controversial concept (Berry, 1980c; Inkeles, 1977), we feel it may provide an approach to understanding the present results in relation to economic-social development.

The only major self-concept findings that are not embraced by the economic-social development concept are those related to diversity of masculinity/femininity; the economic-social development measure was not significantly related to the diversity measure but both the percentage Protestant and values measures were highly related. In countries with relatively high individualism values, the self-concepts and ideal self-concepts of men and women tended to be more diverse along the masculinity/femininity dimension. In other words, in countries where there is the expectation that persons will take care of themselves, self-concepts tend to be more diverse, or more androgynous; in countries where it is expected that the group will take care of the individual, self-concepts tend to be less diverse. If one prefers to emphasize the relation between self-concept diversity and Protestantism, one can point to the relative emphasis on individual persons, their morals, and their behavior in the Protestant tradition (Spence, 1985). Finally, we should also note those theories that relate Protestantism with its emphasis on individualism (e.g., the Protestant work ethic) to socioeconomic development, as this is reflected in the capitalist tradition (Weber, 1958).

Although there are a number of scattered findings that are not embraced by this integration, it appears to us that the major findings of the study related to self-concept can be understood in relation to the economic-social development concept, with the special codicil relating diversity of self-concept to individualistic values and the Protestant tradition.

SUMMARY

In this chapter we summarized the major findings from the project. We first noted the findings related to cross-cultural similarities in the self-concepts and sex-role ideologies of men and women. We then examined the variations across countries in the self-concept and sex-role ideology measures in relationship to each of our cultural comparison variables. We suggested that the findings related to cross-cultural differences can be related, primarily, to economic-social development and, secondarily, to values related to individualism and the Protestant tradition.

NOTES

1. A compelling illustration of this phenomenon is provided by Fenley's (1986) findings that whereas the perceived selves of young male drug addicts and normal controls were strikingly different, the ideal selves of the two groups were indistinguishable.

2. Block (1984) endorsed Bakan's (1966) idea of a relationship between "agentic" personality characteristic and a capitalistic economic orientation. Block's finding that the ideal self-descriptions of Americans were more agentic than those of Swedes and Danes were taken to support this view. To the degree that agentic characteristics are masculine characteristics, as indexed by M% scores, and to the degree that capitalism is associated with economic-social development, the findings of the present study provide no support for a link between agency and capitalism.

3. In addition, it is interesting to consider the possible parallels between the variable of economic-social development studied on an *inter*country basis and the variable of socioeconomic status studied on an *intra*country basis. (See Chapter 9.)

9

RETROSPECT AND PROSPECT: A BROADER VIEW

Cross-cultural psychologists are highly concerned—almost preoccupied—with methodological considerations. This is as it should be. Good cross-cultural research requires careful attention to such matters as comparability of subjects, research instruments, and test conditions across the various cultural groups involved in a particular study. At first glance, it might appear that cross-cultural psychologists face a substantial number of unique problems with which the psychologists working within a single country need not be concerned. On more careful examination, this turns out not to be true. Rather, the nature of the work of cross-cultural psychologists forces them to attend to problems which other psychologists may succeed in minimizing or ignoring.

As an example, take the question of the language employed in questionnaire materials. If an American psychologist wishes to compare university student values in the United States and France, it is immediately obvious that the English-language version of the instrument is inappropriate for use in France, and the researchers must deal with the highly complex task of creating a questionnaire in French that is comparable with the English-language version. Compare this with the situation of another American psychologist who wishes to compare the values among Euro-American and Afro-American university students. Because all of the latter subjects "speak English," the researcher is likely to proceed with the study without concern as to whether the research materials are equally appropriate for both groups of research subjects. In principle, both research psychologists face the same problem: Are the questionnaire materials equally appropriate for the different groups who will respond to them? In fact, the second psychologist may gloss over this issue or, even worse, not recognize that the issue exists. Thus, the "hypersensitivity" of cross-cultural psychologists to methodological issues may best be viewed as a greater sophistication regarding the general vicissitudes involved in psychological research.

In Chapter 3, we attempted a methodological critique of the research procedures employed in the current project. In this chapter, we will return to a consideration of methodological issues with the benefit of the hindsight provided by the findings obtained in the project. After reviewing these methodological matters, we will discuss some of the directions that future research related to self-concept and sex-role ideology may take.

SOME METHODOLOGICAL CONSIDERATIONS

The question of the appropriateness of research instruments for use in different cultures is often addressed in terms of the emic/etic distinction discussed at some length in Chapter 1. Briefly, emic considerations have to do with intracultural validity, whereas etic considerations have to do with intercultural or pancultural validity. Research strategies that involve the use of instruments developed in one country and arbitrarily applied in other countries have been called *imposed etic* (Berry, 1969) or *pseudo etic* (Triandis et al., 1972) approaches. On the other hand, methods that attend appropriately to intracultural considerations and then attempt to make pancultural comparisons are called *derived etic* (Berry, 1980b) approaches. We will use these terms as we reflect again upon the nature of the research questionnaires employed in the current project and discuss these in relation to the general nature of the findings obtained with each.

Sex-Role Ideology

Our findings concerning sex-role ideology were the most robust effects obtained. Substantial variation was found across countries along the traditional to modern dimension. Furthermore, the variation across countries in typical sex-role ideology was found to be significantly related to virtually all of our cultural comparison variables. If one expected to find cross-cultural variation in sex-role ideology, then the observed differences and their relation to cultural comparison variables should prove satisfying and provide much food for thought.

The degree to which one is impressed by the sex-role ideology findings may well depend on the view one takes of the instrument employed. It will be recalled that the SRI measure was initially developed and validated in Canada (Kalin & Tilby, 1978) and subsequently shown to be appropriate for use in England and Ireland (Kalin et al., 1982). Should the use of the SRI in countries as culturally diverse as Nigeria, Japan, and Pakistan be viewed as an imposed etic (bad) method or as a derived etic (good) method?

Let us note, first of all, the matter of the overall dimension along which sex-role ideology was scaled: a traditional position in which men are viewed as dominant and/or more important than women to a modern position in which both sexes are viewed as equally important and neither sex is viewed as generally controlling of the other. We believe that the *dimension* employed in assessing sex-role ideology has wide pancultural validity. It can be argued that, in all of our countries, the historical ideology has tended to be relatively male dominant or traditional. It is our view that in all 14 countries there is a current struggle between the forces of tradition and the forces of modernization, as indexed by socioeconomic development. Thus, we consider it panculturally appropriate to examine sex-role ideology along a traditional/modern dimension.

Even if one agrees as to the legitimacy of the dimension employed, there remain questions concerning the particular items used to locate the position of a country along this dimension. Are the 30 items employed equally valid in all countries for assessing ideology along the traditional/modern dimension? Had we had the opportunity to employ a strictly emic method in each country, we would undoubtedly have found that in some countries there were other behaviors, not included in our measure, which also reflected the traditional/modern dimension.

On the other hand, the reader is reminded that, in our initial approach to the researchers in other countries, we asked each one to consider the 30 SRI items and to modify the item set in order to make it more culturally appropriate. The researchers were invited to do this through the addition of items that might reflect other relevant behaviors and/or by the deletion of items considered culturally inappropriate. Some of our cooperating researchers responded to the latter invitation by deleting items; thus, in Pakistan, three items, all of which referred explicitly to sexual relations, were omitted. On the other hand, none of our cooperating researchers found it necessary to add additional items to the standard set. Hence, it would appear that in the judgment of the participating psychologists in the various countries, the item set was generally adequate for assessing sex-role ideology along the traditional/modern dimension. We must leave it for our readers to decide whether the procedure we followed was adequate to enable the SRI to be viewed as a derived etic measure or whether they choose to view this method as an imposed etic.

Affective Meanings of Self-Concepts

Looking at the Adjective Check List, a methodological purist might quibble over the fact that the 300 items in the pool used to describe self and ideal self were originally selected by American psychologists. Frankly, we are not particularly concerned with this. The item pool is so diverse that it is difficult to imagine persons in any of our countries who could not find relevant traits to describe themselves. This view is supported by the fact that neither in our earlier study involving 25 countries nor in the current project involving 14 countries have either our 40 cooperating researchers or the 6500+ participating university students suggested that the item pool was not appropriate for the descriptions of persons in their countries. Furthermore, the ACL has been used successfully in a number of countries in clinical and organizational settings to describe human personality.

The analysis of the self-concepts and ideal self-concepts of women and men in terms of affective meaning appeared fruitful in both pancultural and cross-cultural terms. For example, there was the pancultural finding that the ideal self-concepts of men and women in all countries were stronger, more active, and more favorable than their self-concepts. Cross-culturally, it was found that affective meaning differences in the self-concepts of men and women varied across countries and were related to a number of cultural comparison variables; for example, the differences between the self-concepts in terms of affective meaning were greater in less developed countries than in more developed countries. Generally, the affective meaning findings were robust on both a pancultural and a cross-cultural basis.

How does the affective meaning analysis fare when examined in terms of the emic/etic distinction? Once again, we need to distinguish between the nature of the concepts being assessed and the details of the scoring system employed. The idea of assessing the self-concepts of men and women in different countries in terms of the three general affective meaning factors seems to us panculturally valid. This view rests upon the work of Osgood and his associates (Osgood et al., 1975) whose investigations conducted in 23 language-culture groups in Europe, Asia, and the Americas indicated that the three-factor affective meaning system was a general one that could be found in the context of all of the languages studied. As our three dimensions (strength, activity, and favorability) were designed to approximate Osgood's three dimensions (potency, activity, and evaluation), we feel on relatively sound ground in comparing the self-concepts of men and women across countries on these three dimensions.

On the other hand, our affective meaning analysis is more vulnerable to criticism in terms of the actual values used to score for strength, activity, and favorability in the project. We have described in Chapter 5 the studies in which the 300 ACL items were scaled along each of the three dimensions by American university students (Best et al., 1980; Williams & Best, 1977). It is these American-based values that were used to score the self-descriptions and ideal self-descriptions of the men and women in all of the countries in the project. This smacks strongly of an imposed etic approach. It would, of course, have been ideal to have scaled the 300 adjectives separately in each of our countries with regard to the three affective meaning dimensions but this was an enterprise far beyond our capabilities.

We noted in Chapter 3 that the nature of the translation process may mitigate, to a degree, the problem of using the American-based scoring system. In choosing second-language "equivalents" for the English-language adjectives, we believe that translators often take affective meanings into account as they fine tune their translated versions. If, at first, it appears that there are three possible options for a given English adjective, the final choice may be influenced by a consideration of the differences in affective meanings among the alternatives. To the degree that this occurs, we can expect substantial affective meaning similarity between the foreign-language adjectives and the corresponding English terms.

The possibility of American bias in the affective meaning scoring system influencing our findings seemed greatest in making direct mean score comparisons between countries. Thus, it seemed precarious to note that the men's self-concepts had a higher mean strength score in Country X than in Country Y and to conclude that the men in Country X had a stronger self-perception than those in Country Y. For this reason, we did little more than report the mean affective meaning scores and, instead, focused our analysis on the *difference* scores between men and women and between self and ideal self in each country; for example, it was only the difference scores that we examined in relation to our cultural comparison variables.

It seems to us that the use of difference scores offsets, at least to a degree, the problem of American bias in the scoring system. After all, the self-descriptions and ideal self-descriptions of the men and women subjects in each country were all being evaluated by a common scoring system. Thus, if we find that the men and women in Country X have a larger difference score in strength of self-concept than do the men and women in Country Y, this is not easily attributable to American bias in the scoring system. Regardless of bias, why are the differences between men's and women's responses in one country greater than those in another country? Why are the affective meaning differences between self and ideal self more dramatic in some countries than in other countries? Although not completely satisfactory, we believe that our emphasis on difference scores in the analysis of the affective meaning data mitigates, in large degree, the possible problem of American bias in the affective meaning scoring system.

Self-Concepts Scored for Masculinity/Femininity

From a purely methodological viewpoint, our best findings are those related to masculinity/femininity. This is attributable to the manner in which masculinity/femininity was assessed. In our previous study of sex stereotypes (Williams & Best, 1982), we determined the degree to which each of the 300 adjectives was differentially associated with men and women in each country. Using this information, we were able to score the self-concepts and ideal self-concepts of the men and women in each country for masculinity/femininity based on culture-specific or emic definitions. The masculinity of men in Finland was judged by Finnish standards, the masculinity of men in Pakistan by Pakistani standards, and so forth.

The analysis of the average or typical masculinity/femininity scores revealed some notable pancultural effects: In all countries the perceived and ideal selves of the men were more masculine than the perceived and ideal selves of the women; in all countries, the ideal self was more masculine than the self for both men and women. Although there were what appeared to be substantial differences in the average masculinity/femininity scores of the men and women across countries, these differences showed little relationship to the cultural comparison variables. On the other hand, the diversity of the masculinity/femininity measure was found to vary cross-culturally and to be greater in countries from the Protestant Christian tradition and in countries where work-related values were relatively high in the individualism and antiauthoritarianism associated with the Protestant tradition.

The lack of relationship between the average masculinity/femininity scores obtained in the different countries and our cultural comparison variables is worthy of special note. This is taken to indicate that, if one judges masculinity/femininity in culture-specific terms, there is no evidence of cultural variation in self-perceptions of masculinity/femininity. It is true that there were *observed* differences in masculinity/femininity from country to country, but the failure of these differences to correlate with our cultural comparison variables casts doubt on the significance or meaning of the observed variations. It is possible, of course, that the observed differences in masculinity/femininity might be related to some *other* cultural differences that are not tapped by our comparison variables (e.g., differences in child-rearing practices). On the other hand, the robust set of relationships between our cultural comparison variables and sex-role ideology suggests that this is not an unreasonable set of variables to examine in relation to differences in masculinity/femininity.

Perhaps the most important general finding to emerge from this study is the fact that both sex-role ideology and self-concept evaluated in terms of affective meaning show cross-cultural variation but masculinity/femininity does not. In countries with traditional ideologies men are in the "one up" position and women are in the "one down" position, as the practices reflected in the ideology present men as more important than women and as being in a position of dominance or control over them. Not surprisingly, we find that in traditional ideology countries the self-concepts of men tend to be stronger and more active relative to women than is true in countries with more modern egalitarian ideologies. In addition, there is the tendency in traditional countries for men to view themselves more positively than women view themselves, whereas in more egalitarian countries this tends to reverse, with women having higher self-esteem than men. In view of these interesting and understandable relationships, it is most surprising to find that there is essentially no relationship between average masculinity/femininity of self-concept and sex-role ideology; men are not appreciably more masculine, nor women more feminine, in traditional countries than in egalitarian countries. To the authors, this is another reflection of the relative "sterility" of the masculinity/femininity concept. The concept fails to account for the many dimensions involved in gender-related self-concepts and the situational factors that influence their development (Deaux, 1984). Despite the great intuitive and popular appeal of the concept of masculinity/femininity, it is apparently of little value in attempting to understand cross-cultural variations in the self-concepts of women and men.

DIRECTIONS FOR FUTURE RESEARCH

In this project, we have made a cross-cultural examination of several psychological variables: perceived self and ideal self, evaluated in terms of affective meaning, average masculinity/femininity, diversity of masculinity/femininity, and sex-role ideology. Let us also add the values measure derived from Hofstede's work, which was psychological in nature.

We have observed the robust nature of the findings relating sex-role ideology to cultural comparison variables. We have also noted the relationships between the self-concept measures scored for affective meaning and a number of cultural comparison variables. We have seen that both sex-role ideology and affective meaning self-concept scores covaried with the values index. Thus, we conclude that there are important relationships among the affective meanings of self-concepts, sex-role ideology, and work-related values that warrant further investigation.

Sex-Role Ideology

The substantial findings obtained with our relatively crude measure of sex-role ideology suggest that a more careful study of this topic might be fruitful. This could be done by selecting a large and relatively diverse group of cultures for study. Within each culture, persons would be asked to specify behaviors that they considered to be indicative of a traditional relationship between men and women and other behaviors that they considered to be indicative of a modern relationship. Frequently mentioned items could then be tested using the "known groups" strategy by examining their endorsement by persons from that culture judged, on an independent basis, to be traditional or modern in their personal views. Having followed this approach in each of the countries, it would then be possible to examine the findings across countries to determine whether there are common factors involved in the definition of traditional and modern ideologies on a pancultural basis. Such an approach might lead to the identification of aspects of traditionalism versus modernism other than those tapped by the measure employed in the present project.

Affective Meaning Scoring Systems

We have noted in several places our concern with regard to the question of American bias in the affective meaning scoring system. The existing system represents the judgments of American university students as to the relative favorability, strength, and activity of the ACL items presented in the English language. Although we have argued that the American scoring system was useful in the context of our study, it is clear that, ideally, each of the foreign-language versions of the ACL should be scaled for the three affective meaning factors using as subjects persons who speak that language. For example, each of the 300 Japanese ACL items would be scaled for favorability, strength, and activity by Japanese persons. The method involved in such scaling studies is relatively straightforward, as summarized in Chapter 5 and as described in detail elsewhere (Best et al., 1980; Williams & Best, 1977).

We have noted elsewhere (Williams & Best, 1983, pp. 165-166) the wide variety of research questions which can be addressed via the ACL item pool:

1. *Descriptions of Individual Persons.* A frequent application is one in which subjects are asked to describe self, significant others (spouse, parent, child, etc.), or persons whom the subjects have observed in particular settings (e.g., therapists describing clients; teachers describing pupils; supervisors describing employees, etc.). The method could be used, for example to compare the manner in which well-known politicians are perceived by the public.
2. *Descriptions of Groups of Persons.* Another common use is to ask subjects to consider groups of persons with whom they have had extensive experience and to indicate the traits which characterize them collectively (e.g., successful employees). A variation of this use is to compare two or more groups and to indicate the traits which are considered differentially characteristic (e.g., clinical type A vs. clinical type B, etc.).
3. *Social Stereotypes.* Related to the foregoing are applications in which subjects are asked to describe their *beliefs* concerning the psychological characteristics of persons classified into broad social groups: ethnic group A vs. ethnic group B; men, in general vs. women, in general; etc.

4. *Historical Figures.* The item pool can be used in psychobiographical studies in which subjects are asked to describe their impressions of historically important persons; e.g., Nehru, Stalin, Roosevelt, Churchill, etc.
5. *Hypothetical Persons.* The method may be employed to delineate the characteristics of various sorts of hypothetical persons. Illustrative here is the use of the item pool to characterize various ideal types such as ideal self, ideal mate, ideal physician, etc.
6. *Personified Concepts.* Subjects may be asked to use the item pool to characterize a variety of non-person concepts which, nevertheless, can be meaningfully personified. Illustrative here are the studies reported by Gough and Heilbrun (1980b, p. 40) comparing the cities of Rome and Paris, and Fiat and Volkswagen automobiles. The ACL would appear to have many other such applications in the areas of environmental and advertising psychology.

If the versatility of the ACL method were combined with emically derived affective meaning scoring systems for a large number of languages, the result would be a research method with great potential for cross-cultural investigation. An illustrative use would be in the further exploration of the favorability of self-concept findings, seen in Table 5.8, which suggested appreciable differences in the relative self-esteem of women and men in some countries. Once such differences were confirmed via emically derived favorability scores, one could pursue the question of why men have higher self-esteem than women in some countries (e.g., Malaysia), and women have higher self-esteem in other countries (e.g., Venezuela).

Relation of Self-Concepts and Gender Roles to Socioeconomic Differences

We have noted the robust relationships between self-concept and sex-role ideology variables and socioeconomic variables studied on a cross-national basis. For example, as one moves from countries that are less developed to those that are more developed, socioeconomically speaking, the self-concepts of women and men become more similar to one another, and the perceived and ideal self-concepts become less similar. These findings are based on "average" differences between countries in economic-social development. When we remind ourselves that, in all countries, there are relative differences among groups of people in socioeconomic status (SES), we can question whether self-concept differences might be found to be related to *intra*country differences in SES in a manner similar to that found for *inter*country differences in economic-social development. If, for example, one had access to high and low SES groups in several different countries, one could determine whether it was generally true that the self-concept differences between SES groups within countries mirrored the self-concept differences related to differences in economic-social development between countries.

Measures of Intraperson Diversity

A relatively novel feature in the present project was that masculinity/femininity was approached not only in terms of the average masculinity/femininity for a particular self-description but also in terms of the diversity of the self-description. This diversity measure, which could be considered to be one way of defining androgyny, was found to be related to a number of other variables of interest; for example, the self-concepts and ideal self-concepts of men and women tended to be less diverse in countries with relatively authoritarian value systems.

Personality psychologists have paid little attention to the question of intraperson diversity on their trait measures. This is attributable to the fact that many measures involve the use of categorical (either/or) items rather than items that have been scaled with regard to the degree of their association with the relevant concept. Few personality psychologists would claim that the items that they use in their procedures are all equally indicative of the psychological dimensions they study, and yet the endorsement of the items are often weighted as if they were equally representative. In constructing a new assessment procedure, it may be relatively easy to scale the degree to which the various items represent the concept or dimension of interest. Once this is done, it becomes possible to compute a diversity measure, similar to the M/F variance measure employed in the present study, as well as to obtain weighted mean scores which may provide a more sensitive measure of central tendency for the concept being studied. If, as in the present study, the diversity measure is found to be largely independent of the measure of central tendency, then one has an additional characteristic of persons to employ in personality research.

Once one has access to several personality measures, each of which yields a variance or diversity measure, one could administer the instruments to a group of persons and then correlate the different variance scores. This would provide evidence as to whether diversity of response is specific to particular psychological domains (e.g., masculinity/femininity) or whether it is a more general characteristic that cuts across tasks (i.e., some people tend to give more diverse self-descriptions than other people regardless of specific content domains). Finding the latter might suggest a new theoretical concept that could be labeled something like *diversity of personality.* This new concept might prove to be related to the concept of *cognitive complexity*, which Triandis (1977) has proposed as an organizing principle of human behavior—a counterpart in the personality domain of the "g" factor in intelligence.

In Triandis's (1977) view, cognitive complexity should be related in a general way to cultural complexity; simpler societies (socially, economically, politically) should produce persons low in cognitive complexity, and more complex societies should produce persons higher in this characteristic. Triandis notes that there are a number of different ways in which cognitive complexity has been operationalized by different groups of researchers, and that further research is needed regarding convergent validity. Nevertheless, Triandis (1977, p. 147) is sufficiently impressed by the evidence for such a construct that he has been willing to offer hypotheses concerning the correlates of cognitive complexity:

> It would seem, then, that highly complex individuals have attitudes and values that are different from individuals low in complexity. As yet there is too little clarity in this literature, but it seems reasonable to hypothesize that the more complex will be less authoritarian, higher in modernity (Inkeles & Smith, 1974), higher in need for achievement (McClelland, 1961) and their social behavior will be determined by *several* rather than a few factors. . . . Another plausible hypothesis is that complex individuals will be characterized by positive self-concepts, and will tend to show more associative, more independent, more coordinate (rather than superordinate or subordinate) and more overt behaviors in many social settings. Finally, it is plausible that complex individuals will be more willing to be intimate in relation to a wider range of others.

Let us assume that our measure of intrapersonal diversity represents at least one aspect of cognitive complexity and see if we have any evidence bearing on Triandis's hypotheses. The high correlations between our values measure and our variance measure (see Table 7.5) are congruent with his expectation that cognitive complexity should be associated with lower authoritarianism. What about Triandis's expectation that complex individuals will have more positive self-concepts? When LeVerrier (1987) administered a self-descriptive ACL to 180 American university students and correlated the M/F diversity measure with the mean affective meaning scores, she found correlations of .19 for favorability, .39 for strength, and .46 for activity, all of which are statistically significant. Taken together, these findings seem consistent with Triandis's expectation. The evidence that the M/F variance scores are related to non-M/F aspects of self-description suggests that further research on the correlates of intrasubject variance may prove profitable.

IN CONCLUSION

The cross-cultural findings concerning psychological masculinity/femininity were very sparse. There was little evidence that the average masculinity/femininity measures were related to cultural variation, as indexed by our cultural comparison variables, nor did average masculinity/femininity appear to be related cross-culturally to sex-role ideology or to work-related values. The diversity measure of masculinity/femininity fared somewhat better, being related to the Protestant Christian religious tradition and also to the work-related values measure.

At the outset of this project, the authors were particularly excited at the prospect of being able to study the masculinity/femininity of self-concepts on a culture-specific basis and viewed the analysis of self-concepts in terms of affective meaning as a secondary matter. The findings from the project have caused us to reverse our thinking about the relative utility of these two approaches. We now conclude that, although there are interesting cross-cultural variations in men and women's self-concepts, it is not particularly useful to approach these differences via locally defined masculinity/femininity. The differences in men's and women's self-perceptions are better understood when conceptualized in terms of other variables (Gill, Stockard, Johnson, & Williams, 1987).

We doubt that we have sounded the death knell for the concept of psychological masculinity/femininity. The concept has so much intuitive appeal for both laypersons and psychologists that it will no doubt continue to be a subject of psychological inquiry. We suggest, however, that there may be more profitable ways to study the self-perceptions and ideal self-perceptions of men and women and the manner in which these concepts vary across cultures.

As a parting thought, we note that the general findings of the present project add to the large and growing body of evidence (Lonner, 1980) that persons from different cultures are much more similar than they are different (i.e., there is a large "human nature" component encountered in people everywhere). Although culture certainly influences psychological processes, the degree of influence often turns out not to be as great as would be expected by persons who are captives of the old "cultural relativism" model.

As scientists, we have been prepared to recognize and accept whatever degree of cultural influence we found in our data, but as persons, we are pleased that the findings from the present project, and the preceding one (Williams & Best, 1982), provide more evidence of pancultural similarities than of culture-specific differences. A strong emphasis on cultural differences—sometimes expressed as a need for "national" psychologies (e.g., Diaz-Guerrero, 1977)—may provide unintended support for political nationalism. An emphasis on pancultural similarities encourages viewing persons from all countries as one people—a perspective which, to us, seems much more conducive to the long-term survival of humankind.

SUMMARY

In this chapter, we took a broader view of the project as it relates to some of the basic problems in cross-cultural psychology, for example, intracultural (emic) versus intercultural (etic) issues related to our assessment procedures and findings. A paradox was noted in our having obtained rather sparse cross-cultural findings from our methodologically superior measure of masculinity/femininity and more robust findings from our methodologically inferior measures of affective meaning and sex-role ideology. Suggestions were offered for future research related to sex-role ideology, affective meaning, and intrapersonal diversity with a possible link suggested between the latter and the concept of cognitive complexity. We observed that self-concept differences between the genders may be better understood by employing concepts other than masculinity/femininity. We concluded by noting that the project provided more evidence of pancultural similarities than culture-specific differences, which encourages a perspective in which persons from all countries are viewed as one people.

Appendixes

Appendix A

Item	Affective Meaning Scores			M% Scores													
	FAV	*STR*	*ACT*	*CAN*	*ENG*	*FIN*	*GER*	*IND*	*ITA*	*JAP*	*MAL*	*NET*	*NIG*	*PAK*	*SIN*	*USA*	*VEN*
1. absent-minded	393	378	425	54	51	88	66	77	80	25	61	90	16	49	65	34	75
2. active	629	651	687	81	90	86	84	76	78	78	88	78	92	75	96	83	65
3. adaptable	634	603	496	48	36	5	13	20	27	59	70	21	65	39	60	41	44
4. adventurous	615	694	695	93	96	94	91	89	94	80	99	94	97	92	96	98	96
5. affected	455	419	479	14	31	1	10	41	41	31	14	2	9	19	8	13	19
6. affectionate	611	571	563	10	3	4	13	8	6	34	4	6	1	10	16	5	25
7. aggressive	504	713	712	94	99	93	81	95	85	77	85	96	62	88	82	98	84
8. alert	631	630	620	66	75	38	51	66	51	38	74	67	84	67	67	59	47
9. aloof	420	405	414	49	44	90	62	74	84	21	35	71	12	54	41	42	58
10. ambitious	599	678	642	86	93	93	86	73	73	91	88	94	93	47	85	89	49
11. anxious	452	506	604	20	10	44	3	21	58	25	9	1	27	40	11	33	43
12. apathetic	369	329	329	42	49	45	72	75	77	46	29	28	28	72	30	62	42
13. appreciative	618	546	488	34	15	6	8	51	40	34	14	34	23	49	24	9	35
14. argumentative	441	619	643	44	57	71	10	42	88	68	55	92	65	69	41	57	59
15. arrogant	376	559	600	80	88	91	77	88	93	67	70	85	31	28	71	68	68
16. artistic	613	506	511	26	28	20	45	20	39	59	36	34	59	46	38	22	34
17. assertive	541	625	620	78	90	94	83	85	99	92	9	92	70	51	71	85	78
18. attractive	620	559	464	7	3	2	6	38	16	12	1	5	2	13	9	9	25
19. autocratic	477	559	551	89	87	91	87	94	91	95	88	94	91	57	82	90	77
20. awkward	394	368	453	59	53	95	45	43	88	64	66	24	60	78	62	71	72
21. bitter	353	459	517	46	44	38	50	61	75	77	38	41	47	67	33	48	47
22. blustery	424	460	587	42	57	48	95	60	97	88	68	98	43	8	38	44	92
23. boastful	369	486	611	90	93	91	93	51	73	32	95	92	78	34	65	93	79
24. bossy	381	521	662	46	34	73	89	74	97	93	67	48	76	93	47	44	80

Item	Affective Meaning Scores			M% Scores													
	FAV	STR	ACT	CAN	ENG	FIN	GER	IND	ITA	JAP	MAL	NET	NIG	PAK	SIN	USA	VEN
25. calm	598	486	300	56	54	45	57	48	58	45	52	73	12	45	69	57	33
26. capable	626	583	486	73	46	88	89	56	72	90	79	94	86	80	81	73	67
27. careless	380	356	442	60	60	66	60	65	81	38	58	59	49	74	70	52	80
28. cautious	551	463	405	24	38	19	23	46	50	28	20	15	33	42	18	29	40
29. changeable	521	448	496	18	16	17	44	34	65	26	31	9	15	53	30	18	29
30. charming	610	527	475	34	44	1	4	10	9	3	12	7	11	19	24	14	22
31. cheerful	641	586	562	14	47	51	18	29	51	31	52	20	20	68	45	9	57
32. civilized	596	513	454	37	54	55	57	53	70	49	54	35	51	51	30	29	54
33. clear-thinking	636	589	480	77	73	75	93	70	56	75	76	82	88	59	75	84	73
34. clever	623	638	558	71	72	35	58	50	94	52	84	64	86	43	72	56	69
35. coarse	398	517	512	92	97	98	96	94	97	90	95	98	80	51	89	97	78
36. cold	365	437	408	67	52	62	71	62	37	36	37	54	19	64	53	52	74
37. commonplace	448	397	380	35	45	55	43	83	42	41	47	41	42	80	58	70	74
38. complaining	359	375	520	9	20	5	21	13	44	21	4	7	5	13	8	11	37
39. complicated	484	546	537	25	28	13	26	54	43	41	18	16	19	27	17	29	38
40. conceited	353	476	555	64	69	81	48	49	87	37	59	46	33	26	44	59	41
41. confident	601	679	563	88	89	95	61	81	51	75	90	86	85	79	88	92	39
42. confused	426	386	478	10	19	18	30	52	73	53	16	40	13	40	9	19	49
43. conscientious	616	600	514	28	29	4	58	61	57	49	25	54	65	43	25	31	55
44. conservative	505	475	374	54	53	40	77	39	98	43	22	65	48	51	25	51	40
45. considerate	636	587	466	14	24	42	63	34	48	40	31	45	24	52	33	26	39
46. contented	582	494	353	37	29	50	44	66	72	42	34	48	57	19	37	31	42
47. conventional	494	432	396	64	64	23	63	39	66	35	21	63	60	23	42	53	51
48. cool	535	465	387	81	67	43	55	68	72	72	59	87	19	40	70	76	52
49. cooperative	613	551	464	38	33	39	70	44	58	56	59	45	42	33	55	40	63
50. courageous	608	725	654	94	91	98	82	82	98	95	84	96	96	85	89	97	51

Item	Affective Meaning Scores			M% Scores												
	FAV	STR	ACT	CAN	ENG	FIN	GER	IND	ITA	JAP	MAL	NET	NIG	PAK	SIN	USA	VEN
51. cowardly	387	314	393	30	63	6	67	43	79	51	18	64	17	15	35	36	53
52. cruel	337	483	613	86	85	90	91	90	61	49	72	92	69	91	78	88	65
53. curious	572	563	588	32	27	19	15	37	16	14	28	3	52	42	24	33	26
54. cynical	403	510	530	60	80	56	69	71	85	38	49	88	57	71	61	74	80
55. daring	547	660	691	90	91	83	92	90	83	74	96	86	55	91	86	93	75
56. deceitful	347	444	550	44	40	31	35	69	71	39	66	55	32	83	51	39	63
57. defensive	440	473	528	38	48	34	25	52	19	31	44	55	81	81	36	47	48
58. deliberate	519	544	511	38	74	72	58	76	53	57	62	79	58	59	41	71	32
59. demanding	453	573	626	65	33	67	60	45	73	13	66	35	7	42	42	64	45
60. dependable	648	641	507	51	63	73	57	35	20	90	57	64	40	54	65	55	58
61. dependent	463	381	345	15	13	24	8	28	19	29	13	5	15	33	15	10	35
62. despondent	418	390	317	40	40	15	8	64	13	68	14	16	43	25	24	29	45
63. determined	603	671	614	76	76	91	87	77	90	85	80	90	95	72	77	78	69
64. dignified	580	583	466	62	45	66	80	40	72	94	49	59	61	86	46	57	42
65. discreet	560	487	382	42	42	33	70	72	32	52	65	51	34	61	40	34	49
66. disorderly	396	480	554	78	65	69	66	88	88	26	77	67	65	75	77	79	87
67. dissatisfied	413	422	488	30	45	28	39	46	49	22	51	29	13	42	46	51	66
68. distractible	436	403	478	30	42	49	25	59	74	34	19	12	32	38	43	53	62
69. distrustful	358	398	462	62	53	36	36	64	42	29	34	41	37	57	48	56	41
70. dominant	462	644	659	92	86	98	90	86	98	92	84	92	85	67	83	92	76
71. dreamy	483	410	328	12	15	10	4	26	26	31	13	11	9	9	9	11	39
72. dull	379	281	284	76	71	18	78	70	73	38	53	26	21	18	56	74	50
73. easy-going	604	481	395	68	69	52	38	55	94	53	81	49	51	40	78	80	59
74. effeminate	438	378	363	31	58	77	65	60	82	39	19	87	9	8	43	38	54
75. efficient	619	629	571	47	48	76	62	59	55	96	86	89	77	75	71	34	60
76. egotistical	389	505	595	88	91	79	83	76	92	62	71	89	57	34	79	84	73

Item	Affective Meaning Scores			M% Scores												
	FAV	*STR*	*ACT*	*CAN*	*ENG*	*FIN*	*GER*	*IND*	*ITA*	*JAP*	*MAL*	*NET*	*NIG*	*PAK*	*SIN*	*USA*	*VEN*
77. emotional	508	513	587	2	6	4	4	10	12	17	9	3	12	51	4	0	32
78. energetic	616	673	708	75	85	64	82	89	24	93	95	81	98	93	89	68	82
79. enterprising	604	648	657	90	82	83	49	83	94	96	88	91	69	70	86	88	76
80. enthusiastic	631	692	699	41	54	56	21	52	19	46	69	38	63	77	54	33	50
81. evasive	422	410	436	36	36	47	49	60	71	40	45	36	45	64	38	31	57
82. excitable	527	557	643	10	17	66	43	35	59	42	15	12	12	86	22	9	38
83. fair-minded	609	519	441	46	55	64	63	65	44	79	60	78	32	66	60	60	53
84. fault-finding	379	371	497	28	38	7	77	38	76	20	22	9	32	22	25	32	24
85. fearful	420	386	436	6	30	11	7	42	23	14	2	5	22	5	11	18	20
86. feminine	530	419	397	1	2	1	8	8	54	15	0	7	2	19	0	3	3
87. fickle	411	354	476	18	23	36	30	52	22	54	15	6	19	45	14	7	35
88. flirtatious	437	422	584	18	16	24	3	60	5	9	72	29	44	81	60	6	11
89. foolish	383	367	486	32	36	9	16	60	24	40	20	32	22	26	25	23	34
90. forceful	475	627	680	95	96	98	77	90	95	98	90	99	94	91	91	98	96
91. foresighted	598	560	503	61	54	84	71	59	3	83	80	82	74	55	75	67	57
92. forgetful	406	360	407	52	51	49	58	67	72	45	53	54	27	48	60	55	73
93. forgiving	632	603	449	15	14	13	29	21	21	95	34	19	36	28	39	28	48
94. formal	484	492	426	46	74	67	92	50	73	60	60	96	48	35	39	37	51
95. frank	596	608	542	74	78	90	34	70	85	70	67	16	80	65	65	83	55
96. friendly	649	602	566	22	47	26	24	47	53	73	48	30	28	53	46	28	52
97. frivolous	445	371	550	10	17	17	28	64	30	24	52	23	39	30	28	8	25
98. fussy	401	354	583	10	14	9	41	25	57	11	4	35	25	29	9	5	38
99. generous	635	597	530	38	54	43	85	62	61	87	55	84	35	68	70	49	27
100. gentle	635	492	362	14	21	13	12	30	12	7	16	23	34	39	27	16	21
101. gloomy	373	363	320	66	74	87	44	76	82	48	35	86	22	25	43	65	65
102. good-looking	609	538	471	52	60	18	30	20	28	26	27	33	13	12	58	52	54

Item	Affective Meaning Scores			M% Scores													
	FAV	STR	ACT	CAN	ENG	FIN	GER	IND	ITA	JAP	MAL	NET	NIG	PAK	SIN	USA	VEN
103. good-natured	654	575	493	49	39	40	52	34	89	71	44	32	28	24	42	66	49
104. greedy	343	443	595	74	81	71	41	67	88	66	57	49	61	47	57	76	63
105. handsome	606	563	487	96	96	97	4	91	19	98	100	18	98	9	97	96	74
106. hard-headed	412	535	567	74	87	79	67	90	57	86	72	85	88	36	70	73	54
107. hard-hearted	372	465	526	79	71	80	85	85	87	43	58	91	79	44	73	81	73
108. hasty	408	470	612	46	45	15	61	67	90	35	48	58	71	42	55	51	59
109. headstrong	450	576	638	70	57	71	86	82	83	48	66	62	80	87	67	76	63
110. healthy	624	598	532	71	73	56	53	73	80	79	79	52	74	92	80	77	71
111. helpful	636	606	557	28	34	22	29	47	39	26	49	27	28	53	43	36	34
112. high-strung	439	473	662	14	13	8	13	66	67	43	8	2	68	22	22	15	53
113. honest	661	621	463	44	54	76	64	52	88	71	44	52	47	45	54	63	54
114. hostile	356	506	630	74	83	76	71	80	61	26	43	67	56	64	51	82	53
115. humorous	619	571	549	75	79	57	90	66	79	75	8	84	51	64	84	75	68
116. hurried	437	441	630	40	34	91	60	70	73	30	48	55	73	38	43	37	62
117. idealistic	541	541	449	51	56	43	65	57	64	59	34	70	66	20	27	37	62
118. imaginative	574	576	504	28	31	26	23	35	46	54	39	22	52	42	27	18	44
119. immature	368	333	453	53	77	47	50	58	86	21	31	26	6	11	62	50	55
120. impatient	385	383	584	60	62	45	51	48	75	37	61	51	35	43	51	67	49
121. impulsive	470	481	64	32	36	43	39	45	77	52	27	18	31	43	40	31	60
122. independent	612	671	603	86	88	84	86	89	83	87	94	88	84	80	83	94	70
123. indifferent	407	410	359	64	80	67	47	80	76	62	63	88	56	76	67	80	63
124. individualistic	609	651	568	77	68	36	75	81	90	69	55	92	49	41	71	79	64
125. industrious	624	675	641	93	68	50	25	75	87	81	63	20	78	83	65	79	30
126. infantile	381	332	407	29	70	43	40	70	85	28	12	26	17	27	38	28	52
127. informal	552	481	439	68	66	25	75	72	52	61	72	23	45	69	63	76	53
128. ingenious	606	610	553	80	69	91	74	86	89	93	5	79	35	54	72	70	54

Item	Affective Meaning Scores			M% Scores													
	FAV	STR	ACT	CAN	ENG	FIN	GER	IND	ITA	JAP	MAL	NET	NIG	PAK	SIN	USA	VEN
129. inhibited	415	405	337	28	41	60	41	63	48	61	85	34	29	18	23	30	42
130. initiative	606	624	589	77	70	71	80	82	87	93	61	81	87	68	87	74	57
131. insightful	608	584	524	51	40	67	29	74	73	85	85	97	69	61	57	47	55
132. intelligent	631	649	538	74	74	80	79	61	78	59	6	91	92	79	80	58	73
133. interests narrow	401	330	358	36	37	29	19	40	36	25	92	13	13	21	18	55	40
134. interests wide	619	630	603	63	72	77	84	75	79	82	92	87	85	81	81	51	60
135. intolerant	375	414	571	59	74	65	70	76	75	38	49	68	35	69	39	77	36
136. inventive	594	603	609	85	77	62	82	87	85	78	87	75	91	96	86	79	57
137. irresponsible	356	368	474	62	66	71	72	76	64	35	73	27	56	58	70	57	69
138. irritable	357	422	566	44	46	66	47	61	69	44	48	46	29	60	42	44	42
139. jolly	613	549	574	74	68	12	39	64	90	64	73	94	39	42	74	88	58
140. kind	645	557	466	12	16	22	29	18	31	42	27	30	20	28	32	26	49
141. lazy	372	316	279	78	85	82	81	71	97	55	88	70	13	29	81	86	69
142. leisurely	529	419	320	50	64	87	85	62	61	57	68	90	15	28	68	56	50
143. logical	599	579	467	76	86	95	92	73	70	74	88	94	86	66	79	91	43
144. loud	429	516	614	74	86	82	86	74	96	72	74	82	70	78	71	85	62
145. loyal	631	608	487	28	47	55	25	47	81	83	10	28	24	18	43	47	40
146. mannerly	591	532	438	32	59	33	10	57	34	61	10	51	20	85	31	38	74
147. masculine	576	616	570	100	96	99	94	95	97	96	97	92	99	79	95	100	99
148. mature	623	665	507	52	63	40	59	61	53	16	70	55	88	75	55	62	49
149. mock	449	346	308	14	19	49	9	32	43	36	9	10	14	25	16	13	36
150. methodical	516	495	466	60	60	65	92	59	72	41	35	94	54	50	53	66	44
151. mild	485	375	307	14	19	6	11	33	35	45	16	8	16	24	24	15	43
152. mischievous	464	506	611	65	52	70	87	65	92	18	80	34	63	76	77	71	68
153. moderate	516	465	443	28	49	49	37	63	52	67	30	62	22	53	28	57	50
154. modest	569	494	389	35	30	36	21	24	57	3	15	22	16	9	27	32	53

Item	Affective Meaning Scores			M% Scores												
	FAV	STR	ACT	CAN	ENG	FIN	GER	IND	ITA	JAP	MAL	NET	NIG	PAK	SIN	USA	VEN
155. moody	407	432	471	23	37	4	28	44	57	46	21	71	22	70	30	31	32
156. nagging	344	416	608	3	5	1	51	22	52	34	5	35	17	73	8	2	62
157. natural	609	560	457	45	49	32	21	67	55	66	59	32	63	43	65	54	60
158. nervous	408	422	595	12	16	29	40	20	76	51	8	10	18	13	9	26	38
159. noisy	399	489	642	62	80	73	84	61	97	33	55	85	40	28	47	74	60
160. obliging	539	471	438	32	42	5	72	41	30	15	49	11	43	34	47	50	53
161. obnoxious	337	481	639	78	88	90	73	88	73	31	80	85	55	83	62	77	49
162. opinionated	469	586	583	64	79	60	57	68	89	76	67	47	59	75	66	69	44
163. opportunistic	535	602	600	86	74	77	68	71	89	62	81	74	46	65	74	81	57
164. optimistic	621	648	572	50	52	50	62	59	79	61	74	44	76	40	75	39	61
165. organized	612	603	533	38	50	75	90	68	81	55	52	94	65	56	61	48	47
166. original	630	610	525	60	65	40	64	83	56	85	72	41	84	54	74	47	63
167. outgoing	627	663	658	63	75	26	83	84	51	55	96	85	62	67	75	48	57
168. outspoken	518	614	671	72	83	70	64	66	89	57	85	10	77	70	71	76	58
169. painstaking	530	529	542	44	33	73	30	41	79	72	27	69	61	59	29	39	42
170. patient	630	560	371	28	21	31	26	36	38	56	26	41	32	28	33	32	42
171. peaceable	620	513	318	24	26	26	35	63	61	19	35	27	29	38	30	40	34
172. peculiar	443	430	454	50	69	54	62	64	53	79	32	48	33	73	38	49	40
173. persevering	580	621	568	51	55	59	78	68	58	74	35	83	68	86	44	70	51
174. persistent	545	633	614	56	47	94	78	66	70	73	56	78	70	69	44	69	52
175. pessimistic	382	400	376	52	60	62	59	63	57	31	29	58	25	62	24	75	51
176. planful	569	524	496	52	53	79	90	74	30	65	73	90	86	44	57	55	53
177. pleasant	619	565	413	16	23	31	27	30	9	18	39	38	15	13	31	20	48
178. pleasure-seeking	559	503	522	66	67	67	36	57	96	53	84	72	23	70	76	76	60
179. poised	594	537	459	18	17	50	57	34	62	39	42	90	47	50	22	16	47
180. polished	570	519	464	35	45	12	82	50	90	44	43	37	26	25	34	38	59

Item	Affective Meaning Scores			M% Scores												
	FAV	STR	ACT	CAN	ENG	FIN	GER	IND	ITA	JAP	MAL	NET	NIG	PAK	SIN	USA	VEN
181. practical	594	535	480	50	51	32	47	69	59	73	78	45	85	76	76	60	67
182. praising	580	532	538	23	25	14	32	45	90	40	45	65	30	69	41	31	51
183. precise	568	562	525	61	62	58	81	81	54	53	75	54	74	66	73	66	61
184. prejudiced	377	433	546	84	69	50	48	36	46	34	18	55	23	64	25	77	33
185. preoccupied	427	398	487	62	54	63	59	74	51	28	41	57	42	25	45	65	52
186. progressive	575	597	617	80	78	57	79	85	72	82	90	76	96	82	84	82	71
187. prudish	402	397	422	22	27	13	3	36	36	13	9	11	47	36	23	5	39
188. quarrelsome	360	430	611	32	42	34	6	32	91	46	27	34	15	26	8	34	63
189. queer	357	403	451	72	86	59	77	61	28	84	43	78	36	84	48	74	45
190. quick	568	573	626	68	69	54	75	73	90	78	88	73	87	53	73	68	66
191. quiet	543	451	296	20	29	43	24	45	36	25	13	62	15	47	26	33	43
192. quitting	358	313	383	40	62	16	20	79	43	56	16	15	26	45	29	45	49
193. rational	591	581	480	72	82	86	82	76	89	67	80	94	71	49	77	90	62
194. rattlebrained	382	360	526	20	26	22	75	65	67	6	33	30	48	21	29	15	37
195. realistic	601	586	496	72	71	66	87	73	81	61	83	89	76	75	72	85	62
196. reasonable	614	560	453	61	56	44	79	59	44	81	71	79	67	66	66	76	71
197. rebellious	432	548	659	56	81	61	71	83	74	47	71	29	47	67	70	78	65
198. reckless	382	494	654	73	86	93	97	87	89	82	78	74	78	72	82	77	64
199. reflective	567	492	378	36	33	78	92	69	48	70	30	81	45	78	45	43	54
200. relaxed	604	487	321	50	58	54	54	69	66	54	71	65	29	56	61	62	58
201. reliable	647	595	470	50	56	74	56	49	98	94	60	74	60	52	67	52	47
202. resentful	373	444	536	34	46	23	19	73	49	56	24	33	23	36	37	46	41
203. reserved	511	435	341	38	43	37	24	43	63	12	29	49	26	36	28	47	49
204. resourceful	611	598	557	68	60	61	70	80	81	74	82	70	79	81	80	58	68
205. responsible	641	646	534	61	70	76	81	63	69	94	63	91	70	74	60	67	48
206. restless	448	456	605	52	58	49	72	63	78	45	45	27	68	43	60	68	69

Item	Affective Meaning Scores			M% Scores												
	FAV	*STR*	*ACT*	*CAN*	*ENG*	*FIN*	*GER*	*IND*	*ITA*	*JAP*	*MAL*	*NET*	*NIG*	*PAK*	*SIN*	*USA*	*VEN*
207. retiring	452	381	449	66	54	36	51	78	58	71	30	36	44	57	49	55	47
208. rigid	415	478	464	59	66	91	86	84	80	64	68	90	75	85	50	63	70
209. robust	559	606	642	74	82	73	92	87	100	93	91	94	21	90	85	83	75
210. rude	342	454	603	84	89	92	98	82	100	77	85	98	32	71	81	89	65
211. sarcastic	405	476	572	56	59	50	92	52	93	20	46	89	34	41	44	53	72
212. self-centered	353	437	497	68	76	67	67	48	91	48	44	58	28	41	54	59	47
213. self-confident	595	648	557	82	85	90	81	76	87	61	88	95	84	59	84	88	65
214. self-controlled	607	640	470	66	60	50	74	60	62	80	69	85	73	29	68	59	61
215. self-denying	494	506	445	39	31	20	38	56	61	56	38	11	61	40	31	36	35
216. self-pitying	372	322	374	22	28	23	28	52	59	35	15	25	18	26	12	34	43
217. self-punishing	394	398	500	34	39	45	40	61	80	69	24	66	58	31	37	56	60
218. self-seeking	464	456	525	60	75	91	76	76	47	41	44	71	40	64	54	51	51
219. selfish	353	375	509	66	78	86	62	64	81	60	34	67	32	73	33	62	49
220. sensitive	592	498	426	5	13	6	9	8	9	45	4	4	17	11	9	11	33
221. sentimental	563	490	370	2	12	4	13	12	19	15	7	3	8	21	14	3	29
222. serious	553	576	442	68	71	89	84	65	87	74	70	84	75	56	66	80	62
223. severe	418	529	568	74	80	90	84	51	95	86	75	84	80	88	69	88	67
224. sexy	594	589	609	11	11	11	3	28	15	9	5	2	37		5	10	39
225. shallow	391	314	370	40	43	28	29	74	28	37	16	24	9	70	15	37	39
226. sharp-witted	591	616	617	69	71	77	93	61	83	65	69	85	59	61	42	66	55
227. shiftless	394	398	484	69	66	7	79	76	82	50	29	12	62	42	46	87	71
228. show-off	384	425	637	85	92	83	91	41	93	64	69	86	18	25	48	84	42
229. shrewd	498	565	582	65	57	43	80	63	84	71	67	61	45	61	47	61	61
230. shy	474	395	299	14	23	45	9	10	54	18	3	10	5	16	18	23	65
231. silent	464	384	278	24	38	52	50	47	51	68	22	24	9	22	28	44	43
232. simple	480	387	347	24	49	29	30	45	55	41	58	15	40	64	41	45	54

Item	Affective Meaning Scores			M% Scores												
	FAV	STR	ACT	CAN	ENG	FIN	GER	IND	ITA	JAP	MAL	NET	NIG	PAK	SIN	USA	VEN
233. sincere	630	573	420	22	45	36	62	45	54	79	41	34	44	32	46	35	52
234. slipshod	420	363	445	56	73	27	16	87	72	56	60	20	53	82	73	86	59
235. slow	418	354	334	48	53	82	50	66	64	42	10	39	3	39	9	61	35
236. sly	449	494	533	66	64	22	73	74	79	48	52	65	35	70	58	57	58
237. smug	400	413	458	62	76	78	86	74	78	44	52	89	49	73	58	63	34
238. snobbish	352	429	497	19	28	64	94	56	77	63	39	79	22	91	36	18	34
239. sociable	599	579	574	35	54	33	59	34	64	50	56	10	52	23	43	27	55
240. soft-hearted	567	478	380	10	19	10	20	17	30	25	7	4	6	12	15	19	38
241. sophisticated	549	543	488	23	18	10	91	28	32	79	39	34	11	13	17	14	40
242. spendthrift	444	443	550	35	44	13	45	59	64	45	56	28	43	27	34	41	60
243. spineless	376	330	368	56	78	61	74	75	87	33	35	41	26	42	45	66	39
244. spontaneous	553	540	616	42	92	21	47	75	52	83	45	6	46	65	58	40	53
245. spunky	579	627	663	46	86	81	57	86	95	78	92	68	40	77	59	42	52
246. stable	585	581	441	82	72	69	85	76	33	81	78	93	80	84	82	88	85
247. steady	598	567	437	80	71	80	70	73	48	88	84	93	74	47	87	85	58
248. stern	456	579	521	86	88	95	91	88	69	67	86	91	89	79	75	97	68
249. stingy	374	433	516	60	80	79	86	65	89	53	31	68	48	70	52	72	46
250. stolid	450	525	483	80	93	75	88	72	64	69	79	85	58	89	72	81	48
251. strong	601	681	605	96	96	97	94	94	94	92	94	96	97	93	94	98	75
252. stubborn	421	533	564	56	70	91	39	63	63	49	54	61	59	83	46	78	63
253. submissive	447	338	317	20	14	5	13	28	16	23	3	4	4	21	11	8	30
254. suggestible	492	438	409	24	31	16	12	60	23	10	15	9	31	36	36	21	30
255. sulky	386	346	371	22	34	98	74	58	60	6	17	8	17	55	19	26	61
256. superstitious	430	398	474	14	6	4	8	17	27	12	5	7	4	16	8	25	29
257. suspicious	422	448	505	25	30	27	55	32	50	19	10	28	10	71	8	41	40
258. sympathetic	603	527	418	6	13	60	7	17	74	27	13	9	11	14	18	11	39

Item	Affective Meaning Scores			M% Scores													
	FAV	STR	ACT	CAN	ENG	FIN	GER	IND	ITA	JAP	MAL	NET	NIG	PAK	SIN	USA	VEN
259. tactful	606	567	489	36	23	51	25	44	88	54	55	32	81	56	58	25	46
260. tactless	379	395	501	62	80	62	81	77	97	31	45	80	25	40	43	81	46
261. talkative	512	492	625	10	22	9	23	12	41	4	15	27	9	10	4	12	55
262. temperamental	425	414	542	20	25	11	17	58	71	43	31	26	22	25	18	25	45
263. tense	411	451	574	37	36	59	57	70	87	57	49	48	52	46	25	54	66
264. thankless	373	371	434	80	80	71	62	81	77	54	82	61	55	73	71	78	43
265. thorough	577	548	546	60	57	72	68	80	75	12	48	89	57	73	54	62	52
266. thoughtful	627	603	470	22	33	65	65	59	68	30	29	60	68	58	37	28	56
267. thrifty	561	521	499	43	39	79	29	67	61	40	28	46	48	29	41	63	43
268. timid	444	384	308	18	16	15	24	28	64	41	3	13	15	10	13	18	44
269. tolerant	598	579	434	38	42	35	21	46	36	78	35	58	49	36	54	47	43
270. touchy	402	422	547	22	30	30	10	16	60	48	5	23	11	33	13	32	44
271. tough	520	644	597	96	97	65	78	96	96	98	97	98	93	91	93	98	55
272. trusting	620	597	459	25	35	31	45	47	35	25	33	64	45	79	37	34	47
273. unaffected	478	452	378	78	69	76	60	79	82	72	73	44	74	81	83	80	52
274. unambitious	388	321	311	22	21	5	33	58	59	48	10	11	3	68	13	28	46
275. unassuming	479	395	359	34	36	24	40	69	56	54	40	20	56	85	41	41	29
276. unconventional	507	540	513	46	66	63	54	86	56	78	76	38	47	77	51	58	52
277. undependable	362	340	425	56	60	35	50	76	67	51	54	48	40	63	44	56	47
278. understanding	638	595	442	24	25	15	39	39	25	71	38	18	52	63	38	27	43
279. unemotional	418	410	339	94	90	82	69	93	70	60	91	90	88	44	90	97	77
280. unexcitable	417	421	309	87	78	56	65	80	53	73	80	92	78	41	70	92	49
281. unfriendly	349	378	412	72	63	79	87	80	54	53	58	90	59	62	56	74	53
282. uninhibited	552	549	609	73	77	42	73	78	88	62	87	62	71	25	76	78	58
283. unintelligent	394	381	395	29	46	19	24	60	52	36	14	11	11	27	19	37	23
284. unkind	349	389	479	84	70	79	80	87	76	63	80	83	75	71	63	82	66

Item	Affective Meaning Scores			M% Scores												
	FAV	*STR*	*ACT*	*CAN*	*ENG*	*FIN*	*GER*	*IND*	*ITA*	*JAP*	*MAL*	*NET*	*NIG*	*PAK*	*SIN*	*USA*	*VEN*
285. unrealistic	385	392	445	26	39	10	27	66	65	44	25	19	22	49	19	27	38
286. unscrupulous	388	406	550	60	87	80	94	87	79	58	58	88	47	67	54	71	59
287. unselfish	622	590	480	31	35	18	23	56	70	48	57	21	52	45	44	33	69
288. unstable	385	370	521	18	27	10	15	64	29	23	21	10	21	31	14	29	46
289. vindictive	399	456	600	45	58	50	42	69	55	18	32	67	60	45	26	56	45
290. versatile	621	627	601	59	56	61	74	80	44	75	68	70	69	77	64	50	41
291. warm	640	581	484	6	12	9	7	35	28	41	36	6	27	78	21	22	59
292. wary	451	430	470	50	48	52	12	60	60	17	24	43	43	79	27	60	55
293. weak	393	273	322	5	23	8	33	29	15	16	5	4	2	11	1	10	28
294. whiny	361	271	411	10	23	8	12	48	16	22	8	2	21	51	15	8	40
295. wholesome	593	567	470	31	56	69	12	77	50	67	73	26	76	84	46	36	68
296. wise	630	656	472	85	88	80	83	68	77	71	87	81	82	81	79	88	71
297. withdrawn	402	357	317	21	41	40	52	67	57	24	20	27	18	17	27	47	39
298. witty	607	581	584	70	82	44	91	50	78	74	66	79	57	51	53	53	54
299. worrying	393	375	503	6	14	22	34	32	66	15	8	13	5	27	6	18	52
300. zany	525	538	671	36	41	92	65	68	97	79	71	79	45	95	46	31	54

Appendix B SRI Item Means for Men (M), Women (W), and Total (T) Subjects in Each Country

		1	2	3	4	5	6	7	8	9	10	11	12	13	14	15	16	17	18	19	20	21	22	23	24	25	26	27	28	29	30
CAN	M	4.1	4.4	5.9	3.7	5.3	4.2	3.7	4.3	3.9	4.5	2.3	3.4	2.9	2.5	3.7	5.0	5.4	3.3	4.4	4.2	2.4	4.6	5.1	4.8	3.9	3.4	2.8	5.2	5.3	3.8
	W	5.3	4.7	6.3	3.9	6.1	5.1	4.1	4.6	5.4	5.8	2.8	3.9	2.9	2.5	3.4	4.8	6.1	4.4	5.1	4.9	3.2	4.5	5.5	6.0	3.7	3.0	2.8	6.0	6.0	4.0
	T	4.7	4.6	6.1	3.8	5.7	4.7	3.9	4.5	4.7	5.2	2.6	3.7	2.9	2.5	3.6	4.9	5.8	3.9	4.8	4.6	2.8	4.6	5.3	5.4	3.8	3.2	2.8	5.6	5.7	3.9
ENG	M	5.1	5.1	6.2	4.4	5.6	4.8	4.5	4.4	5.0	5.4	3.3	3.0	3.5	3.6	3.9	5.3	5.3	4.3	5.0	4.9	4.6	4.2	6.1	5.5	4.6	4.5	3.3	5.6	5.6	4.6
	W	5.4	5.6	6.5	5.2	6.6	5.6	4.9	5.3	5.7	5.9	3.9	3.4	3.5	4.0	5.0	5.3	5.5	5.0	5.8	5.8	4.9	3.9	6.2	6.2	4.1	4.3	3.8	6.4	6.2	4.8
	T	5.3	5.4	6.4	4.8	6.1	5.2	4.7	4.9	5.4	5.7	3.6	3.2	3.5	3.8	4.5	5.3	5.4	4.7	5.4	5.4	4.8	4.1	6.2	5.9	4.4	4.4	3.6	6.0	5.9	4.7
FIN	M	6.3	4.5	6.5	4.9	6.2	4.2	6.0	6.1	5.9	6.0	4.5	5.3	4.3	3.7	4.4	6.1	5.8	4.0	5.6	4.5	5.1	5.2	6.2	6.2	5.8	4.8	4.0	6.1	6.2	4.5
	W	6.6	5.3	6.6	5.2	6.6	5.3	5.9	6.3	6.2	6.5	4.2	5.8	4.7	4.2	5.7	6.1	6.8	4.0	6.1	5.7	5.1	5.1	6.3	6.5	6.4	4.6	4.7	6.6	6.7	5.0
	T	6.5	4.9	6.6	5.1	6.4	4.8	6.0	6.2	6.1	6.3	4.4	5.6	4.5	4.0	5.1	6.1	6.3	4.0	5.9	5.1	5.1	5.2	6.3	6.4	6.1	4.7	4.4	6.4	6.5	4.8
GER	M	6.0	6.3	6.5	5.5	5.9	5.7	6.1	5.8	5.8	6.5	5.5	4.7	4.4	4.6	3.7	5.8	6.3	5.6	2.4	5.3	5.6	4.7	6.4	6.2	4.9	5.4	4.5	3.5	6.1	5.4
	W	6.3	6.3	6.8	5.4	6.3	6.2	6.5	5.6	6.2	6.5	5.7	4.9	4.3	4.6	4.8	5.8	6.5	6.1	3.0	5.6	6.1	4.6	6.7	6.8	5.3	6.0	4.7	3.5	6.3	5.5
	T	6.2	6.3	6.7	5.5	6.1	6.0	6.3	5.7	6.0	6.5	5.6	4.8	4.4	4.6	4.3	5.8	6.4	5.9	2.7	5.5	5.9	4.7	6.6	6.5	5.1	5.7	4.6	3.5	6.2	5.5
IND	M	3.2	2.8	5.3	3.2	4.4	4.4	4.3	3.6	2.9	4.3	5.0	2.9	3.9	2.1	4.2	4.4	5.6	2.5	3.3	2.5	2.5	4.7	4.6	3.8	5.0	4.9	2.9	3.7	3.6	4.2
	W	3.1	2.7	5.8	2.7	5.0	4.7	4.4	3.2	3.5	3.9	4.2	4.1	3.8	2.6	3.7	3.9	5.6	2.6	3.6	3.4	3.2	4.8	4.0	4.0	4.1	5.3	2.4	4.2	3.6	4.6
	T	3.2	2.8	5.6	3.0	4.7	4.6	4.4	3.4	3.2	4.1	4.6	3.5	3.9	2.4	4.0	4.2	5.6	2.6	3.5	3.0	2.9	4.8	4.3	3.9	4.6	5.1	2.7	4.0	3.6	4.4
ITA	M	5.2	5.7	6.3	3.6	5.5	4.5	5.1	4.4	—	5.4	3.6	4.0	3.4	2.4	4.1	5.6	5.6	4.4	5.0	3.8	4.1	3.5	5.6	5.2	2.8	4.0	2.8	5.8	6.0	5.1
	W	5.6	5.9	6.6	3.7	5.9	4.8	5.1	5.2	—	6.3	4.2	4.8	2.3	2.1	4.2	4.9	5.9	4.9	5.4	4.4	4.8	4.1	5.9	6.4	2.4	4.5	3.2	6.3	6.4	4.8
	T	5.4	5.8	6.5	3.7	5.7	4.7	5.1	4.8	—	5.9	3.9	4.4	2.9	2.3	4.2	5.3	5.8	4.7	5.2	4.1	4.5	3.8	5.8	5.8	2.6	4.3	3.0	6.1	6.2	5.0

		1	2	3	4	5	6	7	8	9	10	11	12	13	14	15	16	17	18	19	20	21	22	23	24	25	26	27	28	29	30
MAL	M	3.5	3.2	4.9	2.9	4.4	4.3	3.9	3.8	3.9	4.9	—	3.3	3.6	6.2	3.7	5.1	5.0	3.3	3.3	3.0	3.2	4.0	3.6	4.5	3.7	4.5	2.8	5.0	3.7	—
	W	3.6	3.2	5.4	2.9	5.3	4.5	4.1	4.2	3.8	4.5	—	4.3	2.7	2.2	3.7	4.5	5.5	4.1	3.8	4.2	3.0	4.0	3.8	5.3	2.9	4.5	2.8	4.9	4.5	—
	T	3.6	3.2	5.2	2.9	4.9	4.4	4.0	4.0	3.9	4.7	—	3.8	3.2	4.2	3.7	4.8	5.3	3.7	3.6	3.6	3.1	4.0	3.7	4.9	3.3	4.5	2.8	5.0	4.1	—
NET	M	6.2	6.0	6.6	5.6	5.5	4.3	5.5	6.1	5.8	6.3	5.0	2.8	3.9	3.3	4.9	5.7	6.1	5.3	6.1	5.5	6.4	4.0	6.6	6.6	5.6	5.5	4.6	6.7	6.5	5.3
	W	6.6	6.2	6.8	5.2	6.0	4.8	6.2	6.3	6.0	6.2	4.7	3.9	3.9	3.7	5.8	5.3	6.5	6.0	6.4	5.9	6.0	5.0	6.3	6.5	5.6	5.6	5.1	6.7	6.5	5.4
	T	6.4	6.1	6.7	5.4	5.8	4.6	5.9	6.2	5.9	6.3	4.9	3.4	3.9	3.5	5.4	5.5	6.3	5.7	6.3	5.7	6.2	4.5	6.5	6.6	5.6	5.6	5.4	6.7	6.5	5.4
NIG	M	2.3	2.7	3.0	2.7	2.4	3.4	4.2	3.1	2.6	2.5	2.0	3.0	3.5	2.0	4.5	3.9	3.9	1.7	2.6	2.8	2.2	4.4	2.2	4.0	4.0	3.3	2.4	3.7	4.4	4.2
	W	3.4	3.3	3.7	2.3	3.2	3.6	4.3	4.8	2.5	4.0	2.2	3.2	2.9	2.0	4.0	3.2	4.8	2.4	1.9	3.7	2.2	4.0	2.9	6.2	3.6	3.4	2.0	4.3	5.1	2.6
	T	2.9	3.0	3.4	2.5	2.8	3.5	4.3	4.0	2.6	3.3	2.1	3.1	3.2	2.0	4.3	3.6	4.4	2.1	2.3	3.3	2.2	4.2	2.6	5.1	3.8	3.4	2.2	4.0	4.8	3.4
PAK	M	1.5	2.3	4.3	2.6	2.7	4.4	4.9	3.0	2.9	3.1	4.7	4.0	4.6	2.3	4.9	—	4.9	1.4	2.5	2.3	—	4.2	—	2.6	4.3	3.5	2.1	3.4	2.7	3.7
	W	2.4	2.0	5.6	5.6	2.6	4.1	5.5	2.5	2.6	3.0	4.2	3.5	3.1	2.0	5.2	—	5.1	1.5	2.0	2.7	—	3.7	—	3.3	4.6	4.1	1.5	3.8	2.9	3.9
	T	2.0	2.2	5.0	4.1	2.7	4.3	5.2	2.8	2.8	3.1	4.5	3.8	4.1	2.2	5.1	—	5.0	1.5	2.3	2.5	—	4.0	—	3.0	4.5	5.6	1.8	3.6	2.8	3.8
SIN	M	3.0	2.8	5.1	3.1	4.9	3.5	3.9	4.2	4.0	4.4	—	2.8	3.3	2.0	3.8	3.8	7.7	3.6	3.5	3.4	2.0	4.0	3.0	4.8	3.6	3.5	2.5	4.4	3.7	—
	W	4.4	3.7	5.8	5.1	5.9	4.6	4.5	4.8	4.5	5.3	—	3.6	3.2	3.0	3.9	3.4	5.3	4.9	3.7	4.7	3.0	4.9	3.6	6.0	3.8	4.2	3.1	5.6	4.6	—
	T	3.7	3.3	5.5	4.1	5.4	4.1	4.2	4.5	4.3	4.9	—	3.2	3.3	2.5	3.9	3.6	4.9	4.3	3.6	4.1	2.5	4.5	3.3	5.4	3.7	3.9	2.8	5.0	4.2	—
USA	M	3.5	3.9	5.6	4.0	5.1	4.6	3.7	4.6	3.8	5.3	1.8	1.9	2.8	2.7	3.2	4.9	5.2	3.2	4.5	4.6	2.4	3.9	4.9	4.9	4.4	4.4	2.8	5.1	5.2	3.6
	W	4.9	4.7	6.3	4.2	6.6	5.0	4.4	5.1	5.4	5.5	2.0	2.3	2.8	2.9	4.0	4.7	6.0	4.7	5.1	5.7	2.7	4.1	5.4	5.9	4.2	4.9	3.3	6.3	6.1	4.3
	T	4.2	4.3	6.0	4.1	5.9	4.8	4.1	4.9	4.6	5.4	1.9	2.1	2.8	2.8	3.6	4.8	5.6	4.0	4.8	5.2	2.6	4.0	5.2	5.4	4.3	4.7	3.1	5.7	5.7	4.0
VEN	M	4.7	3.7	5.6	3.5	5.6	5.1	4.4	5.4	5.3	5.5	4.0	3.0	3.4	2.0	4.4	5.9	5.5	3.3	4.7	4.2	3.5	3.7	4.5	5.7	4.6	4.5	3.2	5.7	6.3	4.1
	W	5.8	4.2	6.1	3.8	6.4	5.6	4.8	5.7	5.7	5.9	3.8	4.0	2.7	2.1	4.9	5.6	6.0	4.2	5.6	5.5	4.1	3.7	5.3	6.3	4.4	5.0	3.3	6.6	6.6	3.6
	T	5.3	4.0	5.9	3.7	6.0	5.4	4.6	5.6	5.5	5.7	3.9	5.3	5.1	2.1	4.7	5.8	5.8	3.8	5.2	4.9	4.3	3.7	4.9	6.0	4.5	4.8	3.3	6.2	6.5	3.9

REFERENCES

Adams, F. M., & Osgood, C. E. (1973). A cross-cultural study of the affective meanings of color. *Journal of Cross Cultural Psychology, 4*, 135-156.

Allport, G. W., & Odbert, H. (1936). Trait names: A psycho-lexical study. *Psychological Monographs, 47* (1, Whole No. 211).

Bakan, D. (1966). *The duality of human existence*. Chicago: Rand McNally.

Barrett, D. B. (1982). *World christian encyclopedia*. Oxford, England: Oxford University Press.

Barry, H., III, Bacon, M. K., & Child, I. L. (1957). A cross-cultural survey of some sex differences in socialization. *Journal of Abnormal and Social Psychology, 55*, 327-332.

Basow, S. A. (1980). *Sex-role stereotypes: Traditions and alternatives*. Belmont, CA: Brooks/Cole.

Basow, S. A. (1984). Cultural variations in sex typing. *Sex Roles, 10*, 577-585.

Baumeister, R. F. (1987). How the self became a problem: A psychological view of historical research. *Journal of Personality and Social Psychology, 52*, 163-173.

Bem, S. L. (1974). The measurement of psychological androgyny. *Journal of Consulting and Clinical Psychology, 42*, 155-162.

Bem, S. L. (1977). On the utility of alternative procedures for assessing psychological androgyny. *Journal of Consulting and Clinical Psychology, 45*, 196-205.

Bem, S. L. (1979). Theory and measurement of androgyny: A reply to the Pedhazur-Tetenbaum and Locksley-Cotten critiques. *Journal of Personality and Social Psychology, 37*, 1047-1054.

Berne, E. (1961). *Transactional analysis in psychotherapy*. New York: Grove.

Berne, E. (1966). *Principles of group treatment*. New York: Oxford University Press.

Berry, J. W. (1969). On cross-cultural comparability. *International Journal of Psychology, 4*, 119-128.

Berry, J. W. (1979). Culture and cognitive style. In A. J. Marsella et al. (Eds.), *Perspectives on cross-cultural psychology* (pp. 117-135). New York: Academic Press.

Berry, J. W. (1980a). Ecological analyses for cross-cultural psychology. In N. Warren (Ed.), *Studies in cross-cultural psychology* (Vol. 2, pp. 157-189). New York: Academic Press.

Berry, J. W. (1980b). Introduction to methodology. In H. C. Triandis & J. W. Berry (Eds.), *Handbook of cross-cultural psychology* (Vol. 2, pp. 1-28). Boston: Allyn & Bacon.

Berry, J. W. (1980c). Social and cultural change. In H. C. Triandis & R. W. Brislin (Eds.), *Handbook of cross-cultural psychology* (Vol. 5, pp. 211-279). Boston: Allyn & Bacon.

Berzins, J. I., Welling, M. A., & Wetter, R. E. (1978). A new measure of psychological androgyny based on the Personality Research Form. *Journal of Consulting and Clinical Psychology, 46*, 126-138.

Best, D. L., Field, J. T., & Williams, J. E. (1976). Color bias in a sample of young German children. *Psychological Reports, 38*, 1145-1146.

Best, D. L., Naylor, C. E., & Williams, J. E. (1975). Extension of color bias research to young French and Italian children. *Journal of Cross-Cultural Psychology, 6*, 390-405.

Best, D. L., & Williams, J. E. (1984). A cross-cultural examination of self and ideal self descriptions using Transactional Analysis Ego States. In I. R. Lagunes & Y. H. Poortinga (Eds.), *From a different perspective: Studies of behavior across cultures* (pp. 213-220). Lisse, The Netherlands: Swets and Zeitlinger.

Best, D. L., Williams, J. E., & Briggs, S. R. (1980). A further analysis of the affective meanings associated with male and female sex-trait stereotypes. *Sex Roles, 6*, 735-746.

Best, D. L., Williams, J. E., Cloud, J. M., Davis, S. W., Robertson, L. S., Edwards, J. R., Giles, H., & Fowles, J. (1977). Development of sex-trait stereotypes among young children in the United States, England, and Ireland. *Child Development, 48*, 1375-1384.

Bhana, K. (1980). Sex-trait stereotypes and their evaluation among Indian adults. *South African Journal of Psychology, 10*, 42-45.

Block, J. H. (1979). Another look at sex differentiation in the socialization behavior of mothers and fathers. In J. Sherman & F. L. Denmark (Eds.), *Psychology of women: Future directions of research* (pp. 29-87). New York: Psychological Dimensions.

Block, J. H. (1984). *Sex role identity and ego development*. San Francisco: Jossey-Bass.

Brannon, R. (1978). Measuring attitudes (toward women, and otherwise): A methodological critique. In J. Sherman & F. Denmark (Eds.), *Psychology of women: Future directions in research* (pp. 645-731). New York: Psychological Dimensions.

Brislin, R.W. (1980). Translation and content analysis of oral and written materials. In H. C. Triandis & J. W. Berry (Eds.), *Handbook of cross-cultural psychology* (Vol. 2, pp. 389-444). Boston: Allyn & Bacon.

Brislin, R.W. (1983). Cross-cultural research in psychology. *Annual Review of Psychology, 34*, 363-400.

Bull, D., & David, I. (1986). The stigmatizing effect of facial disfigurement: Nigerian and English nurses' and office workers' ratings of normal and scarred faces. *Journal of Cross Cultural Psychology, 17*, 99-108.

Campbell, D. T. (1964). Distinguishing differences of perception from failures of communication in cross-cultural studies. In F. S. C. Northrop & H. H. Livingston (Eds.), *Cross-cultural understanding: Epistemology in anthropology* (pp. 308-336). New York: Harper & Row.

Campbell, D. T., & Stanley, J. C. (1966). *Experimental and quasi-experimental designs for research*. Chicago: Rand McNally.

Constantinople, A. (1973). Masculinity-femininity: An exception to a famous dictum? *Psychological Bulletin, 80*, 389-407.

Cook, T. D., & Campbell, D. T. (1979). *Quasi-experimentation: Design and analysis issues for field settings*. Chicago: Rand McNally.

Davidson, A. R., & Thomson, E. (1980). Cross-cultural studies of attitudes and beliefs. In H. C. Triandis & R. W. Brislin (Eds.), *Handbook of cross-cultural psychology* (Vol. 5, pp. 25-72). Boston: Allyn & Bacon.

Davis, S. W., Williams, J. E., & Best, D. L. (1982). Sex-trait stereotypes in the self and peer descriptions of third grade children. *Sex Roles, 8*, 315-331.

Deaux, K. (1984). From individual differences to social categories. *American Psychologist, 39* 105-116.

Dermer, M., & Thiel, D. L. (1975). When beauty may fail. *Journal of Personality and Social Psychology, 31*(6), 1168-1176.

Diaz-Guerrero, R. (1977). A Mexican psychology. *American Psychologist, 32*, 936-944.

Dion, K., Berscheid, E., & Walster, E. (1972). What is beautiful is good. *Journal of Personality and Social Psychology, 24*(3), 285-290.

Draguns, J. G. (1979). Culture and personality. In A. J. Marsella, R. G. Tharp, & T. J. Ciborowski (Eds.), *Perspectives on cross-cultural psychology* (pp. 179-207). New York: Academic Press.

Edwards, J. R., & Williams, J. E. (1980). Sex-trait stereotypes among young children and young adults: Canadian findings and cross-national comparisons. *Canadian Journal of Behavioral Science, 12*, 210-220.

Ember, C. R. (1981). A cross-cultural perspective on sex differences. In R. H. Munroe, R. L. Munroe, & B. B. Whiting (Eds.), *Handbook of cross-cultural human development* (pp. 531-380). New York: Garland STPM.

Enriquez, V. G. (1988). The structure of Philippine social values: Towards integrating indigenous values and appropriate technology. In D. Sinha & H. S. R. Kao (Eds.), *Social values and development: Asian Perspectives* (pp. 124-148). Newbury Park, CA: Sage.

Fenley, J. M. (1986). *The relationship of the perceived self and the ideal self among drug addicts and non-addicts*. Unpublished master's thesis, Wake Forest University, Winston-Salem, NC.

Fling, S., & Manosevitz, M. (1972). Sex typing in school children's play interests. *Developmental Psychology, 7*, 146-152.

Gill, S., Stockard, J., Johnson, M., & Williams, S. (1987). Measuring gender differences: The expressive dimension and critique of androgyny scales. *Sex Roles, 17*, 375-400.

Gillen, B. (1981). Physical attractiveness: A determinant of two types of goodness. *Personality and Social Psychology Bulletin, 7*(2), 277-281.

Goodenough, E. W. (1957). Interest in persons as an aspect of sex differences in the early years. *Genetic Psychology Monographs, 55*, 287-323.

Gough, H. G. (1952). Identifying psychological femininity. *Educational and Psychological Measurement, 12*, 427-439.

Gough, H. G. (1966). A cross-cultural analysis of the CPI femininity scale. *Journal of Consulting Psychology, 30*, 136-141.

Gough, H. G., Chun, K., & Chung, Y. E. (1968). Validation of the CPI femininity scale in Korea. *Psychological Reports, 22*, 155-160.

Gough, H. G., & Heilbrun, A. B. (1965). *Adjective check list manual*. Palo Alto, CA: Consulting Psychologists Press.

Gough, H. G., & Heilbrun, A. B. (1980a). *The adjective check list bibliography*. Palo Alto, CA: Consulting Psychologists Press.

Gough, H. G., & Heilbrun, A. B., Jr. (1980b). *The adjective check list manual*. Palo Alto, CA: Consulting Psychologists Press.

Haque, A. (1982). Sex stereotypes among adults and children in Pakistan. In R. Rath, H. S. Asthana, D. Sinha, & J. B. H. Sinha (Eds.), *Diversity and unity in cross-cultural psychology*. Amsterdam, The Netherlands: Swets Publishing Service.

Hartup, W. W., & Moore, S. G. (1965). Avoidance of inappropriate sextyping by young children. *Journal of Consulting Psychology, 27*, 467-473.

Hathaway, S. R., & McKinley, J. C. (1943). *The Minnesota Multiphasic Personality Inventory*. New York: Psychological Corporation.

Heilbrun, A. L. (1976). Measurement of masculine and feminine sex role identities as independent dimensions. *Journal of Consulting and Clinical Psychology, 44*, 183-190.

Heilbrun, A. L. (1981). *Human sex-role behavior*. Elmsford, NY: Pergamon.

Hofstede, G. (1979). Value systems in forty countries: Interpretation, validation and consequences for theory. In L. Eckensberger, W. Lonner, & Y. H. Poortinga (Eds.), *Cross-cultural contributions to psychology* (pp. 389-407). Lisse, The Netherlands: Swets & Zeitlinger.

Hofstede, G. (1980). *Culture's consequences: International differences in work-related values*. Beverly Hills, CA: Sage.

Inkeles, A. (1977). Understanding and misunderstanding individual modernity. *Journal of Cross-Cultural Psychology, 8*, 135-176.

Inkeles, A., & Smith, D. H. (1974). *Becoming modern: Individual change in sex developing countries*. Cambridge, MA: Harvard University Press.

Insko, C. A., & Schopler, J. (1972). *Experimental social psychology*. New York: Academic Press.

Iwawaki, S., Sonoo, K., Williams, J. E., & Best, D. L. (1978). Color bias among young Japanese children. *Journal of Cross-Cultural Psychology, 9*(1), 61-74.

Jackson, D. N. (1967). *Manual for the Personality Research Form*. Goshen, NY: Research Psychologists Press.

Jackson, L. A. (1983). The perception of androgyny and physical attractiveness: Two is better than one. *Personality and Social Psychology Bulletin, 9*(3), 405-413.

Jahoda, G. (1980). Cross-cultural comparisons. In M. H. Bornstein (Ed.), *Comparative methods in psychology* (pp. 105-148). Hillsdale, NJ: Lawrence Erlbaum.

Jahoda, G. (1984). Do we need a concept of culture? *Journal of Cross-Cultural Psychology, 15*, 139-151.

Jones, E. E., & Pittman, T. S. (1982). Toward a general theory of strategic self-presentation. In J. Suls (Ed.), *Psychological perspectives on the self* (Vol. 1, pp. 231-262). Hillsdale, NJ: Lawrence Erlbaum.

Kalin, R., Heusser, C., & Edwards, J. (1982). Cross-national equivalence of a sex-role ideology scale. *Journal of Social Psychology, 116*, 141-142.

Kalin, R., & Tilby, P. (1978). Development and validation of a sex-role ideology scale. *Psychological Reports, 42*, 731-738.

Kaplan, A. G., & Bean, J. P. (Eds.). (1976). *Beyond sex-role stereotypes: Readings toward a psychology of androgyny*. Boston: Little, Brown.

Kaschak, E., & Sharratt, S. (1983). A Latin American sex role inventory. *Cross Cultural Psychology Bulletin, 18*, 3-6.

Kelly, J. A., Caudill, S., Hathorn, S., & O'Brien, C. G. (1977). Socially undesirable sex-correlated characteristics: Implications for androgyny and adjustment. *Journal of Consulting and Clinical Psychology, 45*, 1186-1187.

Kelly, J. A., Furman, W., & Young, V. (1978). Problems associated with the typological measurement of sex roles and androgyny. *Journal of Consulting and Clinical Psychology, 46*, 1574-1576.

Kelly, J. A., & Worell, J. A. (1977). New formulations of sex roles and androgyny: A critical review. *Journal of Consulting and Clinical Psychology, 45*, 1101-1115.

Lansky, L. M. (1967). The family structure also affects the model; sex role attitudes in parents of preschool children. *Merrill-Palmer Quarterly, 1*(2), 147-154.

Lara-Cantu, M. A., & Navarro-Arias, R. (1987). Self-descriptions of Mexican college students in response to the Bem Sex Role Inventory and other sex role items. *Journal of Cross-Cultural Psychology, 18*, 331-344.

LeVerrier, L. C. (1987). *Theoretical and methodological issues related to masculinity and femininity*. Unpublished master's thesis, Wake Forest University, Winston-Salem, NC.

Levin, J., & Karni, E. S. (1971). A comparative study of the CPI femininity scale: Validation in Israel. *Journal of Cross-Cultural Psychology, 2*, 387-391.

Lewis, M., & Weinraub, M. (1979). Origins of early sex-role development. *Sex Roles, 5*, 135-153.

Liebert, R. M., & Spiegler, M. D. (1987). *Personality: Strategies and issues*. Homewood, IL: Dorsey Press.

Lonner, W. J. (1979). Issues in cross-cultural psychology. In A. J. Marsella, R. G. Tharp, & T. J. Ciborowski (Eds.), *Perspectives on cross-cultural psychology* (pp. 17-45). New York: Academic Press.

Lonner, W. J. (1980). The search for psychological universals. In H. C. Triandis & W. W. Lambert (Eds.), *Handbook of cross-cultural psychology* (Vol. 1, pp. 143-204). Boston: Allyn & Bacon.

Lonner, W. J., & Berry, J. W. (1986). Sampling and surveying. In W. J. Lonner & J. W. Berry (Eds.), *Field methods in cross-cultural research* (pp. 85-110). Beverly Hills, CA: Sage.

Lucker, G. W., Beane, W. E., & Helmreich, R. L. (1981). The strength of the halo effect in physical attractiveness research. *The Journal of Psychology, 107*, 69-75.

Malpass, R. S., & Poortinga, Y. H. (1986). Strategies for design and analysis. In W. J. Lonner & J. W. Berry (Eds.), *Field methods in cross-cultural research* (pp. 47-86). Beverly Hills: Sage.

Margalit, B. A., & Mauger, P. A. (1985). Aggressiveness and assertiveness: A cross-cultural study of Israel and the United States. *Journal of Cross-Cultural Psychology, 16*, 497-511.

McCauley, C., Stitt, C., & Segal, M. (1980). Stereotyping: From prejudice to prediction. *Psychological Bulletin, 87*, 195-208.

McClelland, D. C. (1961). *The achieving society*. Princeton: Van Nostrand.

Mead, G. H. (1934). *Mind, self, and society*. Chicago: University of Chicago Press.

Milo, T., Badger, L. W., & Coggins, D. R. (1983). Conceptual analysis of the sex-role ideology scale. *Psychological Reports, 53*, 139-146.

Morris, M. D. (1979). *Measuring the condition of the world's poor: The physical quality of life index*. Elmsford, NY: Pergamon.

Moss, H. A. (1974). Early sex differences and mother-infant interaction. In R. C. Friedman, R. M. Richart, & R. L. Vande Wiele (Eds.), *Sex differences in behavior* (pp. 149-163). New York: John Wiley.

Munroe, R. L., & Munroe, R. H. (1980). Perspectives suggested by anthropological data. In H. C. Triandis, & W. W. Lambert (Eds.), *Handbook of cross-cultural psychology (Vol. 1, pp. 253-318). Boston: Allyn & Bacon.*

Munroe, R. H., Shimmin, H. S., & Munroe, R. L. (1984). Gender understanding and sex role preference in four cultures. *Developmental Psychology, 20*, 673-682.

Myers, A. M., & Gonda, G. (1982). Utility of the masculinity-femininity construct: Comparison of traditional androgyny approaches. *Journal of Personality and Social Psychology, 43*, 514-522.

Myers, A. M., & Sugar, J. (1979). A critical analysis of scoring the BSRI: Implications for conceptualization. *JSAS Catalog of Selected Documents in Psychology, 9*, 24. (Ms. No. 1833).

Nishiyama, I. (1975). Validation of the CPI femininity scale in Japan. *Journal of Cross-Cultural Psychology, 5*, 482-489.

Osgood, C. E., May, W. H., & Miron, M. S. (1975). *Cross-cultural universals of affective meaning*. Urbana: University of Illinois Press.

Packer, M. J. (1985). Hermeneutic inquiry in the study of human conduct. *American Psychologist, 40*, 1081-1093.

Parsons, T., & Bales, R. F. (1955). *Family, socialization and interaction process*. New York: Free Press.

Pitariu, H. (1981). Validation of the CPI femininity scale in Romania. *Journal of Cross Cultural Psychology, 12*(1), 111-117.

Poortinga, Y. H. (1975). Limitations on intercultural comparisons of psychological data. *Nederlands Tijdschrift van de Psychologie, 30*, 23-39.

Poortinga, Y. H., & Malpass, R. S. (1986). Making inferences from cross-cultural data. In W. J. Lonner & J. W. Berry (Eds.), *Field methods in cross-cultural research* (pp. 17-46). Beverly Hills, CA: Sage.

Ramanaiah, N. V., & Martin, H. J. (1984). Convergent and discriminant validity of selected masculinity and femininity scales. *Sex Roles, 10*, 493-504.

Rogers, C. R. (1951). *Client-centered therapy*. Boston: Houghton Mifflin.

Rohner, R. P. (1984). Toward a conception of culture for cross-cultural psychology. *Journal of Cross-Cultural Psychology, 15*, 111-138.

Rosenkrantz, P. S., Vogel, S. R., Bee, H., Broverman, I. K., & Broverman, D. M. (1968). Sex-role stereotypes and self-concepts in college students. *Journal of Consulting and Clinical Psychology*, *32*, 287-295.

Ruble, D. N., & Ruble, T. L. (1982). Sex stereotypes. In A. G. Miller (Ed.), *In the eye of the beholder: Contemporary issues in stereotyping* (pp. 188-252). New York: Praeger.

Ruby, A. J. (1968). Sex-role perceptions in early adolescence. *Adolescence*, *3*, 453-470.

Runge, T. E., Frey, D., Gollwitzer, P. M., Helmreich, R. L., & Spence, J. T. (1981). Masculine (instrumental) and feminine (expressive) traits: A comparison between students in the United States and West Germany. *Journal of Cross Cultural Psychology*, *12*, 141-162.

Sedney, M. A. (1981). Comments on median split procedures for scoring androgyny measures. *Sex Roles*, *1*(1), 217-222.

Segall, M. H. (1984). More than we need to know about culture but are afraid not to ask. *Journal of Cross-Cultural Psychology*, *15*, 153-162.

Segall, M. H. (1986). Culture and behavior: Psychology in global perspective. *Annual Review of Psychology*, *37*, 523-564.

Sewell, J. W. and the staff of the Overseas Development Council. (1980). *The United States and world development: Agenda 1980*. New York: Praeger.

Sivard, R. L. (1982). *World military and social expenditures*. Leesburg, VA: World Priorities.

Spence, J. T. (1984). Masculinity, femininity and gender-related traits: A conceptual analysis and critique of recent research. In D. A. Maher & W. B. Maher (Eds.), *Progress in experimental personality research* (Vol. 13, pp. 1-97). New York: Academic Press.

Spence, J. T. (1985). Achievement American style: The rewards and costs of individualism. *American Psychologist*, *40*(12), 1285-1295.

Spence, J. T., Deaux, K., & Helmreich, R. L. (1985). Sex roles in contemporary American society. In G. Lindzey & E. Aronson (Eds.), *The handbook of social psychology* (3rd ed., pp. 149-178). New York: Random House.

Spence, J. T., & Helmreich, R. (1972). The Attitudes Towards Women Scale: An objective instrument to measure attitudes towards the rights and roles of women in contemporary society. *JSAS Catalog of Selected Documents in Psychology*, *2*, 66.

Spence, J. T., & Helmreich, R. (1973). A short version of the Attitude Toward Women Scale (AWS). *Bulletin of the Psychonomic Society*, *2*, 219-220.

Spence, J. T., & Helmreich, R. L. (1978). *Masculinity and femininity: Their psychological dimensions, correlates, and antecedents*. Austin: University of Texas Press.

Spence, J. T., & Helmreich, R. L. (1980). Masculine instrumentality and feminine expressiveness: Their relationships with sex role attitudes and behaviors. *Psychology of Women Quarterly*, *5*, 147-163.

Spence, J. T., & Helmreich, R. L. (1981). Androgyny versus gender schema: A comment on Bem's gender schema theory. *Psych Review*, *88*, 365-368.

Spence, J. T., Helmreich, R. L., & Holahan, C. K. (1979). Negative and positive components of masculinity and femininity and relations to self-reports of neurotic and acting out behaviors. *Journal of Personality and Social Psychology*, *37*, 1673-1682.

Spence, J. T., Helmreich, R., & Stapp, J. (1974). The Personal Attributes Questionnaire: A measure of sex-role stereotypes and masculinity-femininity. *JSAS Catalog of Selected documents in Psychology*, *4*, 43.

Spence, J. T., Helmreich, R. L., & Stapp, J. (1975). Ratings of self and peers on sex role attributes and their relation to self esteem and conceptions of masculinity and femininity. *Journal of Personality and Social Psychology*, *32*, 29-39.

Strodtbeck, F. L. (1964). Considerations of metamethod in cross-cultural studies. *American Anthropologist* (Special publication), *66* (3, part 2), 223-229.

Strong, E. K. (1936). Interests of men and women. *Journal of Social Psychology*, *7*, 49-67.

Tajfel, H. (1969). Cognitive aspects of prejudice. *Journal of Social Issues*, *25*, 79-97.

Tarrier, N., & Gomes, L. (1981). Knowledge of sex-trait stereotypes: Effects of age, sex and social class on Brazilian children. *Journal of Cross-Cultural Psychology, 12*, 81-93.

Terman, L., & Miles, C. C. (1936). *Sex and personality*. New York: McGraw-Hill.

Triandis, H. C. (1977). Cross-cultural social and personality psychology. *Personality and Social Psychology Bulletin, 3*, 145-158.

Triandis, H. C. (1980). Introduction of handbook of cross-cultural psychology. In H. C. Triandis & W. W. Lambert (Eds.), *Handbook of cross-cultural psychology* (Vol. 1). Boston: Allyn & Bacon.

Triandis, H. C., & Berry, J. W. (Eds.) (1980). *Handbook of cross-cultural psychology* (Vol. 2). Boston: Allyn & Bacon.

Triandis, H. C., Malpass, R. S., & Davidson, A. (1972). Cross-cultural psychology. *Biennial Review of Anthropology*, 1-84.

Ward, C. (1985). Sex-trait stereotypes in Malaysian children. *Sex Roles, 12*, 35-45.

Ward, C., & Sethi, R. R. (1986). Cross-cultural validation of the Bem Sex Role Inventory: Malaysian and South African research. *Journal of Cross-Cultural Psychology, 17*, 300-314.

Ward, C., & Williams, J. E. (1982). A psychological needs analysis of male and female sex trait stereotypes in Malaysia. *International Journal of Psychology, 17*, 369-381.

Weber, M. (1958). *The Protestant work ethic and the spirit of capitalism* (Talcott Parsons, Translator). New York: Academic Press.

Whiting, B. (1976). The problem of the packaged variable. In K. F. Riegel & J. A. Meacham (Eds.), *The developing individual in a changing world.* The Hague, The Netherlands: Mouton.

Williams, J. E., & Bennett, S. W. (1975). The definition of sex stereotypes via the adjective check list. *Sex Roles, 1*, 327-337.

Williams, J. E., & Best, D. L. (1977). Sex stereotypes and trait favorability on the adjective check list. *Educational and Psychological Measurement, 37*, 101-110.

Williams, J. E., & Best, D. L. (1982). *Measuring sex stereotypes: A thirty-nation study.* Beverly Hills, CA: Sage. (Revised edition: *Measuring sex stereotypes: A multination study*, 1990. Newbury Park, CA: Sage.)

Williams, J. E., & Best, D. L. (1983). The Gough-Heilbrun Adjective Check List as a cross-cultural research tool. In J. B. Deregowski, S. Dziurawiec, & R. C. Annis (Eds.), *Expiscations in cross-cultural psychology* (pp. 163-173). Lisse, The Netherlands: Swets & Zeitlinger.

Williams, J. E., Best, D. L., Haque, A., Pandey, J., & Verma, R. K. (1982). Sex-trait stereotypes in India and Pakistan. *Journal of Psychology, 111*, 167-181.

Williams, J. E., Best, D. L., Tilquin, C., Keller, H., Voss, H. G., Bjerke, T., & Baarda, B. (1981). Traits associated with men and women: Attribution by young children in France, Germany, Norway, the Netherlands and Italy. *Journal of Cross-Cultural Psychology, 12*, 327-346.

Williams, J. E., Daws, J. T., Best, D. L., Tilquin, C., Wesley, F., & Bjerke, T. (1979). Sex-trait stereotypes in France, Germany, and Norway. *Journal of Cross-Cultural Psychology, 10*, 133-156.

Williams, J. E., Giles, H., & Edwards, J. R. (1977). Comparative anâlysis of sex-trait stereotypes in the United States, England, and Ireland. In Y. H. Poortinga (Ed.), *Basic problems in cross-cultural psychology* (pp. 241-246). Amsterdam, The Netherlands: Swets Publishing Service.

Williams, J. E., Giles, H., Edwards, J. R., Best, D. L., & Daws, J. T. (1977). Sex-trait stereotypes in England, Ireland, and the United States. *British Journal of Social and Clinical Psychology, 16*, 303-309.

Williams, J. E., & Morland, J. K. (1976). *Race, color, and the young child.* Chapel Hill: University of North Carolina Press.

Williams, K. B., & Williams, J. E. (1980). The assessment of transactional analysis ego states via the adjective check list. *Journal of Personality Assessment, 44*(2), 120-129.

Wilson, R. F., & Cook, E. P. (1984). Concurrent validity of four androgyny instruments. *Sex Roles, 11*(9/10), 813-837.

World book encyclopedia. (1963). Chicago: Field Enterprises.

Wylie, R. C. (1968). The present status of self theory. In E. F. Borgatta & W. W. Lambert (Eds.), *Handbook of personality theory and research*. Chicago: Rand McNally.

Wylie, R. C. (1974). *The self concept (Revised edition) volume one: A review of methodological considerations and measuring instruments*. Lincoln: University of Nebraska Press.

Wylie, R. C. (1979). *The self concept (Revised edition) volume two: Theory and research on selected topics*. Lincoln: University of Nebraska Press.

Yearbook of labor statistics. (1976). Geneva: International Labor Office.

AUTHOR INDEX

ABOUT THE AUTHORS

John E. Williams is Professor of Psychology and Chairman of the Department of Psychology at Wake Forest University in Winston-Salem, North Carolina. He holds a B.A. degree from the University of Richmond and M.A. and Ph.D. degrees from the University of Iowa. Prior to coming to Wake Forest in 1959, he was on the faculty at Yale University and the University of Richmond. Author of over 80 scholarly papers in personality, social, and developmental psychology, his book, *Race, Color, and the Young Child*, coauthored with J. K. Morland, was published by the University of North Carolina Press in 1976. In addition to his academic duties, he is director of Spectrum, an organization that provides psychological services to individuals and businesses in the Winston-Salem area.

Deborah L. Best is Professor of Psychology at Wake Forest University in Winston-Salem, North Carolina. She received her B.A. and M.A. degrees from Wake Forest University and her Ph. D. from the University of North Carolina at Chapel Hill. Her primary research interests are in developmental and personality psychology, and she has published over 40 articles in these areas. Along with her academic responsibilities, she has provided clinical services for children and their parents and has been involved in a number of applied development projects. She is coauthor with Williams of *Measuring Sex-Stereotypes: A Thirty-Nation Study*, published by Sage in 1982.